Python Social Media Analytics

Analyze and visualize data from Twitter, YouTube, GitHub, and more

Siddhartha Chatterjee
Michal Krystyanczuk

BIRMINGHAM - MUMBAI

Python Social Media Analytics

First published: July 2017

Production reference: 1260717

Published by Packt Publishing Ltd.
Livery Place
35 Livery Street
Birmingham
B3 2PB, UK.
ISBN 978-1-78712-148-5

www.packtpub.com

Credits

Authors
Siddhartha Chatterjee
Michal Krystyanczuk

Copy Editor
Safis Editing

Reviewer
Rubén Oliva Ramos

Project Coordinator
Nidhi Joshi

Commissioning Editor
Amey Varangaonkar

Proofreader
Safis Editing

Acquisition Editor
Divya Poojari

Indexer
Tejal Daruwale Soni

Content Development Editor
Cheryl Dsa

Graphics
Tania Dutta

Technical Editor
Vivek Arora

Production Coordinator
Arvindkumar Gupta

About the Authors

Siddhartha Chatterjee is an experienced data scientist with a strong focus in the area of machine learning and big data applied to digital (e-commerce and CRM) and social media analytics.

He worked between 2007 to 2012 with companies such as IBM, Cognizant Technologies, and Technicolor Research and Innovation. He completed a Pan-European Masters in Data Mining and Knowledge Management at Ecole Polytechnique of the University of Nantes and University of Eastern Piedmont, Italy.

Since 2012, he has worked at OgilvyOne Worldwide, a leading global customer engagement agency in Paris, as a lead data scientist and set up the social media analytics and predictive analytics offering. From 2014 to 2016, he was a senior data scientist and head of semantic data of Publicis, France. During his time at Ogilvy and Publicis, he worked on international projects for brands such as Nestle, AXA, BNP Paribas, McDonald's, Orange, Netflix, and others. Currently, Siddhartha is serving as head of data and analytics of Groupe Aéroport des Paris.

Michal Krystyanczuk is the co-founder of The Data Strategy, a start-up company based in Paris that builds artificial intelligence technologies to provide consumer insights from unstructured data. Previously, he worked as a data scientist in the financial sector using machine learning and big data techniques for tasks such as pattern recognition on financial markets, credit scoring, and hedging strategies optimization.

He specializes in social media analysis for brands using advanced natural language processing and machine learning algorithms. He has managed semantic data projects for global brands, such as Mulberry, BNP Paribas, Groupe SEB, Publicis, Chipotle, and others.

He is an enthusiast of cognitive computing and information retrieval from different types of data, such as text, image, and video.

Acknowledgments

This book is a result of our experience with data science and working with huge amounts of unstructured data from the web. Our intention was to provide a practical book on social media analytics with strong storytelling. In the whole process of analytics, the scripting of a story around the results is as important as the technicalities involved. It's been a long journey, chapter to chapter, and it would not have been possible without our support team that has helped us all through. We would like to deeply thank our mentors, Air commodore TK Chatterjee (retired) and Mr. Wojciech Krystyanczuk, who have motivated and helped us with their feedback, edits, and reviews throughout the journey.

We would also like to thank our co-author, Mr. Arjun Chatterjee, for sharing his brilliant technical knowledge and writing the chapter on *Social Media Analytics at Scale*. Above all, we would also like to thank the Packt editorial team for their encouragement and patience with us. We sincerely hope that the readers will find this book useful in their efforts to explore social media for creative purposes.

About the Reviewer

Rubén Oliva Ramos is a computer systems engineer with a master's degree in computer and electronic systems engineering, teleinformatics, and networking specialization from University of Salle Bajio in Leon, Guanajuato, Mexico. He has more than five years of experience in developing web applications to control and monitor devices connected with Arduino and Raspberry Pi using web frameworks and cloud services to build Internet of Things applications.

He is a mechatronics teacher at University of Salle Bajio and teaches students studying the master's degree in Design and Engineering of Mechatronics Systems. He also works at Centro de Bachillerato Tecnologico Industrial 225 in Leon, Guanajuato, Mexico, teaching electronics, robotics and control, automation, and microcontrollers at Mechatronics Technician Career. He has worked on consultant and developer projects in areas such as monitoring systems and datalogger data using technologies such as Android, iOS, Windows Phone, Visual Studio .NET, HTML5, PHP, CSS, Ajax, JavaScript, Angular, ASP .NET databases (SQlite, MongoDB, and MySQL), and web servers (Node.js and IIS). Ruben has done hardware programming on Arduino, Raspberry Pi, Ethernet Shield, GPS, and GSM/GPRS, ESP8266, and control and monitor systems for data acquisition and programming.

I would like to thank my savior and lord, Jesus Christ, for giving me strength and courage to pursue this project, to my dearest wife, Mayte, our two lovely sons, Ruben and Dario. To my father, Ruben, my dearest mom, Rosalia, my brother, Juan Tomas, and my sister, Rosalia, whom I love, for all their support while reviewing this book, for allowing me to pursue my dream, and tolerating not being with them after my busy day job.

www.PacktPub.com

For support files and downloads related to your book, please visit www.PacktPub.com. Did you know that Packt offers eBook versions of every book published, with PDF and ePub files available? You can upgrade to the eBook version at www.PacktPub.com and as a print book customer, you are entitled to a discount on the eBook copy. Get in touch with us at service@packtpub.com for more details. At www.PacktPub.com, you can also read a collection of free technical articles, sign up for a range of free newsletters and receive exclusive discounts and offers on Packt books and eBooks.

https://www.packtpub.com/mapt

Get the most in-demand software skills with Mapt. Mapt gives you full access to all Packt books and video courses, as well as industry-leading tools to help you plan your personal development and advance your career.

Why subscribe?

- Fully searchable across every book published by Packt
- Copy and paste, print, and bookmark content
- On demand and accessible via a web browser

Customer Feedback

Thanks for purchasing this Packt book. At Packt, quality is at the heart of our editorial process. To help us improve, please leave us an honest review on this book's Amazon page at `https://www.amazon.com/dp/1787121488`.

If you'd like to join our team of regular reviewers, you can email us at `customerreviews@packtpub.com`. We award our regular reviewers with free eBooks and videos in exchange for their valuable feedback. Help us be relentless in improving our products!

Table of Contents

Preface

Social media in the last decade has taken the world by storm. Billions of interactions take place around the world among the different users of Facebook, Twitter, YouTube, online forums, Pinterest, GitHub, and others. All these interactions, either captured through the data provided by the APIs of these platforms or through custom crawlers, have become a hotbed of information and insights for organizations and scientists around the world. *Python Social Media Analytics* has been written to show the most practical means of capturing this data, cleaning it, and making it relevant for advanced analytics and insight hunting. The book will cover basic to advanced concepts for dealing with highly unstructured data, followed by extensive analysis and conclusions to give sense to all of the processing.

What this book covers

Chapter 1, *Introduction to the Latest Social Media Landscape and Importance*, covers the updated social media landscape and key figures. We also cover the technical environment around Python, algorithms, and social networks, which we later explain in detail.

Chapter 2, *Harnessing Social Data - Connecting, Capturing, and Cleaning*, introduces methods to connect to the most popular social networks. It involves the creation of developer applications on chosen social media and then using Python libraries to make connections to those applications and querying the data. We take you through the advantages and limitations of each social media platform, basic techniques to clean, structure, and normalize the data using text mining and data pre-processing. Finally, you are introduced to MongoDB and essential administration methods.

Chapter 3, *Uncovering Brand Activity, Emotions, and Popularity on Facebook*, introduces the role of Facebook for brand activity and reputation. We will also introduce you to the Facebook API ecosystem and the methodology to extract data. You will learn the concepts of feature extraction and content analysis using keywords, hashtags, noun phrases, and verbatim extraction to derive insights from a Facebook brand page. Trend analysis on time-series data, and emotion analysis via the AlchemyAPI from IBM, are also introduced.

Chapter 4, *Analyzing Twitter Using Sentiment Analysis and Entity Recognition*, introduces you to Twitter, its uses, and the methodology to extract data using its REST and Streaming APIs using Python. You will learn to perform text mining techniques, such as stopword removal, stemming using NLTK, and more customized cleaning such as device detection. We will also introduce the concept and application of sentiment analysis using a popular Python library, VADER. This chapter will demonstrate the classification technique of machine learning to build a custom sentiment analysis algorithm.

Chapter 5, *Campaigns and Consumer Reaction Analytics on YouTube - Structured and Unstructured*, demonstrates the analysis of both structured and unstructured data, combining the concepts we learned earlier with newer ones. We will explain the characteristics of YouTube and how campaigns and channel popularity are measured using a combination of traffic and sentiment data from user comments. This will also serve as an introduction to the Google developer platform needed to access and extract the data.

Chapter 6, *The Next Great Technology - Trends Mining on GitHub*, introduces you to GitHub, its API, and characteristics. This chapter will demonstrate how to analyze trends on GitHub to discover projects and technologies that gather the most interest from users. We use GitHub data around repositories such as watchers, forks, and open issues to while making interesting analysis to infer the most emerging projects and technologies.

Chapter 7, Scraping and Extracting Conversational Topics on Internet Forums, introduces public consumer forums with real-world examples and explains the importance of forum conversations for extracting insights about people and topics. You will learn the methodology to extract forum data using Scrapy and BeautifulSoup in Python. We'll apply the preceding techniques on a popular car forum and use Topic Models to analyze all the conversations around cars.

Chapter 8, *Demystifying Pinterest through Network Analysis of Users Interests*, introduces an emerging and important social network, Pinterest, along with the advanced social network analysis concept of Graph Mining. Along with the Pinterest API, we will introduce the technique of advanced scraping using Selenium. You will learn to extract data from Pinterest to build a graph of pins and boards. The concepts will help you analyze and visualize the data to find the most influential topics and users on Pinterest. You will also be introduced to the concept of community detection using Python modules.

Chapter 9, *Social Data Analytics at Scale - Spark and Amazon Web Services*, takes the reader on a tour of distributed and parallel computing. This chapter will be an introduction to implementing Spark, a popular open source cluster-computing framework. You will learn to get Python scripts ready to run at scale and execute Spark jobs on the Amazon Web Services cloud.

What you need for this book

The goal of the book is to explain the concept of social media analytics and demonstrate its applications using Python. We use Python 3 for the different concepts and projects in the book. You will need a Linux/macOS or Windows machine with Python 3 and an IDE of your choice (Sublime Text 2, Atom, or gedit). All the libraries presented in the chapters can be easily installed with pip package manager. It is advisable to use the Python library Jupyter to work in notebook mode.

The data will be stored in MongoDB, which is compatible with all operating systems. You can follow the installation instruction on the official website (`https://www.mongodb.com`).

Lastly, a good internet connection is a must to be able to process big volumes of data from social networks.

Who this book is for

If you are a programmer or a data analyst familiar with the Python programming language and want to perform analyses of your social data to acquire valuable business insights, this book is for you. The book does not assume any prior knowledge of any data analysis tool or process.

Conventions

In this book, you will find a number of text styles that distinguish between different kinds of information. Here are some examples of these styles and an explanation of their meaning.

Code words in text, database table names, folder names, filenames, file extensions, pathnames, dummy URLs, user input, and Twitter handles are shown as follows: "Let's first create a project called `tutorial`."

A block of code is set as follows:

```
#import packages into the project
from bs4 import BeautifulSoup
from urllib.request import urlopen
import pandas as pd
```

Any command-line input or output is written as follows:

```
mkdir tutorial
cd tutorial
scrapy startproject tutorial
```

New terms and **important words** are shown in bold.

Words that you see on the screen, for example, in menus or dialog boxes, appear in the text like this: "On a forum, usually the depth of pages is between three and five due to the standard structure such as **Topics** | **Conversations** | **Threads**, which means the spider usually has to travel three to five levels of depth to actually reach the conversational data."

 Warnings or important notes appear like this.

 Tips and tricks appear like this.

Reader feedback

Feedback from our readers is always welcome. Let us know what you think about this book-what you liked or disliked. Reader feedback is important for us as it helps us develop titles that you will really get the most out of. To send us general feedback, simply e-mail feedback@packtpub.com, and mention the book's title in the subject of your message. If there is a topic that you have expertise in and you are interested in either writing or contributing to a book, see our author guide at www.packtpub.com/authors.

Customer support

Now that you are the proud owner of a Packt book, we have a number of things to help you to get the most from your purchase.

Downloading the example code

You can download the example code files for this book from your account at http://www.packtpub.com. If you purchased this book elsewhere, you can visit http://www.packtpub.com/support, and register to have the files e-mailed directly to you. You can download the code files by following these steps:

1. Log in or register to our website using your e-mail address and password.
2. Hover the mouse pointer on the **SUPPORT** tab at the top.

3. Click on **Code Downloads & Errata**.
4. Enter the name of the book in the **Search** box.
5. Select the book for which you're looking to download the code files.
6. Choose from the drop-down menu where you purchased this book from.
7. Click on **Code Download**.

Once the file is downloaded, please make sure that you unzip or extract the folder using the latest version of:

- WinRAR / 7-Zip for Windows
- Zipeg / iZip / UnRarX for Mac
- 7-Zip / PeaZip for Linux

The code bundle for the book is also hosted on GitHub at `https://github.com/PacktPublishing/Python-Social-Media-Analytics`. We also have other code bundles from our rich catalog of books and videos available at `https://github.com/PacktPublishing/`. Check them out!

Errata

Although we have taken every care to ensure the accuracy of our content, mistakes do happen. If you find a mistake in one of our books-maybe a mistake in the text or the code-we would be grateful if you could report this to us. By doing so, you can save other readers from frustration and help us improve subsequent versions of this book. If you find any errata, please report them by visiting `http://www.packtpub.com/submit-errata`, selecting your book, clicking on the **Errata Submission Form** link, and entering the details of your errata. Once your errata are verified, your submission will be accepted and the errata will be uploaded to our website or added to any list of existing errata under the Errata section of that title. To view the previously submitted errata, go to `https://www.packtpub.com/books/content/support`, and enter the name of the book in the search field. The required information will appear under the **Errata** section.

Piracy

Piracy of copyrighted material on the Internet is an ongoing problem across all media. At Packt, we take the protection of our copyright and licenses very seriously. If you come across any illegal copies of our works in any form on the Internet, please provide us with the location address or website name immediately so that we can pursue a remedy. Please contact us at copyright@packtpub.com with a link to the suspected pirated material. We appreciate your help in protecting our authors and our ability to bring you valuable content.

Questions

If you have a problem with any aspect of this book, you can contact us at questions@packtpub.com, and we will do our best to address the problem.

1
Introduction to the Latest Social Media Landscape and Importance

Have you seen the movie *The Social Network*? If you have not, it could be a good idea to see it before you read this book. If you have, you may have seen the success story around Mark Zuckerberg and his company Facebook. This was possible due to power of the platform in connecting, enabling, sharing, and impacting the lives of almost two billion people on this planet.

The earliest social networks existed as far back as 1995; such as Yahoo (Geocities), theglobe.com, and tripod.com. These platforms were mainly to facilitate interaction among people through chat rooms. It was only at the end of the 90s that user profiles became the in thing in social networking platforms, allowing information about people to be discoverable, and therefore, providing a choice to make friends or not. Those embracing this new methodology were Makeoutclub, Friendster, SixDegrees.com, and so on.

MySpace, LinkedIn, and Orkut were thereafter created, and the social networks were on the verge of becoming mainstream. However, the biggest impact happened with the creation of Facebook in 2004; a total game changer for people's lives, business, and the world. The sophistication and the ease of using the platform made it into mainstream media for individuals and companies to advertise and sell their ideas and products. Hence, we are in the age of social media that has changed the way the world functions.

Since the last few years, there have been new entrants in the social media, which are essentially of different interaction models as compared to Facebook, LinkedIn, or Twitter. These are Pinterest, Instagram, Tinder, and others. Interesting example is Pinterest, which unlike Facebook, is not centered around people but is centered around interests and/or topics. It's essentially able to structure people based on their interest around these topics. CEO of Pinterest describes it as a *catalog of ideas*. Forums which are not considered as regular social networks, such as Facebook, Twitter, and others, are also very important social platforms. Unlike in Twitter or Facebook, forum users are often anonymous in nature, which enables them to make in-depth conversations with communities. Other non-typical social networks are video sharing platforms, such as YouTube and Dailymotion. They are non-typical because they are centered around the user-generated content, and the social nature is generated by the sharing of these content on various social networks and also the discussion it generates around the user commentaries. Social media is gradually changing from being platform centric to focusing more on experiences and features. In the future, we'll see more and more traditional content providers and services becoming social in nature through sharing and conversations. The term social media today includes not just social networks but every service that's social in nature with a wide audience.

To understand the importance of social media, it's interesting to look at the statistics of these platforms. It's estimated that out of around 3.4 billion internet users, 2.3 billion of them are active social media users. This is a staggering number, reinforcing the enormous importance of social media. In terms of users of individual social media platforms, Facebook leads the way with almost 1.6 billion active users. You must have heard the adage that if Facebook were a country, it would be second largest one after China and ahead of India. Other social platforms linked to Facebook are also benefiting from this user base, such as WhatsApp, hosting 1 billion users on its chat application, and Instagram, with 400 million on its image sharing social network.

Among other platforms, Tumblr and Twitter lead the way with 550 million and 320 million active users respectively. LinkedIn, the world's most popular professional social media has 100 million active users. Pinterest, which is a subject of a later chapter, also has 100 million active users. Seina and Weibo, the equivalents of Facebook and Twitter in China, alone host 222 million active users. In terms of growth and engagement, Facebook is still the fastest growing social media, way ahead of the rest. If we look at engagement, millennials (age group 18-34) spend close to 100 minutes on average per person per month on Facebook. The number is way lower for others. Among user-generated content and sharing platforms, YouTube is a leader with 300 hours of video uploaded every minute and 3.25 billion hours of video watched every month.

In this chapter, we will cover the following topics:

- Social graph
- Introduction to the latest social media landscape and importance
- What does social data mean in the modern world?
- Tools and their specificities to mine the social web (Python, APIs, and machine learning)

Introducing social graph

A **social graph** is created through this widespread interaction and exchange of information on social media. A social graph is a massive network that illustrates the relations between individuals and information on the internet. Facebook owns the largest social graph of relations of 1.5 billion users. Every social media has its own social graph. The nature of social graph and its utility can be of various types, based on the types of relations described as follows. We will show a concrete example of a piece of the social graph and how to analyze it.

- **User graph**: This is a network that shows the relationships between users or individuals connected to each other.
- **Content graph**: As there are billions of content being uploaded on social media, there is a relationship existing between different types of content (text, images, videos, or multimedia). These relations could be based on semantic sense around those content, or in-bond or out-bond links between them, like that of the Google's page rank.
- **Interest graph**: The interest graph takes the original graphs a step further, where individuals on the social media or the internet are not related based on their mere links, like being added as a friend or followed on Twitter, but on their mutual interests. This has a huge advantage over standard social graph, in the sense that it leads to finding communities of people with similar interests. Even if these people have no interaction or know each other personally, there is an inherent link based on their interests and passions.

Notion of influence

This massive growth and interaction on the social web is leading the way to understand these individuals. Like in a society there are influencers, the same phenomenon is getting replicated on the social web. There are people who have more influence over other users. The process of finding influencers and calculating influence is becoming an important science. If you have used a service called Klout, you'll know what we are talking about. Klout gives a 'social influence score' based on your social media activities. There are questions about the relevance of such scores, but that's only because the influence of a person is a very relative topic. In fact, in our view, no one is an influencer while everyone's an influencer. This can sound very confusing but what we are trying to say is that influence is relative. Someone who is an influencer to you may not be an influencer to another. If you need admission of your child to a school, the principal of the school is an influencer, but if you are seeking admission to a university, the same principal is not an influencer to you. This confusion makes the topic super exciting; trying to understand human dynamics and then figuring out who influences whom and how. Merely having thousands of followers on Twitter doesn't make one an influencer but the influencer of his or her followers and the way they are influenced to take action, sure does. Our book will not get into detailed aspects of influence but it's important to keep in mind this notion while trying to understand social media analytics.

Social impacts

Social media is already having a profound influence on both society and business. The societal impact has been both psychological and behavioral. Various events, crises, and issues in the world have received a boost because of the use of social media by millions of people. Stating a few examples would be that of the Arab Spring and the refugee crisis. In environmental crisis, such as earthquakes, social media like Twitter has proved in accelerating information and action because of its immediacy of dissemination and spread.

Platforms on platform

Social media companies like Facebook started presenting their technology as a platform, where programmers could build further tools to give rise to more social experiences, such as games, contests, and quizzes, which in turn gave rise to social interactions and experiences beyond mere conversational interaction. Today, there is a range of tools that allows one to build over the platforms. Another application of this is to gather intelligence through the data collected from these platforms. Twitter shares a lot of its data around the usage of its platform with programmers and companies. Similarly, most of the popular social networks have started sharing their data with developers and data warehousing companies. Sharing their data serves revenue growth, and is also a very interesting source for researchers and marketers to learn about people and the world.

Delving into social data

The data acquired from social media is called **social data**. Social data exists in many forms.

The types of social media data can be information around the users of social networks, like name, city, interests, and so on. These types of data that are numeric or quantifiable are known as **structured data**.

However, since social media are platforms for expression, a lot of the data is in the form of texts, images, videos, and such. These sources are rich in information, but not as direct to analyze as structured data described earlier. These types of data are known as **unstructured data**.

The process of applying rigorous methods to make sense of the social data is called **social data analytics**. In the book, we will go into great depth in social data analytics to demonstrate how we can extract valuable sense and information from these really interesting sources of social data. Since there are almost no restrictions on social media, there are lot of meaningless accounts, content, and interactions. So, the data coming out of these streams is quite noisy and polluted. Hence, a lot of effort is required to separate the information from the noise. Once the data is cleaned and we are focused on the most important and interesting aspects, we then require various statistical and algorithmic methods to make sense out of the filtered data and draw meaningful conclusions.

Understanding semantics

A concept important to understand when handling unstructured data is **semantics**. Dictionaries define the term as *the branch of linguistics and logic concerned with meaning*.

It is a concept that comes from linguistic science and philosophy, to deal with the study and research of meaning. These meanings are uncovered by understanding the relationship between words, phrases, and all types of symbols. From a social media point of view, symbol could be the popular emoticons, which are not exactly formal language but they signify emotions. These symbols can be extended to images and videos, where patterns in their content can be used to extract meanings. In the later chapters, we will show few techniques that can help you to get meaning out of textual data. Extracting meaning or sense from images and videos is out of scope for the book. Semantic technology is very central to effectively analyzing unstructured social data.

For effectively extracting sense out of social data, semantic technologies have underlying artificial intelligence or machine learning algorithms. These algorithms allow you to find patterns in the data, which are then humanly interpreted. That's why social data analytics is so exciting, as it brings together knowledge from the fields of semantics and machine learning, and then binds it with sociology for business or other objectives.

Defining the semantic web

The growth of the internet has given rise to platforms like websites, portals, search engines, social media, and so on. All of these have created a massive collection of content and documents. Google and other search engines have helped to organize these documents and make them accessible to everyday users. So, today we are able to search our questions and select websites or pages that are linked to the answer. Even social media content is more and more accessible via search engines. You may find a tweet that you created two years back suddenly showing on a Google result. The problem of organization of web content is almost a solved problem. However, wouldn't it be more exciting if you asked a question on Google, Bing, or another search engine and it directly gave you the answer, just like a friend with the required knowledge? This is exactly what the future web would look like and would do. Already, for example, if you put the query on Google about *what's the temperature in Paris?* or *who is the wife of Barack Obama?*, it gives you the right answer. The ability of Google to do this is inherently semantic technology with natural language processing and machine learning. Algorithms that Google has behind its search engine creates links between queries and content by understanding relation between words, phrases, and actual answers.

However, today only a fixed number of questions can be answered, as there is big risk of inferring wrong answers on multiple questions. The future of the internet will be an extension to the World Wide Web, which is the semantic web. The term was coined by the creator of the World Wide Web, Tim Berners-Lee. The semantic web is a complex concept on a simple idea of connecting entities (URLs, pages, and content) on the web through relations, but the underlying implementation is difficult at scale, due to the sheer volume of entities present on the internet. New markup languages called **Resource Description Framework** (**RDF**) and **Web Ontology Language** (**OWL**) will be used to create these links between pages and content, based on relations. These new languages will allow creators of content to add meaning to their documents, which machines could process for reasoning or inference purposes, allowing automating many tasks on the web. Our book is not about explaining the underlying concepts of the semantic web, but just for your knowledge about where the web is heading and to appreciate the needs to mine the web more intelligently, as you'll learn in the later chapters.

Exploring social data applications

Now that you know where the future of the web is heading, let's shift our focus back to our discussion on the purpose of analyzing the social web data. We have discussed about the nature of social media and the social data, structured and unstructured, but you must be curious as to how this is used in the real world. In our view, restricting the application of social data analytics to certain fields or sectors is not entirely fair. Social data analytics leads you to the learning or discovery of facts or knowledge. If acquiring knowledge can't be restricted to a few fields, neither can be social media analytics. However, there are some fields that are prospering more from this science, such as marketing, advertising, and research communities. Social media data is being integrated more and more in existing digital services to provide a much more personalized experience through recommendations. You must have seen that most online services allow you to register using your social profiles along with added information. When you do so, the service is able to mine your social data and recommend products or catalogs aligned with your interests. Entertainment services like Spotify and Netflix, or e-commerce ones like Amazon, eBay, and others, are able to propose personalized recommendations based on social data analytics and other data sources. More traditional companies selling consumer products derive value from social data in their marketing of products and brands. People use social networks as a means to both connect with companies and to express about their products and services. Hence, there is a huge amount of data on the social web that contains customer preferences and complaints about companies. This is an example of unstructured-social data, since it's mostly textual or images in format. Companies are analyzing this data to understand how consumers feel and use their services or campaigns, and then are using this intelligence to integrate it in their marketing and communications.

A similar approach has been applied in political campaigns to understand the opinion of people on various political issues. Analysts and data scientists have gone as far as trying to predict election results using sentiments of people about the concerned politicians. There are certainly many data scientists using social media data to predict the results of Clinton and Trump elections. There have been attempts to predict the stock market using social data but this has not been very successful, as financial data is highly sensitive and volatile and so is social data, and combining the two is still a big challenge.

In the later chapters, you'll see how we can analyze the Facebook page of a brand to understand their relation with their consumers. In Chapter 7, *Scraping and Extracting Conversational Topics on Internet Forums* about analyzing forums, you'll see how we are able to understand deeper conversations regarding certain subjects. Building recommendation engines is beyond the scope of the book, but you'll know enough about social data in order to integrate it for your recommender system projects.

Now that you know enough about social media, social data, and their applications, we will dive into the methods to get on top of social data. Among the many techniques used to analyze social data, machine learning is one of the most effective ones.

Understanding the process

Once you are familiar with the topic of social media data, let us proceed to the next phase. The first step is to understand the process involved in exploitation of data present on social networks. A proper execution of the process, with attention to small details, is the key to good results. In many computer science domains, a small error in code will lead to a visible or at least correctable dysfunction, but in data science, it will produce entirely wrong results, which in turn will lead to incorrect conclusions.

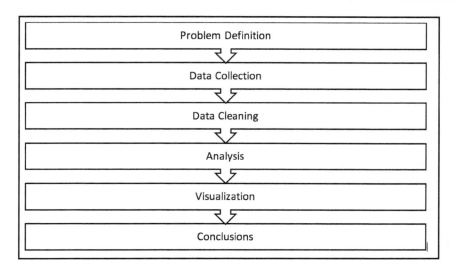

The very first step of data analysis is always **problem definition**. Understanding the problem is crucial for choosing the right data sources and the methods of analysis. It also helps to realize what kind of information and conclusions we can infer from the data and what is impossible to derive. This part is very often underestimated while it is key to successful data analysis.

Any question that we try to answer in a data science project has to be very precise. Some people tend to ask very generic questions, such as *I want to find trends on Twitter*. This is not a correct problem definition and an analysis based on such statement can fail in finding relevant trends. By a naïve analysis, we can get repeating Twitter ads and content generated by bots. Moreover, it raises more questions than it answers. In order to approach the problem correctly, we have to ask in the first step: *what is a trend? what is an interesting trend for us? and what is the time scope?* Once we answer these questions, we can break up the problem in multiple sub problems: *I'm looking for the most frequent consumer reactions about my brand on Twitter in English over the last week* and *I want to know if they were positive or negative*. Such a problem definition will lead to a relevant, valuable analysis with insightful conclusions.

The next part of the process consists of *getting the right data* according to the defined problem. Many social media platforms allow users to collect a lot of information in an automatized way via **APIs (Application Programming Interfaces)**, which is the easiest way to complete the task. However, other platforms, such as forums or blogs, usually require a customized programming approach (scraping), which will be explained in later chapters.

Once the data is stored in a database, we perform the *cleaning*. This step requires a precise understanding of the project's goals. In many cases, it will involve very basic tasks such as duplicates removal, for example, retweets on Twitter, or more sophisticated such as spam detection to remove irrelevant comments, language detection to perform linguistic analysis, or other statistical or machine learning approaches that can help to produce a clean dataset.

When the data is ready to be analyzed, we have to choose what kind of analysis and structure the data accordingly. If our goal is to understand the sense of the conversations, then it only requires a simple list of verbatims (textual data), but if we aim to perform analysis on different variables, like number of likes, dates, number of shares, and so on, the data should be combined in a structure such as data frame, where each row corresponds to an observation and each column to a variable.

The choice of the analysis method depends on the objectives of the study and the type of data. It may require statistical or machine learning approach, or a specific approach to time series. Different approaches will be explained on the examples of Facebook, Twitter, YouTube, GitHub, Pinterest, and Forum data, subsequently in the book.

Once the analysis is done, it's time to **infer conclusions**. We can derive conclusions based on the outputs from the models, but one of the most useful tools is visualization technique. Data and output can be presented in many different ways, starting from charts, plots, and diagrams through more complex 2D charts, to multidimensional visualizations. These techniques are shown in example chapters as well as the reasoning process to infer insightful conclusions.

Once the process is clear enough, we can start setting up the programming environment.

Working environment

The choice of the right tools is decisive for the smooth execution of the process. There are some important parts of the environment which facilitate data manipulation and algorithm implementation, but above all, they make the data science reproducible. We have selected the main components, which are widely used by data scientists all over the world, related to programming language, integrated development environment, and version control system.

Defining Python

Python is one of the most common programming languages among data scientists, along with R. The main advantage of Python is its flexibility and simplicity. It makes the data analysis and manipulation easy by offering a lot of packages. It shows great performance in analyzing unstructured textual data and has a very good ecosystem of tools and packages for this purpose.

For the purposes of the book, we have chosen Python 3.5.2. It is the most up-to-date version, which implements many improvements compared to Python 2.7. The main advantage in text analysis is an automatic management of Unicode variables. Python 2.7 is still widely used by programmers and data scientists due to a big choice of external libraries, documentation, and online resources. However, the new version has already reached a sufficient level of compatibility with packages, and on top of it, offers multiple new features.

We will use the `pip` command tool for installation of all libraries and dependencies.

Selecting an IDE

The choice of **IDE** (**Integrated Development Environment**) is mostly a matter of personal preferences. The most common choices are PyCharm, Sublime Text, or Atom. PyCharm is a very complete development environment while Sublime Text is a lightweight text editor which allows us to install additional plugins. Its main advantage is the fact that the user can choose the tools that he needs for his development. Atom is the newest software of all three, similar to Sublime Text. It was developed by GitHub and integrates by default the git version control system. In the book, we will use Sublime Text as the simplest and the easiest solution to start data analysis and development.

Illustrating Git

A version control system is one of the main elements of programming process. It helps to manage different versions of the code over time and reverse the changes in case of errors or wrong approach. The most widespread and easy-to-use version control system is Git and we will use it in our examples.

Getting the data

Data harvesting is the entry point for any social media analysis project. There are two main ways to collect data for an analysis: by connecting to APIs or by crawling and scraping the social networks. It is crucial to understand how the data was collected in order to be aware of the bias that might introduced. Different harvesting techniques will require customized approaches to data preprocessing and analysis workflow, which we will explain in further chapters.

Defining API

A widely used term, **API (Application Programming Interface)** is defined as a set of instructions and standards to access a web based software application. But what does it mean in real life? Firstly, APIs allow users to send a request for a particular resource, such as Facebook or Twitter , and receive some data in response. It is worth noting that all API providers fix some limitations on the quantity or type of data which users can obtain. APIs give access data processing resources, such as AlchemyAPI that receives in a request verbatim (textual data) and sends in response all results of the analysis, such as nouns, verbs, entities, and so on. In our case, the APIs are used either to get data from social networks or to execute some complex processing on them.

In order to access and manipulate APIs, we have to install the `urllib2` library:

```
pip3 install urllib2
```

In some cases, if you fail to perform the installation. You can also try using the `request` library, which is compatible with Python 2.x and 3.x.

```
pip3 install request
```

Scraping and crawling

Scraping (or web scraping) is a technique to extract information from websites. When we do not have access to APIs, we can only retrieve visible information from HTML generated on a web page. In order to perform the task, we need a scraper that is able to extract information that we need and structure it in a predefined format. The next step is to build a crawler—a tool to follow links on a website and extract the information from all sub pages. When we decide to build a scraping strategy, we have to take into consideration the terms and conditions, as some websites do not allow scraping.

Python offers very useful tools to create scrapers and crawlers, such as `beautifulsoup` and `scrapy`.

```
pip3 install bs4, scrapy
```

Analyzing the data

In this section, we briefly introduce the main techniques which lie behind the social media analysis process and bring intelligence to the data. We also present how to deal with reasonably big amount of data using our development environment. However, it is worth noting that the problem of scaling and dealing with massive data will be analyzed in `Chapter 9`, *Social Data Analytics at Scale - Spark and Amazon Web Services*.

Brief introduction to machine learning

The recent growth in the volume of data created by mobile devices and social networks has dramatically impacted the need for high performance computation and new methods of analysis. Historically, large quantities of data (big data) were analyzed by statistical approaches which were based on sampling and inductive reasoning to derive knowledge from data. A more recent development of artificial intelligence, and more specifically, machine learning, enabled not only the ability to deal with large volume of data, but it brought a tremendous value to businesses and consumers by extracting valuable insights and hidden patterns.

Machine learning is not new. In 1959, Arthur Samuel defined machine learning as:

> *Field of study that gives computers ability to learn without being specifically programmed for it.*

Within the field of data analytics, machine learning is a method used to devise complex models and algorithms that allow to This approach is similar to a person who increases his knowledge on a subject by reading more and more books on the subject. There are three main approaches in machine learning: **supervised learning**, **unsupervised learning**, and **reinforcement learning.**

Supervised learning assumes that we know what the outputs are of each data point. For example, we learn that a car that costs $80,000, which has an electric engine and acceleration of 0-100 km/h in 3 seconds, is called Tesla; another car, which costs $40,000, has a diesel engine, and acceleration of 0-100 km/h in 9.2 seconds, is called Toyota; and so on. Then, when we look for the name of a car which costs $35,000, has acceleration of 0-100 km/h in 9.8 seconds, and has a diesel engine, it is most probably Toyota and not Tesla.

Unsupervised learning is used when we do not know the outputs. In the case of cars, we only have technical specifications: acceleration, price, engine type. Then we cluster the data points into different groups (clusters) of similar cars. In our case, we will have the clusters with similar price and engine types. Then, we understand similarities and differences between the cars.

The third type of machine learning is **reinforcement learning**, which is used more in artificial intelligence applications. It consists of devising an algorithm that learns how to behave based on a system of rewards. This kind of learning is similar to the natural human learning process. It can be used in teaching an algorithm how to play chess. In the first step, we define the environment—the chess board and all possible moves. Then the algorithm starts by making random moves and earns positive or negative rewards. When a reward is positive, it means that the move was successful, and when it is negative, it means that it has to avoid such moves in the future. After thousands of games, it finishes by knowing all the best sequences of moves.

In real-life applications, many hybrid approaches are widely used, based on available data and the complexity of problems.

Techniques for social media analysis

Machine learning is a basic tool to add intelligence and extract valuable insights from social media data. There exist other widespread concepts that are used for social media analysis: Text Analytics, Natural Language Processing, and Graph Mining.

The first notion allows to retrieve non trivial information from textual data, such as brands or people names, relationships between words, extraction of phone numbers, URLs, hashtags, and so on. Natural Language Processing is more extensive and aims at finding the meaning of the text by analyzing text structure, semantics, and concepts among others.

Social networks can also be represented by graph structures. The last mining technique enables the structural analysis of such networks. These methods help in discovering relationships, paths, connections and clusters of people, brands, topics, and so on, in social networks.

The applications of all the techniques will be presented in following chapters.

Setting up data structure libraries

In our analysis, we will use some libraries that enable flexible data structures, such as pandas and `sframe`. The advantage of `sframe` over pandas is that it helps to deal with very big datasets which do not fit RAM memory. We will also use a `pymongo` library to pull collected data from MongoDB, as shown in the following code:

```
pip3 install pandas, sframe, pymongo
```

All necessary machine learning libraries will be presented in corresponding chapters.

Visualizing the data

Visualization is one of the most important parts of data science process. It helps in the initial steps of analysis, for example, to choose the right method or algorithm according to the structure of the data, but essentially to present in a simple way the obtained results. Python ecosystem proposes many interesting libraries, such us `plotly`, `matplotlib`, and `seaborn`, among others, as follows. In the following chapters, we will focus on three of them.

```
pip3 install plotly, matplotlib, seaborn
```

Getting started with the toolset

Once you set up the whole environment, you can create your first project. If you use Linux or macOS machine, you can open a terminal and go to your working directory. Then, use the following command to create your project directory:

```
mkdir myproject
```

On Windows machines, you can create the directory in the usual way without terminal.

At the same time, we initialize an empty repository in Git (in terminal on Linux or macOS, or in Git bash on Windows):

```
cd myproject
git init
```

Then, you can open your directory in Sublime Text 2 using its **GUI** (**Graphical User Interface**) and create your first Python file. Now it's time to start working on a real project.

Summary

The avalanche of social network data is a result of communication platforms being developed for the last two decades. These are the platforms that evolved from chat rooms to personal information sharing and finally, social and professional networks. Among many, Facebook, Twitter, Instagram, Pinterest, and LinkedIn have emerged as the modern day social media. These platforms collectively have reach of more than a billion individuals across the world, sharing their activities and interaction with each other. Sharing of their data by these media through APIs and other technologies has given rise to a new field called social media analytics. This has multiple applications, such as in marketing, personalized recommendations, research, and societal. modern data science techniques such as machine learning and text mining are widely used for these applications. Python is one of the most programming languages used for these techniques. However, manipulating the *unstructured-data* from social networks requires a lot of precise processing and preparation before coming to the most interesting bits.

In the next chapter, we will see the way this data from social networks can be harnessed, processed, and prepared to make a sandbox for interesting analysis and applications in the subsequent chapters.

2
Harnessing Social Data - Connecting, Capturing, and Cleaning

The first step to realize the promise of social data, which we went through in `Chapter 1`, *Introduction to the Latest Social Media Landscape and Importance*, is by harnessing it. A proper harnessing strategy can help to remove obstacles to and expedite processing. As we saw in the last chapter, many sources of social data can be used through the **Application Protocol Interfaces** (**APIs**) of these platforms. However, the data coming from APIs is not readily usable for multiple cases, hence it requires several steps before the data is ready to be analyzed and then applied. Therefore, we have dedicated a chapter that explains in detail how to do this. We have briefly touched upon the technical notion of an API in the first chapter. Here we intend to go deeper into it and help you to understand its types and usage. We also want to delve into its advantages and disadvantages so that you know exactly what to expect.

In the first chapter, we have seen the impact of social media on society at large. One of the best events in social media has been the ability to grow through the use of platforms and APIs. The sharing of data on social media platforms to third-party developers has resulted in thousands of creative applications of this data. It not only is a source of great learning for people, but also innovative use cases that impact the lives of millions of people. APIs also allow the creators of social media platforms to focus and build their platforms to perfection and let the creative applications of their data be exploited by anyone interested in them.

In this chapter, we will cover the following topics:

- Introduction to APIs and web services
- Introduction to authentication techniques
- Parsing API outputs
- Basic cleaning techniques
- Basic MongoDB administration

APIs in a nutshell

An API is the medium that allows the exchange of data points between a service and the programmer or user. API concepts have been widely used in the software industry when we needed different software to exchange data with with another. Mobile and internet applications have been using web services and APIs to enrich information from external sources. Social media also started creating APIs to share their data with third-party application developers. The popularity of data science has made APIs emerge also as a source for mining and knowledge creation. The nature of all social media is different, so are their APIs. The steps involved in making a connection may not differ greatly, but the data points we capture do.

Different types of API

Currently, two types of API are available. They are as follows:

- RESTful API
- Stream API

RESTful API

This is the most common type of API that most social media provides. The information from a REST API is static and is from historical data. The back history of data can vary from platform to platform. Facebook calls its REST API service Graph API.

Facebook, Twitter, and Pinterest among others have given access to their APIs to the public through robust data infrastructures. Another real-time version of the RESTful API of Twitter is the Streaming API. The two are inherently similar, but with different usages. We will explore the standard RESTful APIs of the most common platforms and also the Streaming API of Twitter.

REST stands for **Representational State Transfer** and it relies on the HTTP protocol for data transfer between machines. It has been created to simplify the transfer of data between machines unlike previous web services such as CORBA, RPC, and SOAP. Since the architecture of REST uses the HTTP protocol, it would be fair to assume that the WWW itself is based on RESTful design. Two of the most important uses of RESTful services are:

- `Get`: Procedure to receive data from a distant machine
- `Post`: Procedure to write data to a distant machine

Almost all the functionalities of a REST API can be used through the preceding two methods.

Stream API

You need a Stream API when the requirement is to collect data in real time, instead of back-dated from the platform. The Stream API of Twitter is widely used to collect real-time data from Twitter. The output is quite similar to that of a REST API apart from the real-time aspect. We'll see examples of the Twitter Stream API and its outputs.

Advantages of social media APIs

Social media APIs have many advantages. The main advantages are:

- **Social data**: APIs allow you to extract valuable data around Social Media users and content that is used for behavioral analysis and user insights.
- **App development**: Thousands of software and applications have been built using Social Media APIs that provide additional services on top of Social Media platforms.
- **Marketing**: Social media APIs are useful in automating marketing activities such as social media marketing by posting on platforms. It also helps in enriching marketing data through Social Data acquired about customers.

Limitations of social media APIs

However, there are some limitations too, which are:

- **Rate limits**: Social media companies need to take into account the amount of data that enters or leaves their systems. These are rules based on their infrastructural limitations and business objectives. We must not think of acquiring unlimited amounts of data at our own speeds. The amount of data and the speed of receiving are clearly stated by most social media platforms. We have to read them carefully and include them in our extraction strategy.
- **API changes**: This is one of the biggest challenges to deal with when developing applications or analysis using social data. Social media platforms are free to change or stop their API services own will. Such kinds of change or stoppage could severely impact development or analytics strategies. The only advice in such situations is to be prepared for it and have flexible systems to be able to adapt to the changes.
- **Legal**: This challenge is mainly in the use cases around social media APIs. The rules and regulations for social media platforms are strict about the type of usage of its data and services. We have to be conscious of the legal framework before thinking of our usage and applications. Any use of data from APIs that doesn't conform to the stipulated regulations risks legal implications.

Connecting principles of APIs

Connecting to social media platforms and using their API data services require a few steps to be configured before usage. There are nuanced differences between different platforms, but the following are the general steps that are applicable to almost all:

- **APP registration:** Almost every social media platform needs you to register your application on their website. It involves entering personal information and the objectives in using their API services. This step results in the generation of certain keys, which are called authentication and consumer keys.
- **Authentication**: Use the consumer keys (also called authentication keys) generated from the previous step to authenticate your application.
- **API endpoint hunting**: The API endpoints will be different for each provider, so it is necessary to read the provided documentation to identify which end points best correspond to your needs.

Introduction to authentication techniques

Getting data from different APIs requires a good understanding of the data structure and authentication techniques that allow external users to access the resources served by an API. Historically, there were multiple ways of accessing API resources, but nowadays there is one common protocol used by all the main social media networks. When you get into the developer documentation you will most probably encounter the problem of authentication referred to by an enigmatic term, OAuth.

What is OAuth?

OAuth is simply an authorization protocol that allows users to share data with an application without sharing the password. It is a way to obtain a secure authorization scheme based on a token-based authorization mechanism. There are two API authentication models using OAuth:

- User authentication
- Application authentication

User authentication

This is the most common form of resource authentication implementation. The signed request both identifies an application's identity in addition to the identity accompanying granted permissions of the end user making API calls on behalf of, represented by the user's access token.

Application authentication

Application authentication is a form of authentication where the application makes API requests on its own behalf, without a user context. API calls are often rate limited per API method, but the pool each method draws from belongs to your entire application at large, rather than from a per-user limit.

For the purposes of social media analysis, we will use in most cases application authentication by creating an application on each social media platform that will query the related API.

There are several steps that are required to put in place a client with OAuth authorization:

1. **Creating a user/developer account**: First of all, you have to register a user/developer account and provide personal information such as a valid email address, name, surname, country, and in many cases a valid telephone number (the verification process is done by sending you a text message with a code).

2. **Creating an application**: Once you create your account, you will have access to a dashboard, which is very often called a developer console. It provides all the functionalities to manage your developer account, create and delete applications, or monitor your quota. In order to obtain access credentials you will have to create your first application via this interface.

3. **Obtaining access tokens**: Then, you generate access tokens for your application and save them in a safe place. They will be used in your code to create an OAuth connection to the API.

4. **Authorizing HTTP requests (optional)**: Some APIs require HTTP request authorization, which means that a request has to contain an additional authorization header that provides the server with information about the identity of the application and permission scope.

5. **Setting up permission scopes (optional)**: Some APIs have the notion of multilevel permissions. In that case when you generate your API key you need to specify the scope for the key. Scope here refers to a set of allowed actions. Therefore, in cases where an application attempts an action that is out of its scope, it will be refused. This is designed as an additional security layer. Ideally one should use multiple API keys, each with restricted scopes, so that in the scenario where your API key is hijacked, due to the restrictions in its scope the level of potential harm is restricted.

6. **Connecting to the API using obtained access tokens**: When all the preceding steps are configured, you can make requests using your access tokens. Now, the only limitation is the request quota, which depends on each platform.

Why do we need to use OAuth?

Social media networks APIs aim to provide full interaction with third-party applications allowing all kinds of access within rate limits. Thus, applications can perform actions on behalf of their users and access their data. The main advantage of this protocol is full security and the fact that the connection protocol is standardized. Therefore, there are standard ways of writing code and using request libraries.

Moreover, an OAuth connection is the most proper and reliable technique that adheres to the developer policy defined by social network companies. The main advantage for the user is that it gives the highest available quota and very often more API endpoints to collect the data.

Connecting to social network platforms without OAuth

Although it is still possible to connect to multiple platforms without using OAuth, we strongly recommend using the presented approach. Even if you can generate a temporary access key that will help you to instantly collect some interesting data it may cause some issues on production code. Furthermore, as mentioned before, the quota will be much lower.

OAuth1 and OAuth2

You might find different version of OAuth on social media platforms: OAuth1 and OAuth2. OAuth2 is a fully rewritten improved version of OAuth1. It defines four roles for client, authorization server, resource server and resource owner while OAuth1 uses different concepts to describe the roles. There are also multiple technical differences related for example to cryptography, but a complete analysis is beyond the scope of this chapter. We can conclude that OAuth2 is slightly less complicated and easier to use.

Practical usage of OAuth

In this part of the chapter, we will see how to connect to the main social media using OAuth and how to get and parse the data. There are many libraries in Python 3 implementing the OAuth protocol. For the purposes of this book, we will show how to use a library called `requests`.

The `requests` library implements the whole range of authentication protocols and allows you to execute HTTP requests such as GET or POST.

Firstly, you have to import the library in your code:

```
import requests
```

If you are using the OAuth protocol, you import the related library:

```
from requests_oauthlib import OAuth1
```

Then, you have to create your authenticated connection using access tokens and application keys that you will find in the developer console:

```
auth = OAuth1('YOUR_APP_KEY', 'YOUR_APP_SECRET', 'USER_OAUTH_TOKEN',
'USER_OAUTH_TOKEN_SECRET')
```

Then, you can make GET requests:

```
r = requests.get('https://api.sampleurl.org/get',auth=auth)
```

Pass these parameters:

```
payload = {'key1': 'value1', 'key2': 'value2'}
r = requests.get('http://sampleurl.org/get', params=payload)
```

POST requests:

```
r = requests.post('http://sampleurl.org/post', data = {'key':'value'})
```

Also, a whole range of additional requests:

```
r = requests.put('http://sampleurl.org/put', data = {'key':'value'})
r = requests.delete('http://sampleurl.org/delete')
r = requests.head('http://sampleurl.org/get')
r = requests.options('http://sampleurl.org/get')
```

In order to parse the outputs, you can use different methods such as:

- `r.text()` This gets a string with request outputs
- `r.json()`: This gets JSON with request outputs
- `r.econding()`: This checks the encoding of the output

Parsing API outputs

The following subchapter will show you how to connect to different social networks and how to retrieve sample data.

Twitter

Twitter proposes three main APIs: the REST API, Streaming API, and the Ads API. We will be focused on the first two APIs, which provide respectively on-demand or stream data.

Creating application

As explained in the section about OAuth, you have to obtain credentials to be able to collect data from Twitter. There are some simple steps to perform this action:

1. Create a Twitter account or use your existing one.
2. Go to `https://apps.twitter.com/` and log in with your account.
3. Click on **Create your app** and submit your phone number. A valid phone number is required for the verification process. You can use your mobile phone number for one account only.
4. Fill the form, agree to the terms and conditions, and create your Twitter application.
5. Go to the **Keys and Access Tokens** tab, save your API key, and API secret and then click on **Create my access token** to obtain the Access token and Access token secret. These four elements will be required to establish a connection with the API.

Selecting the endpoint

An endpoint indicates where a particular resource can be accessed. It is represented by an URL that contains the name of the action. Even though there are multiple endpoints for each API, we will focus on those used in the next chapters of the book. All other endpoints/actions you can find in the official API documentation.

The Twitter REST API allows clients to retrieve a sample of tweets based on search criteria. The search request is made up of a Boolean query with some additional optional parameters (`to`, `from`, `list`, `url`, and `filter`). We will store the endpoint URL for this resource in a `url` variable:

```
url_rest = "https://api.twitter.com/1.1/search/tweets.json"
```

Similarly, we will use an endpoint URL for the Streaming API that returns a random sample stream of statuses:

```
url_streaming = "https://stream.twitter.com/1.1/statuses/sample.json"
```

We will use both variables to retrieve and parse the data.

Using requests to connect

Firstly, we include all necessary libraries. We have added the `json` library to be able to parse easily the outputs of the Twitter API and `urllib.parse`, which encodes a query string into a proper request URL:

```
import requests
from requests_oauthlib import OAuth1
import json
from urllib.parse import urlparse
```

In the first place, we define parameters that will be used to establish connections with the Twitter API and we create an OAuth client connection:

```
params = {
'app_key':'YOUR_APP_KEY',
 'app_secret':'YOUR_APP_SECRET',
 'oauth_token':'USER_OAUTH_TOKEN',
 'oauth_token_secret':'USER_OAUTH_TOKEN_SECRET'
}

auth = OAuth1(
params['app_key'],
    params['app_secret'],
    params['oauth_token'],
    params['oauth_token_secret']
)
```

 The structure of the queries depends on the definitions of the API. It is important to read the respective documentations to best exploit the APIs.

Firstly, we encode our query. We have chosen to search for three car brands: BMW, Mercedes, and Audi:

```
q = urlparse('BMW OR Mercedes OR Audi')
```

Then we execute a search request using our query and OAuth client:

```
results = requests.get(url_rest, auth=auth)
```

The request returned a list of tweets with all the meta information. We will convert it to JSON and print the content of each tweet we find under the `text` field.

```
for tweet in results.json():
print (tweet['text'])
```

Similarly, we make a request to the Streaming API to get all recent tweets.

```
stream_results = requests.get(url_streaming, stream=True)
```

We keep iterating through all the lines that are being returned.

```
for line in stream_results.iter_lines():
if line:
    decoded_line = line.decode('utf-8')
print(json.loads(decoded_line)['text'])
```

If the line exists we decode it to UTF-8 to make sure we manage the encoding issues and then we print a field `text` from JSON.

We will use both methods to get and pre-process data in a practical example in `Chapter 4`, *Analyzing Twitter Using Sentiment Analysis and Entity Recognition*.

Facebook

Facebook provides three APIs for different purposes:

- **Atlas API**: API for partners and advertisers
- **Graph API**: The primary way for apps to read and write to the Facebook social graph
- **Marketing API**: To build solutions for marketing automation with Facebook's advertising platform

In our data mining exercise will only focus on Graph API, which gives us access to our point of interest, which is the content posted by users: comments, shares, likes, photos, and so on. It is the primary way to collect data from Facebook platform using requests to query data. It also enables the automation of all the actions available on Facebook such as data uploads (photos or videos), likes, shares, and account management, among others. However, our focus is on data collection and not on account management.

The name Graph API is related to the structure of the platform, which in fact represents a social graph composed of:

- **Nodes**: All the main elements such as user, photo, page, and comment
- **Edges**: Relationships between nodes such as user photos and comments in posts
- **Fields**: Attributes that these nodes or edges can have such as location, name, birthday date, time, and so on

Creating an app and getting an access token

We show the following procedure to get access tokens that never expire.

1. Go to the website: `https://developers.facebook.com/apps/`.
2. Create an application.
3. Go to `https://developers.facebook.com/tools/explorer`.
4. Select your application from the **Graph API Explorer** drop-down menu.
5. Click on the **Get Access Token** button.
6. Select permissions from the form.
7. In the **Access token** input field click on the blue exclamation point icon. It will open a pop-up window.
8. In the pop-up window, click on **Open in Access Token Tool**. You will see token details. At this stage the token is valid for around one hour.
9. Click on the **Extend Access Token** button to get a token that will never expire.

You can save the token and use it in your application to collect data from Facebook. It is worth noticing that you will only have access to public information on Facebook. Your application has to have the right to access the data you wish to collect. In our case it is straightforward, because we will analyze public conversation around brands.

Selecting the endpoint

The main endpoint for Graph API which permits to access the Facebook resources. However, we have to specify which node we want to query and the other parameters we send to the API.

```
url = 'https://graph.facebook.com/v2.8/'
```

We will use version 2.8 of Facebook Graph API. There are small differences between versions, mostly in available endpoints, resources, and parameters. We use the basic functionalities of this API so switching between versions should not cause any problems in terms of endpoints and resources, but we have to check the documentation to pass the right arguments.

The are several scenarios we might be interested in. The first one is retrieving all the comments from a public page of a brand:

```
page_url = 'https://graph.facebook.com/v2.8/{page-id}/feed'
```

An example using Mercedes Benz France:

```
page_url = 'https://graph.facebook.com/v2.8/MercedesBenzFrance/feed'
```

In some cases, `{page-id}` may be represented by a number.

We can use the same logic to access another kind of resource such as photos for example:

```
page_url = 'https://graph.facebook.com/v2.8/{page-id}/photos'
```

All available resources are described in the official documentation for the API.

Connect to the API

The following are the steps to connect to the API:

1. Firstly, we import the required libraries as follows:

   ```
   import requests
   import json
   ```

2. Create a params variable that contains your access token.

   ```
   params = {'access_token': 'YOUR_ACCESS_TOKEN'}
   ```

3. Make a request to the feed for the Mercedes Benz page.

   ```
   page_url =
   'https://graph.facebook.com/v2.8/MercedesBenzFrance/feed'
   result = requests.get(page_url, params = params)
   ```

4. Parse the results as a JSON.

   ```
   data = result.json()
   ```

The `data` field contains a list of messages with the following fields: `message`, `created_at`, and `id`. We will print the content of messages.

```
for element in data['data']:
  print(element['message']
```

This simple method helps us access the content of conversations on Facebook pages. We will use this information to perform data mining and extract insights in `Chapter 3`, *Uncovering Brand Activity, Emotions, and Popularity on Facebook*.

GitHub

GitHub is one of the most important platforms for computer programmers and hobbyists. Its main goal is to host source code repositories and empower open source communities to work together on new technologies. The platform contains lots of valuable information about what is happening in the community of technology enthusiasts, what the trends are, what programming languages have started to emerge, and much more. We will use the data from GitHub to predict the trending technologies of the future.

Obtaining OAuth tokens programmatically

In order to start working with the GitHub API we are required to obtain the access token. This time we will obtain it programmatically, instead of manually in the developer console with the following steps:

1. In the first step import all the necessary libraries.

   ```
   import requests
   import json
   ```

2. You can define your access credentials.

   ```
   username = 'YOUR_GITHUB_USERNAME'
   password = 'YOUR_GITHUB_PASSWORD'
   ```

3. You send a POST request through the secure protocol HTTPS, using the following information as arguments: `username`, `password`, `scopes`, and `note`. Scopes define different access rights for your token. In our example, we will use the scopes `user` and `repo`. The `note` field is compulsory and gives a short description of your application.

```
url = 'https://api.github.com/authorizations'
note = 'my test application'

post_data = {'scopes':['user','repo'],'note': note }

response = requests.post(
    url,
    auth = (username, password),
    data = json.dumps(post_data),
    )
```

4. You can check if the API response was correct.

```
print ("API response:", response.text)
```

5. And save your token, which you can find in the `token` field of your response JSON.

```
token = response.json()['token']
```

Application tokens can also be generated manually via the user interface under the section settings/applications: `https://github.com/settings/applications`.

You can also manage all the generated tokens and revoke access.

Selecting the endpoint

The queries in our further project will be mostly based on searches within different repositories. In order to obtain results based on our criteria we will use the following endpoint:

```
url = "https://api.github.com/search/repositories"
```

The argument list is divided into three parts:

- `q`: Query
- `sort`: Field to sort on
- `order`: Ascending or descending

Within the query part we can add multiple additional arguments: we will use language (programming language the code is written in), created (the date it was created on) and pushed (the date of the last update in the repository).

Finally, the endpoint will contain all the arguments used for query:

```
url =
"https://api.github.com/search/repositories/q=QUERY+language:LANG+created:>
START_DATE +pushed:>PUSHED_DATE &sort=stars&order=desc"
```

We pass several variables in parameters of the GET request:

- `q=QUERY`: A string with keywords to match in the repository descriptions and names
- `language=LANG`: A programming language we are looking for
- `created:>START_DATE`: Filter repositories to get only the ones created after `START_DATE`
- `pushed:>PUSHED_DATE`: The date of the last push
- `sort=stars`: Sort by the number of stars
- `order=desc`: Descending order.

We will use this URL to query all GitHub public repositories.

Connecting to the API

Connecting to the API is very straightforward:

1. As usual, import all the relevant libraries.

    ```
    import requests
    import json
    ```

2. You define your access token obtained in the previous step.

    ```
    ACCESS_TOKEN = 'YOUR_ACCESS_TOKEN'
    ```

3. You add it as a parameter to the URL.

```
access_token_str = '&access_token= + ACCESS_TOKEN'
```

In this example, we used the parameters explained in the previous section:

```
url =
"https://api.github.com/search/repositories/q=QUERY+language:LANG+c
reated:>START_DATE+pushed:>PUSHED_DATE&sort=stars&order=desc"
```

4. We obtain a list of results in a response that we will parse as a JSON.

```
response = requests.get(url + access_token_str)
result = response.json()
```

In our project, we will use multiple fields of the results list elements.

YouTube

YouTube is certainly the most popular video sharing social network and helps users to share and monetize their media content. It has a very rich content ranging from amateur users to professionals recording quality videos. On top of the media content it contains different kinds of data such as comments, statistics, or captions automatically extracted from video sound. The main advantage of YouTube is the number of users and the volume of new videos uploaded every day. These numbers are huge and increase every day, making a data goldmine of this social media platform.

Creating an application and obtaining an access token programmatically

There are multiple ways to access YouTube data. We will focus on the most secure approach using OAuth authentication to access YouTube Data API resources. You can use the following steps:

1. The first step is to create a project on the Google Developer console (`https://console.developers.google.com/apis/`)
2. Then, you go to **Credentials**, click on **Create Client ID**, and choose **Other**.
3. You will get a Client ID and a Client Secret that you will use for the next step.

4. Firstly, we will use the `oauth2client` library to perform the first step in authorization:

```
from oauth2client.client import OAuth2WebServerFlow
```

5. Then, we use the credentials obtained in the previous step and we obtain the authorization URI:

```
client_id = 'YOUR_CLIENT_ID'
client_secret = 'YOUR_CLIENT_SECRET'

flow = OAuth2WebServerFlow(client_id=client_id,
client_secret=client_secret,
scope='https://gdata.youtube.com',
redirect_uri='YOUR_APP_URL')
auth_uri = flow.step1_get_authorize_url()
```

6. Then, you go to the following website in order to change the authorization token into an access token: `https://developers.google.com/oauthplayground/`.

You save the access token, which will be used to collect the data.

Selecting the endpoint

We have selected two endpoints that cover all the data needed for our analysis. We will use version 3 of the YouTube API, which introduced major changes compared to the previous versions regarding all aspects: endpoints, limitations, parameters, and so on.

The `search` method allows us to list all the videos related to the search query:

```
url = 'https://www.googleapis.com/youtube/v3/search'
```

The `commentThread` method gives us access to comments under each video:

```
url = 'https://www.googleapis.com/youtube/v3/commentThreads'
```

It's worth noticing that in the past you were only allowed to extract up to 1,000 comments per video, but the recent changes in the API allow you to extract as many as you need. The only requirement is to have enough credits (number of requests allowed per day) to perform the task. If you want to extract more content you will have to buy additional credits.

Connecting to the API

You can use the following steps to connect to the API:

1. In the first place, you import the required libraries.

    ```
    import requests, json
    ```

2. Then, you define the access token from the previous step.

    ```
    access_token = "YOUR_ACCESSS_TOKEN"
    ```

3. The next task consists of creating a search query in the YouTube database that will give you a list of videos that match the search criteria:

    ```
    query = 'YOUR_BOOLEAN_QUERY'

    url = 'https://www.googleapis.com/youtube/v3/search'

    params = {'part': 'snippet', 'q': query, 'type': 'video',
    'videoCaption': 'closedCaption', 'access_token': access_token}
    ```

4. You execute the request and get the data in response. The response is then converted into JSON to facilitate access to the data.

    ```
    response = requests.get(url, params = params)

    data = response.json()
    ```

5. You can print some sample data to see the results.

    ```
    for r in data['items']:
      print(r['snippet']['title'])
    ```

6. To illustrate the second endpoint, we use the results from the first example. We create a `video_id` variable and then we execute a request that retrieves all the comments for this resource.

    ```
    video_id = r['id']['videoId']


    url = 'https://www.googleapis.com/youtube/v3/commentThreads'
    params = {'part': 'snippet', 'videoId': video_id  , 'access_token':
    access_token}

    response = requests.get(url, params = params)
    ```

```
data = response.json()
```

7. We print all top-level comments.

```
for r in data['items']:
    print(r['snippet']['topLevelComment']['snippet']['textDisplay'])
```

We will combine these methods in the following chapters.

Pinterest

Pinterest has become one of the most important photo sharing platforms over the last few years. It allows users to share photos found on the internet with other users by creating pins. In our further analysis we will analyze the content and relationships between users.

In order to gather content, we have to establish a connection to the Pinterest API.

Creating an application

Like in other cases, the very first step is to create an application and obtain an access token in following steps:

1. Create a Pinterest account or use an existing one.
2. Go to `https://developers.pinterest.com/`.
3. Go to **Apps**.
4. Create a new app (you have to agree to the terms and conditions first).
5. You will be redirected to the app management interface where you can find your access token.
6. Save it for further use in your code.

Selecting the endpoint

There are multiples endpoints that we will be useful for network analysis. There are three main objects that we can get with the Pinterest API:

- User
- Board
- Pins

You can use the following steps:

1. Get the user information:

    ```
    /v1/<user>/
    ```

2. Get the user's followers:

    ```
    https://api.pinterest.com/v1/<user>/followers/
    ```

3. Get the user's friends:

    ```
    https://api.pinterest.com/v1/<user>/following/users/
    ```

4. Get user's boards:

    ```
    https://api.pinterest.com/v1/<user>/boards/
    ```

5. Get pins attached to a board:

    ```
    https://api.pinterest.com/v1/boards/<board>/pins/
    ```

We will use all the presented methods for the analysis.

Connecting to the API

In order to connect to the Pinterest API we follow the same logic as in the previous examples with the following steps:

1. Firstly, we import the libraries and define an access token and parameters.

    ```
    import requests

    access_token = 'YOUR_ACCESS_TOKEN'

    params = {'access_token': access_token, 'fields' : 'counts, bio,
    first_name, last_name'}
    ```

2. Then, we create a function that will make requests and parse the response as JSON.

    ```
    def pinterest(url, params):

      response = requests.get(url = url, params = params)

      return response.json()
    ```

3. We use the `pinterest` function to retrieve information from various endpoints.

```
me = pinterest(url = 'https://api.pinterest.com/v1/me', params =
{'access_token': access_token})

followers = pinterest(url =
'https://api.pinterest.com/v1/me/followers/', params =
{'access_token': access_token, 'fields': 'counts,
username'})['data']

following = pinterest(url =
'https://api.pinterest.com/v1/me/following/users/', params =
{'access_token': access_token, 'fields': 'counts,
username'})['data']
```

Once the OAuth framework becomes clear all the connections to the APIs look similar and follow the same logic. However, there are some nuances that may cause some problems for quick implementations. All the presented methods help to retrieve all necessary data and in the next step we will learn what data we get, how to clean it, and how to store it.

Basic cleaning techniques

Social media contains different types of data: information about user profiles, statistics (number of likes or number of followers), verbatims, and media. Quantitative data is very convenient for an analysis using statistical and numerical methods, but unstructured data such as user comments is much more challenging. To get meaningful information, one has to perform the whole process of information retrieval. It starts with the definition of the data type and data structure. On social media, unstructured data is related to text, images, videos, and sound and we will mostly deal with textual data. Then, the data has to be cleaned and normalized. Only after all these steps can we delve into the analysis.

Data type and encoding

Comments and conversation are textual data that we retrieve as strings. In brief, a string is a sequence of characters represented by code points. Every string in Python is seen as a Unicode covering the numbers from 0 through 0x10FFFF (1,114,111 decimal). Then, the sequence has to be represented as a set of bytes (values from 0 to 255) in memory. The rules for translating a Unicode string into a sequence of bytes are called encoding.

Encoding plays a very important role in natural language processing, because people use more and more characters such as emojis or emoticons, which replace whole words and express emotions ✍. Moreover, in many languages there are accents that go beyond the regular English alphabet. In order to deal with all the processing problems that might be caused by these we have to use the right encoding, because comparing two strings with different encodings is actually like comparing apples and oranges. The most common one is UTF-8, used by default in Python 3, which can handle any type of character. As a rule of thumb always normalize your data to Unicode UTF-8.

Structure of data

Another question we'll encounter is, What is the right structure for our data? The most natural choice is a list that can store a sequence of data points (verbatims, numbers, and so on). However, the use of lists will not be efficient on large datasets and we'll be constrained to use sequential processing of the data. That is why a much better solution is to store the data in a tabular format in pandas dataframe, which has multiple advantages for further processing. First of all, rows are indexed, so search operations become much faster. There are also many optimized methods for different kinds of processing and above all it allows you to optimize your own processing by using functional programming.

Moreover, a row can contain multiple fields with metadata about verbatims, which are very often used in our analysis.

It is worth remembering that the dataset in pandas must fit into RAM memory. For bigger datasets we suggest the use of SFrames.

Pre-processing and text normalization

Preprocessing is one of the most important parts of the analysis process. It reformats the unstructured data into uniform, standardized form. The characters, words, and sentences identified at this stage are the fundamental units passed to all further processing stages. The quality of the preprocessing has a big impact of the final result on the whole process.

There are several stages of the process: from simple text cleaning by removing white spaces, punctuation, HTML tags and special characters up to more sophisticated normalization techniques such as tokenization, stemming, or lemmatization. In general, the main aim is to keep all the characters and words that are important for the analysis and, at the same time, get rid of all others, and the text corpus should be maintained in one uniform format.

We import all necessary libraries.

```
import re, itertools
import nltk
from nltk.corpus import stopwords
```

When dealing with raw text, we usually have a set of words including many details we are not interested in, such as whitespace, line breaks, and blank lines. Moreover, many words contain capital letters so programming languages misinterpret for example, "go" and "Go" as two different words. In order to handle such distinctions, we can convert all words to lowercase format with the following steps:

1. Perform basic text mining cleaning.
2. Remove all whitespaces:

```
verbatim = verbatim.strip()
```

   Many text processing tasks can be done via pattern matching. We can find words containing a character and replace it with another one or just remove it. Regular expressions give us a powerful and flexible method for describing the character patterns we are interested in. They are commonly used in cleaning punctuation, HTML tags, and URLs paths.

3. Remove punctuation:

```
verbatim = re.sub(r'[^\w\s]','',verbatim)
```

4. Remove HTML tags:

```
verbatim = re.sub('<[^<]+?>', '', verbatim)
```

5. Remove URLs:

```
verbatim = re.sub(r'^https?:\/\/.*[\r\n]*', '', verbatim,
flags=re.MULTILINE)
```

   Depending on the quality of the text corpus, sometimes there is a need to implement some corrections. This refers to the text sources such as Twitter or forums, where emotions can play a role and the comments contain multiple letters words for example, "happpppy" instead of "happy".

6. Standardize words (remove multiple letters)

```
verbatim = ''.join(''.join(s)[:2] for _, s in
itertools.groupby(verbatim))
```

After removal of punctuation or white spaces, words can be attached. This happens especially when deleting the periods at the end of the sentences. The corpus might look like: "the brown dog is lostEverybody is looking for him". So there is a need to split "lostEverybody" into two separate words.

7. Split attached words

```
verbatim = " ".join(re.findall('[A-Z][^A-Z]*', verbatim))
```

Stop words are basically a set of commonly used words in any language: mainly determiners, prepositions, and coordinating conjunctions. By removing the words that are very commonly used in a given language, we can focus only on the important words instead, and improve the accuracy of the text processing.

8. Convert text to lowercase, `lower()`:

```
verbatim = verbatim.lower()
```

9. Stop word removal:

```
verbatim = ' '.join([word for word in verbatim.split() if word not
in (stopwords.words('english'))])
```

10. **Stemming and lemmatization**: The main aim of stemming and lemmatization is to reduce inflectional forms and sometimes derivationally related forms of a word to a common base form. Stemming reduces word forms to so-called **stems**, whereas lemmatization reduces word forms to linguistically valid lemmas.
    - Some examples of stemming are cars -> car, men -> man, and went -> go
    - Such text processing can give added value in some domains, and may improve the accuracy of practical information extraction tasks

11. **Tokenization**: Tokenization is the process of breaking a text corpus up into words (most commonly), phrases, or other meaningful elements, which are then called tokens. The tokens become the basic units for further text processing.

    ```
    tokens = nltk.word_tokenize(verbatim)
    ```

    Other techniques are spelling correction, domain knowledge, and grammar checking

Duplicate removal

Depending on data source we might notice multiple duplicates in our dataset. The decision to remove duplicates should be based on the understanding of the domain. In most cases, duplicates come from errors in data collection process and it is recommended to remove them in order to reduce bias in our analysis, with the help of the following:

```
df = df.drop_duplicates(subset=['column_name'])
```

Knowing basic text cleaning techniques, we can now learn how to store the data in an efficient way. For this purpose, we will explain how to use one of the most convenient NoSQL databases—MongoDB.

Capture: Once you have made a connection to your API you need to make a special request and receive the data at your end. This step requires you go through the data to be able to understand it. Often the data is received in a special format called **JavaScript Object Notation** (**JSON**). JSON was created to enable a lightweight data interchange between programs. The JSON resembles the old XML format and consists of a key-value pair.

Normalization: The data received from platforms are not in an ideal format to perform analysis.

With textual data there are many different approaches to normalization. One can be stripping whitespaces surrounding verbatims, or converting all verbatims to lowercase, or changing the encoding to UTF-8. The point is that if we do not maintain a standard protocol for normalization, we will introduce many unintended errors. The goal of normalization is to transform all your data in a consistent manner that ensures a uniform standardization of your data.

It is recommended that you create wrapper functions for your normalization techniques, and then apply these wrappers on all your data input points so as to ensure that all the data in your analysis go through exactly the same normalization process.

For example if you choose the following for normalization:

- Stripping surrounding whitespaces
- Lowercasing all verbatims
- Setting encoding to UTF-8

Then ideally you should have a normalization wrapper function as follows:

```
def encode_verbatim(text):
  return text.decode('utf-8')

def to_lowercase(text):
  return text.lower()

def strip_whitespace(text):
   return ' '.join(text.split())

def normalize_verbatim(verbatim):
   """
  Wrapper for the normalization protocol
   """
  return encode_verbatim(
    to_lowercase(
      strip_whitespaces(verbatim)
    )
  )
```

This is recommended practice because then we can simply apply the wrapper function on all the data input sources.

For example:

- Reading data from a file into a list:

```
lines = open('filename', 'r').readlines()
verbatims = [normalize_verbatim(v) for v in lines]
```

- Reading data from a file into pandas:

```
import pandas as pd
df = pd.DataFrame(open('filename', 'r').readlines(),
columns=['verbatim'])
df.verbatims.apply(normalize_verbatim)
```

- Reading data from a Mongo database to pandas:

```
from pymongo import MongoClient
import pandas as pd
c = MongoClient('localhost:27017')
docs = [d for d in c.database.collection.find()]
df = pd.DataFrame(docs, columns=['verbatim'])
df.verbatims.apply(normalize_verbatim)
```

Cleaning: We know that social data can be noisy. Noise is a very subjective topic. It's highly dependent on the objective of our analytics topic. What is considered noise for one objective could be information for another objective. Even though we cannot generalize cleaning we'll show common cleaning practices.

In general, one should always perform the following cleaning steps:

1. **Normalize the textual content**: Normalization generally contains at least the following steps:
    1. Stripping surrounding whitespaces.
    2. Lowercasing the verbatim.
    3. Universal encoding (UTF-8).
2. Remove special characters (example: punctuation).
3. **Remove stop words**: Irrespective of the language stop words add no additional informative value to the analysis, except in the case of deep parsing where stop words can be bridge connectors between targeted words.
4. Splitting attached words.
5. **Removal of URLs and hyperlinks**: URLs and hyperlinks can be studied separately, but due to the lack of grammatical structure they are by convention removed from verbatims.
6. **Slang lookups**: This is a relatively difficult task, because here we would require a predefined vocabulary of slang words and their proper reference words, for example: luv maps to love. Such dictionaries are available on the open web, but there is always a risk of them being outdated.

In the case of studying words and not phrases (or n-grams), it is very important to do the following:

- Tokenize verbatim
- **Stemming and lemmatization (Optional)**: This is where different written forms of the same word do not hold additional meaning to your study

Some advanced cleaning procedures are:

- **Grammar checking**: Grammar checking is mostly learning-based, a huge amount of proper text data is learned, and models are created for the purpose of grammar correction. There are many online tools that are available for grammar correction purposes. This is a very tricky cleaning technique because language style and structure can change from source to source (for example language on Twitter will not correspond with the language from published books). Wrongly correcting grammar can have negative effects on the analysis.

- **Spelling correction**: In natural language, misspelled errors are encountered. Companies, such as Google and Microsoft have achieved a decent accuracy level in automated spell correction. One can use algorithms such as the Levenshtein Distances, Dictionary Lookup, and so on, or other modules and packages to fix these errors. Again take spell correction with a grain of salt, because false positives can affect the results.

- **Storing**: Once the data is received, normalized, and/or cleaned, we need to store the data in an efficient storage database. In this book we have chosen MongoDB as the database as it's a modern and scalable database. It's also relatively easy to use and get started. However, other databases such as Cassandra or HBase could also be used depending on expertise and objectives.

MongoDB to store and access social data

According to Wikipedia:

> *MongoDB (from humongous) is a cross-platform document-oriented database. Classified as a NoSQL database, MongoDB eschews the traditional table-based relational database structure in favor of JSON-like documents with dynamic schemas (MongoDB calls the format BSON), making the integration of data in certain types of applications easier and faster. Released under a combination of the GNU Affero General Public License and the Apache License, MongoDB is free and open-source software.*

Even though the objective of the chapter is not to explore the architecture of MongoDB in depth we are however going to explain the points that justify the use of MongoDB.

Along with ease of use, MongoDB is recognized for the following advantages:

- **Schema-less design**: Unlike traditional relational databases, which require the data to fit its schema, MongoDB provides a flexible schema-less data model. The data model is based on documents and collections. A document is essentially a JSON structure and a collection is a group of documents.

  One links data within collections using specific identifiers. The document model is quite useful in this subject as most social media APIs provide their data in JSON format.

- **High performance**: Indexing and GRIDFS features of MongoDB provide fast access and storage.
- **High availability**: Duplication feature that allows us to make various copies of databases in different nodes confirms high availability in the case of node failures.
- **Automatic scaling**: The Sharding feature of MongoDB scales large data sets automatically.

All the chapters in the book work with datasets that are manageable in memory and don't require the scaling feature of MongoDB; however, you can access information on implementation of Sharding in the official documentation of MongoDB: `https://docs.mongodb.com/v3.0/sharding/`.

In the last chapter, which is dedicated to social media analytics at scale, we'll learn about distributed processing and analytics using Spark

Installing MongoDB

MongoDB can be downloaded and installed from the following link: `http://www.mongodb.org/downloads?_ga=1.253005644.410512988.1432811016`.

Setting up the environment

MongoDB requires a data directory to store all the data. The directory can be created in your working directory:

```
md \data\db
```

Starting MongoDB

We need to go to the folder where `mongod.exe` is stored and and run the following command:

```
cmd bin\mongod.exe
```

Once the MongoDB server is running in the background, we can switch to our Python environment to connect and start working.

MongoDB using Python

MongoDB can be used directly from the shell command or through programming languages. For the sake of our book we'll explain how it works using Python. MongoDB is accessed using Python through a driver module named PyMongo.

 We will not go into the detailed usage of MongoDB, which is beyond the scope of this book. We will see the most common functionalities required for analysis projects. We highly recommend reading the official MongoDB documentation.

PyMongo can be installed using the following command:

```
pip install pymongo
```

Then the following command imports it in the Python script

```
from pymongo import MongoClient
client = MongoClient('localhost:27017')
```

The database structure of MongoDB is similar to SQL languages, where you have databases, and inside databases you have tables. In MongoDB you have databases, and inside them you have collections. Collections are where you store the data, and databases store multiple collections. As MongoDB is a NoSQL database, your tables do not need to have a predefined structure, you can add documents of any composition as long as they are a JSON object. But by convention is it best practice to have a common general structure for documents in the same collections.

Once you have the client object initiated you can access all the databases and the collections very easily.

To access a database named `scrapper` we simply have to do the following:

```
db_scrapper = db.scrapper
```

To access a collection named `articles` in the database scrapper we do this:

```
db_scrapper = db.scrapper
collection_articles = db_scrapper.articles
```

Now, we will see how to perform different operations:

- **Insert**: To insert a document into a collection we build a list of new documents to insert into the database:

  ```
  docs = []
  for _ in range(0, 10):
      # each document must be of the python type dict
      docs.append({
        "author": "...",
        "content": "...",
        "comment": ["...", ... ]
  })
  ```

  Inserting all the docs at once:

  ```
  db.collection.insert_many(docs)
  ```

  Or you can insert them one by one:

  ```
  for doc in docs:
      db.collection.insert_one(doc)
  ```

 Find more detailed documentation at:
  `https://docs.mongodb.com/v3.2/tutorial/insert-documents/`.

- **Find**: To fetch all documents within a collection:

  ```
  # as the find function returns a cursor we will iterate over the
  cursor to actually fetch
  # the data from the database
  docs = [d for d in db.collection.find()]
  ```

To fetch all documents in batches of 100 documents:

```
batch_size = 100
Iteration = 0
count = db.collection.count()  # getting the total number
 of documents in the collection

while iteration * batch_size < count:
  docs = [d for d in db.collection.find().skip(batch_size *
 iteration).limit(batch_size)]
  Iteration += 1
```

To fetch documents using search queries, where the author is `Jean Francois`:

```
query = {'author': 'Jean Francois'}
docs = [d for d in db.collection.find(query)]
```

Where the `author` field exists and is not null:

```
query = {'author': {'$exists': True, '$ne': None}}
docs = [d for d in db.collection.find(query)]
```

There are many other different filtering methods that provide a wide variety of flexibility and precision; we highly recommend taking your time going through the different search operators.

Find more detailed documentation at:
https://docs.mongodb.com/v3.2/reference/method/db.collection.find/.

- **Update**: To update a document where the author is `Jean Francois` and set the attribute published as `True`:

```
query_search = {'author': 'Jean Francois'}
query_update = {'$set': {'published': True}}
db.collection.update_many(query_search, query_update)
```

Or you can update just the first matching document:

```
db.collection.update_one(query_search, query_update)
```

Find more detailed documentation at:
https://docs.mongodb.com/v3.2/reference/method/db.collection.update/.

- **Remove**: Remove all documents where the author is `Jean Francois`:

```
query_search = {'author': 'Jean Francois'}
db.collection.delete_many(query_search, query_update)
```

Or remove the first matching document:

```
db.collection.delete_one(query_search, query_update)
```

 Find more detailed documentation at:
`https://docs.mongodb.com/v3.2/tutorial/remove-documents/`.

- **Drop**: You can drop collections by the following:

```
db.collection.drop()
```

Or you can drop the whole database:

```
db.dropDatabase()
```

Summary

Harnessing social data is of vital importance for any worthwhile application. Public data from social media APIs is messy, noisy, and voluminous, and requires a precise and smart strategy to keep the surface away from the noise. The first step in harnessing social data is to collect it by following the steps to connect it to various RESTful APIs and following authentication techniques. Each social network has variations of its API but the basic rules of app creation and authentication remain a common method. Once we successfully make connection to an API we need to parse the JSON data that is collected. The data arriving at the programmers end through the APIs need to be cleaned through basic text mining such as tokenization, duplicate removal, and normalization techniques. Social media data is often unstructured and in various formats, so traditional relational databases are not suitable for these use cases. Finally, we need a flexible and scalable system to stock thousands of social data points; we use MongoDB for the rest of the book. MongoDB is selected for its document type data structure (highly adaptive for JSON), easy to install, use, and scalability. All the preceding points are explained in a step-by-step manner in the chapter.

The next chapter will deal with a real-world application of social data to use training to practice the concepts learnt so far. We will learn about analyzing a brand's activity through its content on Facebook.

3
Uncovering Brand Activity, Popularity, and Emotions on Facebook

From the time we wake up in the morning until we go to sleep, brands play a big part in our lives. The brands such as those that produce toothbrushes, coffee, cars, and clothing, among others, are all vital for our day to day living. There is one brand that is not in the same bracket, but is equally important, Google. Our lives are incomplete without searching on Google. We search for all kinds of information on Google regarding our day to day necessities. While such information adds to our knowledge, conversely, it also means that Google also gets to know a lot about us. However, it could be interesting to know a bit about Google. According to Interbrand, a brand consultancy company, Google is among the world's top brands along with Apple, Facebook, and Coca-Cola. In this chapter, we will explore how to use social media analytics to learn about brands. Facebook is a leading platform that the world's foremost brands use to communicate with their consumers. From new products, services, company news, and so on, a lot of information is shared by brands to keep their fans and consumers informed. However, in this flow of messages in the formats of text, image, and videos, we lose the gist of all that is being spoken about. The goal of this chapter is to put in a nutshell all that a brand communicates to its audience, the reaction and emotions of the audience, and the measure of popularity of the brand. At the end of this chapter, we will be able to apply the same to any brand of our choice. Having learned about the basics of social data processing and an overview of different APIs we will dig deep into the Facebook API from a brand perspective. We will understand the functionalities and utilities of connecting, extracting, and analyzing the data from the Facebook fan page API.

In this chapter, we will cover the following topics:

- Facebook API and fan pages
- Time series analysis of content
- Emotion analysis using the Alchemy API

Facebook brand page

The best way to familiarize ourselves with the brand activity on Facebook is to check out the actual brand page on Facebook. If you use Facebook, any brand page can be accessed using the search box, as we've done for the case of Google in the following screenshot. We will eventually extract data for from this page using the Facebook API for our analysis.

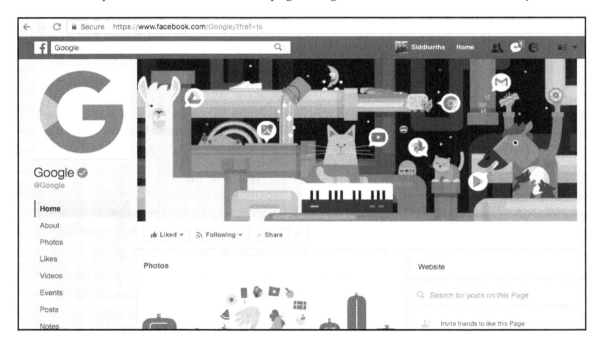

As shown in the following screenshot, there is content that is posted by both Google and its fans:

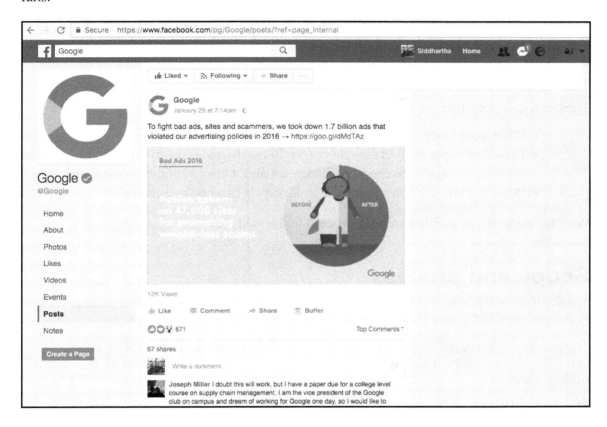

The Facebook API

As explained in `Chapter 2`, *Harnessing Social Data - Connecting, Capturing, and Cleaning*, the Facebook API consists of multiple functionalities. For the purpose of this chapter, we will use the Facebook Graph API.

Project planning

Analysis of content on social media can get very confusing due to difficulty of working on a large amount of data and also trying to make sense out of it. For this reason, it's extremely important to ask the right questions in the beginning to get the right answers. Even though this is an exploratory approach, and getting exact answers may be difficult, the right questions allow you to define the scope, process, and the time.

The main questions that we will be working on are the following:

- What does Google post on Facebook?
- How do people react to Google posts? (likes, shares, and comments)
- What do Google's Facebook audience say about Google and its ecosystem?
- What are the emotions expressed by Google's Facebook audience?

With these questions in mind we will proceed to the next steps.

Scope and process

The analysis will consist of analyzing the feed of posts and comments on the official Facebook page of Google.

The process of information extraction is organized in a data flow. It starts with data extraction from an API, data pre-processing and wrangling, and is followed by a series of different analyses.

The analysis becomes actionable only after the last step of results interpretation.

In order to arrive at retrieving the preceding information, we need to do the following:

- Extract all the posts of Google permitted by the Facebook API
- Extract the metadata for each post: Timestamp, number of likes, number of shares, and number of comments
- Extract the user comments under each post and the metadata
- Process the posts to retrieve the most common keywords, bi-grams, and hashtags
- Process the user comments using the Alchemy API to retrieve the emotions
- Analyze the all results obtained from the preceding steps to derive conclusions

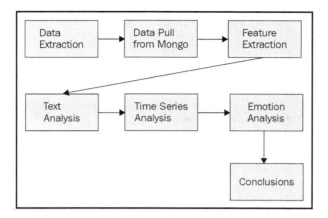

Data type

The main part of information extraction comes from an analysis of textual data (posts and comments). However, in order to add quantitative and temporal dimension, we process numbers (likes and shares) and dates (date of creation).

Analysis

Now that we have defined precisely the process and the techniques that we apply, we will move to the actual exercise of generating the code for the data analysis life cycle of extracting the data, storing it, cleaning it, and applying text mining techniques to analyze the content on the Facebook page of both Google and its users.

Step 1 – data extraction

In the first step, we will define Facebook endpoints, which will be used to retrieve the data from Facebook. We need two different endpoints in order to be able to extract all the posts and comments from the Google Facebook page. Creation of an access token was explained in `Chapter 2`, *Harnessing Social Data - Connecting, Capturing, and Cleaning* and it is a prerequisite for connection to the Graph API. The access token should be stored in a dictionary *params* under a key access token.

The first endpoint will be used to extract all the posts:

```
page_url =
'https://graph.facebook.com/v2.8/Google/feed?fields=id,message,reactions,sh
ares,from,caption,created_time,likes.summary(true)'
```

In new versions of Graph API, all the fields have to be explicitly specified. We have chosen a subset of all available fields that might be useful for our analysis:

- `id`: The ID of the post
- `message`: The content of the post
- `reactions`: A list of reactions to that post
- `shares`: The number of shares
- `from`: The author name
- `caption`: Caption of the post
- `created_time`: A timestamp
- `likes.summary(true)`: An object with a summary of likes

We have added a `summary()` function to the field *likes* in order to get the total number. If we don't apply the `summary()` function, the Graph API will return the first 25 likes objects.

Moreover, it is required to use a second endpoint to extract all the comments, because the feed endpoint fetches maximum 25 comments per post. In order to retrieve all of them we have to call a `comment` endpoint for each post:

```
comments_url =
'https://graph.facebook.com/v2.8/{post_id}/comments?filter=stream&limit=100
'
```

In `comments_url` we defined two fields: `filter=stream` and `limit=100`. The first parameter allows us to get paginated results and insert all of them to our database and the latter sets the limit to the maximum allowed level by the API.

Then we can launch the whole pipeline to get all the data and insert it into MongoDB. The script follows the logic of pagination:

1. Get the first page of posts:

```
posts = requests.get(page_url, params = params)
posts = posts.json()
```

2. Until the response is not empty (there are more posts in response) try to get all the posts and related comments:

```
while True:
    try:
    ###Retrieve one post
        for element in posts['data']:
            collection_posts.insert(element)
            ####Retrieve all comments for this post
            this_comment_url =
comments_url.replace("{post_id}",element['id'])
            comments = requests.get(this_comment_url, params =
params).json()
#loop through all comments until the response is empty (there are
no more comments)
            while ('paging' in comments and 'cursors' in
comments['paging'] and 'after' in comments['paging']['cursors']):
                ###Iterate through all comments
                for comment in comments['data']:
                    comment['post_id'] = element['id']
                    collection_comments.insert(comment)
                comments = requests.get(this_comment_url +
'&after=' + comments['paging']['cursors']['after'], params =
params).json()

            ####Go to the next page in feed
            posts = requests.get(posts['paging']['next']).json()
```

3. Once there are no more pages, break from loop, print error, and end script:

```
except KeyError, e:
    print(e)
    break
```

This process should fetch more than 1,500 posts and 300,000 comments from the Facebook page of Google; all the data is stored in MongoDB, which had been configured before launching the script.

Step 2 – data pull

The process of data extraction might take from a few minutes to an hour depending on multiple factors (Internet connection speed, database location, Graph API response time, and so on). Once all the data is ready in our database we can start the data science workflow by creating data structures that are convenient and efficient for the analysis.

In the first step, we will collect all the data stored in collections: `collection_posts` and `collection_comments` and put them into two lists: `posts_data` and `comments_data`:

```
posts_data = []
comments_data = []
```

We iterate through the MongoDB cursor and get all fields that are needed for the analysis. In the case of posts, these are: `message`, `created_time`, `number of likes`, `number of shares`, and `id`. In case there is no message (text) in a post we print an error message and skip it, because our analysis is focused only on textual data (no images or videos):

```
for doc in collection_posts.find({}):
    try:
    posts_data.append((doc['message'],doc['created_time'],doc['likes']['summary
']['total_count'],doc['shares']['count'],doc['id']))
    except:
        print("No message")
        pass
```

We execute the same process for comments keeping message, `created_time`, and `posts_id` as fields:

```
for comment in collection_comments.find({}):
    try:
    comments_data.append((comment['message'],comment['created_time'],comment['p
ost_id']))
    except:
        pass
```

In the next step, we create pandas `DataFrame` objects filling them with the data from our two lists. We give names to the columns for easy access in further analysis:

```
df_posts = pd.DataFrame(posts_data)
df_posts.columns = ['message','created_time','likes','shares','post_id']
df_comments = pd.DataFrame(comments_data)
df_comments.columns = ['message','created_time','post_id']
```

Finally, we end up with two data frames that will be used for further processing. The first one will be used to analyze the content of the brand and the second one will provide us insights about consumers.

Step 3 – feature extraction

Our data frames contain raw data that we gathered from Graph API. It contains all kinds of characters that we can find in posts and comments. We have to pre-process them and perform initial information extraction to be able to understand what actual consumers say.

We define the feature extraction process as a pipeline that makes different kinds of transformation in a sequence. The goal at this stage is to extract hashtags, keywords, and noun phrases from posts and comments.

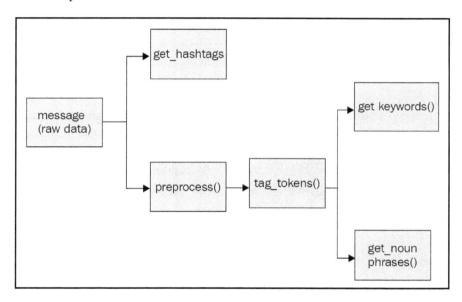

The `preprocess()` function cleans a raw verbatim (field message in our dataset) from white spaces, punctuation, and converts to lowercase. Then, it splits the text into tokens and returns a list of tokens:

```
def preprocess(text):

    #Basic cleaning
    text = text.strip()
    text = re.sub(r'[^\w\s]','',text)
    text = text.lower()

    #Tokenize single comment:
    tokens = nltk.word_tokenize(text)

    return(tokens)
```

The `get_hashtags()` function uses regular expressions to extract a list of hashtags from raw messages. It is applied directly on raw verbatims to avoid losing hash symbols during the cleaning process:

```
def get_hashtags(text):
    hashtags = re.findall(r"#(\w+)", text)
    return(hashtags)
```

`Tag_tokens()` uses the `nltk pos_tag()` function to tag a part of speech on pre-processed text. It returns a list of tokens with their respective parts of speech code. It uses the default Penn Treebank tagset. The results of this step will be used to extract information from sentence structure:

```
def tag_tokens(preprocessed_tokens):
    pos = nltk.pos_tag(preprocessed_tokens)
    return(pos)
```

The `Get_keywords()` function uses the outputs of tagging and returns a list of parts of speech selected by user. In our case it might be nouns, verbs, adjectives or all of them at the same time. These parts of speech are the most insightful ones, but it is very easy to have another one, such as adverb or preposition, depending on the goal of analysis:

```
def get_keywords(tagged_tokens,pos='all'):

    if(pos == 'all'):
        lst_pos = ('NN','JJ','VB')
    elif(pos == 'nouns'):
        lst_pos = 'NN'
    elif(pos == 'verbs'):
        lst_pos = 'VB'
    elif(pos == 'adjectives'):
        lst_pos = 'JJ'
    else:
        lst_pos = ('NN','JJ','VB')

    keywords = [tup[0] for tup in tagged_tokens if
tup[1].startswith(lst_pos)]

    return(keywords)
```

The last function that we will use at this stage of analysis aims to extract noun phrases. A noun phrase is defined as a phrase that has a noun as its head word. We can very often get interesting insights about what people talk about on the web by extracting this kind of syntactic structure.

For this purpose, we first define a pattern that has an optional DT (determiner) and multiple adjectives (JJ) and nouns (NN)

We parse the text with our pattern and then extract noun phrases that contain more than one word:

```
def get_noun_phrases(tagged_tokens):

    grammar = "NP: {<DT>?<JJ>*<NN>}"
    cp = nltk.RegexpParser(grammar)
    tree = cp.parse(tagged_tokens)

    result = []
    for subtree in tree.subtrees(filter=lambda t: t.label() == 'NP'):
        ###We only take phrases not single words
        if(len(subtree.leaves())>1):
            outputs = [tup[0] for tup in subtree.leaves()]
            outputs = " ".join(outputs)
            result.append(outputs)

    return(result)
```

We execute the whole pipeline in order to create two data frames with extracted hashtags, keywords, and noun_phrases. We apply previously defined functions on all the posts and comments:

```
def execute_pipeline(dataframe):
    # #Get hashtags
    dataframe['hashtags'] = dataframe.apply(lambda x:
get_hashtags(x['message']),axis=1)
    #Pre-process
    dataframe['preprocessed'] = dataframe.apply(lambda x:
preprocess(x['message']),axis=1)
    #Extract pos
    dataframe['tagged'] = dataframe.apply(lambda x:
tag_tokens(x['preprocessed']),axis=1)
    #Extract keywords
    dataframe['keywords'] = dataframe.apply(lambda x:
get_keywords(x['tagged'],'all'),axis=1)
    #Extract noun_phrases
    dataframe['noun_phrases'] = dataframe.apply(lambda x:
get_noun_phrases(x['tagged']),axis=1)

    return(dataframe)

df_posts = execute_pipeline(df_posts)
df_comments = execute_pipeline(df_comments)
```

As a result we obtain two data frames: `df_posts` and `df_comments`, which contain all the information required for further steps.

We can now start the most exciting part of the workflow—the analysis itself.

Step 4 – content analysis

In the following section, we will focus on the analysis of the content of posts and consumer comments. The content analysis will be done by using three entities: keywords, hashtags, and parts of speech (nouns and verbs). For each of the entities, we will compare the brand content (Google) and the fan content (users).

In the first stage, we will compare the most frequent keywords used by the brand with keywords used by consumers. In order to facilitate the interpretation, we will use a popular visualization method: `wordcloud`.

Firstly, we define a function that takes as argument a data frame that we want to analyze and a name of a column that will be visualized:

```
def viz_wordcloud(dataframe,column_name):

#Count words or phrases

    lst_tokens =
list(itertools.chain.from_iterable(dataframe[column_name]))
    lst_phrases = [phrase.replace(" ","_") for phrase in lst_tokens]
    wordcloud = WordCloud(font_path='/Library/Fonts/Verdana.ttf',
    background_color="white", max_words=2000, max_font_size=40,
    random_state=42).generate(" ".join(lst_phrases))

    # Display the generated image:
    # the matplotlib way:
    plt.figure()
    plt.imshow(wordcloud)
    plt.axis("off")
    plt.show()
```

Before plotting the wordcloud, our algorithm has to compute the frequency of tokens in our dataset, so we transform a data frame column containing multiple tokens in a single row into a list of tokens (lst_tokens). Then, we replace spaces with underscores to be able to process phrases containing many words, and we create a WordCloud object using the following parameters:

- font_path='/Library/Fonts/Verdana.ttf': Optional argument containing an absolute path to fonts (not always required on Linux machines, necessary on macOS)
- background_color="white": Background color
- max_words=2000: Maximum number of words
- max_font_size=40: Font maximum size
- random_state=42: Seed for random state, it can be any integer

Keywords

In the first place, we generate wordclouds for most frequent keywords for posts and consumer comments on the whole dataset.

In the following screenshot, you can see the most frequent keywords in brand posts:

In the following screenshot, you can see the most frequent keywords used in comments:

We can easily notice that the keywords are polluted by lots of comments related to political and religious issues. As we don't want to focus our analysis on these topics, we'll create a filtering method to remove all the irrelevant words.

We define a list of keywords associated with comments considered as noise in a global variable, CLEANING_LST. Our list can be also saved in a file and loaded to the variable:

```
CLEANING_LST = ['gulf','d','ban','persic' ...]
```

Cleaning irrelevant words is an iterative process and you can add any other word considered as a noise with respect to the subject that you are supposed to analyze. We did a few iterations ourselves to reduce the corpus to our topics of interest.

To be more specific, noise is a relative context around the topic you're focusing on. If you're interested in analyzing things that are related to the brand business, words about politics could be considered as noise. On the other hand, if you're analyzing politics, then it's not noise.

We add a following line to the `viz_wordcloud` function in order to filter out all phrases containing irrelevant words:

```
lst_phrases = [phrase for phrase in lst_phrases if not any(spam in
phrase.lower() for spam in CLEANING_LST)]
```

We also noticed that our wordcloud contains one letter tokens that are useless for our analysis. We add the following line to the `viz_wordcloud` function to remove them:

```
lst_phrases = [phrase.replace(" ","_") for phrase in lst_phrases if
len(phrase) > 1 ]
```

Finally, we obtain a cleaned wordcloud, as shown in the following screenshot; we obtain the most frequent keywords in comments after cleaning:

Another way to be more precise is to look at top 10 keywords and their frequencies in the following table format and then extract the posts:

User comments	Frequency	Brand posts	Frequency
google	123986	google	516
cancel	62846	new	155

play	62729	search	130
ever	30538	day	96
be	16089	today	95
plz	15447	world	94
change	13431	doodle	92
history	12665	check	91
hey	11562	see	91
anyone	11027	get	87

In the above table, we see the most frequent keywords for both the brand and the users. Among the users, words such as cancel, play, plz, change among others are the most frequent. In the case of the brand new, search, world, doodle are among the top 10 keywords the most frequent.

Now to get more context on the keywords we extract some of the actual verbatims for the brand and users. Extracting for all the keywords is beyond the scope of this chapter.

Extracting verbatims for keywords

We define a simple function that helps us to visualize verbatims associated with a keyword. The first argument df requires a data frame containing a column 'message', the second one the number of verbatims to show, and the third one is a keyword:

```
def print_verbatims(df,nb_verbatim,keyword):

    verbatims = df[df['message'].str.contains(keyword)]
    for i,text in verbatims.head(nb_verbatim).iterrows():
        print(text['message'])
```

We can do simple searches by using the following syntax:

```
print_verbatims(df_comments,5,'google')
```

 It is worth noting that some short keywords might be a part of a longer string, so in order to get precise tokens, we use a regex word boundaries \b:

```
print_verbatims(df_comments,5,'\\bgoogle\\b')
```

In the process of verbatim extraction, an interactive process helps to select the verbatims that make sense and ignoring the ones that don't (spammy). On social media a lot of users post interesting, constructive posts and others not as much. After applying the previous code to generate verbatims, we take examples of verbatims on some of the keywords as follows to get more context:

User keywords

The following are examples of some user keywords:

Google:

- "Ok Google", how big are polar bears? (`http://goo.gl/RcjL0q`)
- Winter is long and awful. Let's talk tips for planning spring and summer travel with Google Flights (`http://g.co/go/9cj5a`).
- Pick up your wand and experience the magic of the wizarding world with a little help from Google and #FantasticBeasts: `https://landing.google.com/fantasticbeasts/#/`.

Cancel:

- Why can't I cancel my Google Play Music subscription?
- I keep getting charged by Google for a Pandora account I created and I don't know how to cancel.

Change:

- Recently I received a text for a code to change my password and I did not ask for one.
- I hate change and what i hate is the ignorance of ease to fix things rather then just make things look nice.. and guess wat? i just disabled ur stupid doodle logo so take that!!! some plp need to get fof that google wagon. u got markers all over your face and it aint prety anymore.. adios doodle.. thanx adblock!!

Brand posts

The following are examples of some brand posts:

Google:

- Tributes by you. Phone by google. #Pixel
- G is for google... and games. From dinosaurs to Doodles to drawing join Nat and Lo for the lowdown on what to play (`https://goo.gl/1q1f1f`)
- Experience Day of the Dead traditions in a new google Arts and Culture exhibition: `http://goo.gl/ulZczW`, #VivoDiaDeMuertos

Search:

- We're deeply saddened by the recent violence in Brussels and Turkey. To help we're offering free calls via Hangouts to Belgium and Turkey as well as info in search for people in Brussels. Find Hangouts on Android (`https://goo.gl/75u3GM`) and iOS (`https://goo.gl/FDOfq`)
- Data helps Google search and find the right answers for you. Learn how we keep your data private and safe: `https://goo.gl/gAvaUA`.
- Your vote matters. But with deadlines and methods varying by state registering can be tricky. search Google and get state-by-state voter registration information to ensure your voice can be heard (`https://goo.gl/jyVuJY`).

World:

- Grab Google Cardboard for a narrated VR trek of the iconic facade of Petra one of the great wonders of the world (`https://petravr.withgoogle.com/`).
- Today at Google I/O we previewed Android M introduced the new Google Photos and talked about how we're putting our technology to work to solve complex problems in today's mobile world. Read a summary of this morning's announcements `http://g.co/go/io2015blog`.
- #EveryoneSpeaksFood paired #GoogleTranslate with cuisines from around the world for a very tasty experiment. See how it unfolded

The world clouds of the keywords allow us to visualize the content diffused by Google around search, apps, doodle, homepage, and so on. The users of google are posting mainly content about Google Play, changing, canceling, history, and using requesting words such as please, plz, and help. There are certain lesser frequent keywords by users such as golf and holiday

The word clouds give a visual representation of the content by both the brand and users.

Secondly, we generate wordclouds for most frequent hashtags found in posts and consumer comments on the whole dataset.

The following screenshot shows most frequent keywords in consumer posts:

The following screenshot shows the most frequent hashtags in consumer posts:

User comments	Frequency	Brand posts	Frequency
android_makdous	3518	GoogleDoodle	24
doodleofshivray	2191	GoogleTrends	24
google	457	WorldCup	21
daredtodream	109	YearInSearch	21
19thfeb	92	GoogleSearch	13
doodleofshivaray	91	madebygoogle	10
19Feb	59	OkGoogle	9
doodle	55	HiddenWorlds	8
blogger_for_wp8	51	Zeitgeist2013	7
blogger_for_symbian	50	slightlysuperhuman	7

Similarly, we look more precisely at the top 10 hashtags and the associated content. It is worth noting that hashtags are not so frequently used on Facebook (only in around 3-4% of comments).

User hashtags

Following are examples of some user hashtags:

Android_Makdous:

- Hello Google We would like your company from the respectable name the new generation of Android "android makdous" This name will generate a major revolution in the world of Android has the importance of the Arab peoples that use Android phones Thank you
- We want #Android_makdous

DoodleOfShivray:

- The Emperor of Peoples Pride - Chhatrapati Shivray #doodleofshivray
- Accept Shivajimaharaj as a passion not as a fashion. Google #doodleofshivray

DareToDream:

- Google you turn ideas and dreams into reality that makes a huge difference in lives of millions of people every day. Let's CURE worldwide cities together! I believe I have major key solutions. #daredtodream
- Hello Google! Could you tell if you have received my major key letter addressed to Mountain View to you? It was sent in the yellow A4-size envelope with the sticker #daredtodream.

YearinSearch:

- Breathe easy Don—after seven seasons your secret remains safe. #yearinsearch `http://goo.gl/Z06xCK`
- Meet the Doodlers! Nat and Lo get artsy with the #googledoodle team in a new episode `http://goo.gl/Z06xCK`
- Today's #googledoodle is an ode to this season of togetherness. Happy Thanksgiving! `https://goo.gl/igG8J4`
- "We cannot walk alone." Today's #googledoodle marks #MLKDay and honors Dr. King's legacy of unity nonviolence and love. `https://goo.gl/nzVMRH`

GoogleTrends:

- Breathe easy Don-after seven seasons your secret remains safe. #yearinsearch `http://goo.gl/Z06xCK`
- Before we ring in 2017 let's take a look back through the moments that defined 2016. #yearinsearch `http://g.co/2016`
- Street food reached an all-time high in 2016 with fish and chips ice cream and tacos searched more than ever. #yearinsearch `http://g.co/2016`

From the previous wordclouds, we can clearly compare the main content of both the brand and its users. Google is using hashtags about its features such as Doodle, Search, and also important events such as the World Cup, Olympics, Election, and so on. Users of Google are using hashtags that are more specific such as DoodleofShivaray, Android Makdous, and are also expressing their spirit with the hashtag DaredToDream.

Noun phrases

Finally, we generate wordclouds for the most frequent noun phrases found in posts and consumer comments on the whole dataset. A noun phrase is defined as a phrase that has a noun (or indefinite pronoun) as its head word. It is useful to see what comments talk about.

The following screenshot shows the most frequent noun phrases in brand posts:

The following screenshot shows the most frequent noun phrases in comments:

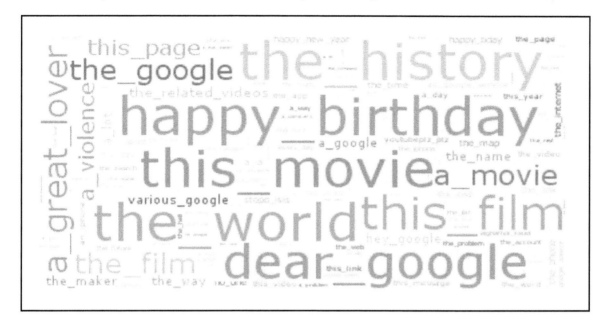

User comments	Frequency	Brand posts	Frequency
the_history	11017	the_google	87
the_world	4117	the_world	61
happy_birthday	4090	this_year	21
this_movie	2578	the_web	17
dear_google	2069	ok_google	14
this_film	1307	the_internet	13
a_great_lover	1291	a_look	13
the_google	1288	this_holiday	12
a_movie	1284	the_year	12
the_film	1283	a_day	11

Brand posts

The previous wordcloud with the noun phrases shows that Google has posted content for its users such as "this holiday", "the world", and "the web". Let's look at some of the verbatim:

this holiday:

- Nowruz Mobarak! Originating in ancient Persia this holiday marks the first day of the spring equinox right down to the tee! Every year the moment the sun crosses the celestial equator is determined giving observers the exact time to start their celebrations. #GoogleDoodle
- When Santa calls you pick up! Watch how #GoogleDuo calls are off the hook this holiday `https://duo.google.com`

the world:

- Did you take the #GoogleDoodle Earth Day quiz? Check out the results distribution from around the world. If you can chip in to help protect wildlife before 11:59 pm ET today and Google.org will match your donation. See where to donate here—it's the last day to have your contribution matched: `http://goo.gl/10oxmV`
- Street art doesn't last forever but you can see it before it disappears. Explore more than 10 000 images from around the world and learn the stories behind them on the Art Project powered by Google. `http://g.co/streetart` #StreetArtProject

the web:

- Data makes Google Photos work better for you. By learning from the content of images across the web we can automatically create and organize your photos into private albums - instantly. (`https://privacy.google.com/`)
- Google Translate helps you explore the world. It learned 100+ languages by using data from translated content across the web. ⊙⊙⊙⊙⊙. `http://goo.gl/y5DrMf`

User comments

The noun phrases of user posts are different from those of Google, but there are some common phrases such as "the world" and "the web":

the history:

- This was the most Evil year and violent in the history of my 60 years on earth right here on American soil at the hands of a Muslim PRESIDENT and a Black widow HILLARY CLINTON what a shame But the Best is yet to come with our New President DONALD TRUMP 2017

- So Google the largest search engine (paid placement engine) in the history of man kind. Absolutely famous for their doodles. On Christmas eve day the doodle links to a Christmas album released in 2000 "tis the season" by Vince Gill and Olivia Newton-John. I DON'T GET IT? I DON'T GET IT? I DON'T GET IT? This is the best Google could do?

the world:

- Dear Google you are outrageous. How dare you suspend my Google Voice for no reason & WHAT COMPANY MAKES YOU PAY TO TALK TO THEIR CUSTOMER SERVICE?! GOOGLE YOU ARE ONE OF THE RICHEST COMPANIES IN THE world—ARE YOU KIDDING ME?! Enemy to small businesses everywhere. Not to mention this video is bogus.

- Users of the Brazilian Internet we need help want to take away our freedom our only window to the world making our internet fixed in pacode data which achieved a certain consumption we are blocked without access! are depriving us of traveling by our monitors Brazilian Internet needs help!

the web:

- Hi and congrats on the video. I have a suggestion why don't you develop a specific search engine just for kids? such as google scholar (which is great for us academic). A search engine like that (which you could name google kids or google schools) would weed out non-education info for kids and it would enable young kids (I am thinking 5 to 12 Primary school mostly) to surf the web freely and safely. Also if done well you really could revolutionaze education.

Detecting trends in time series

In previous sections, we have analyzed the most frequent keywords and phrases without taking into account the time frame. However, a brand can benefit from a temporal dimension and dynamic analysis of the content of posts and comments.

Our goal in this section is to analyze in time series the moments of highest engagement to posts in terms of likes and shares and then see what those posts were about.

Firstly, we convert a string with a date into a datetime object:

```
df_comments['date'] = df_comments['created_time'].apply(pd.to_datetime)
```

The next operation transforms the data frame into a time series and creates an index on a datetime object:

```
df_comments_ts = df_comments.set_index(['date'])
```

Finally, we subset our data frame to only get the verbatims since the beginning of 2015:

```
df_comments_ts = df_comments_ts['2015-01-01':]
```

We have to execute the same operation on our data frame containing the post to be able to make comparisons:

```
df_posts['date'] = df_posts['created_time'].apply(pd.to_datetime)
df_posts_ts = df_posts.set_index(['date'])
df_posts_ts = df_posts_ts['2015-01-01':]
```

In the next step, we will visualize the results to see what are the weeks where brand posts had the highest and lowest number of shares and likes.

 The choice of weeks instead of days or months is purely arbitrary.

We create a data frame that contains the average number of likes and shares per week:

```
dx = df_posts_ts.resample('W').mean()
dx.index.name = 'date'
dx = dx.reset_index()
```

Then, we plot a chart showing the progression of likes over time:

```
p = ggplot(dx, aes(x='date', y = 'likes')) + geom_line(
p = p + xlab("Date") + ylab("Number of likes") + ggtitle("Facebook Google
Page")
print(p)
```

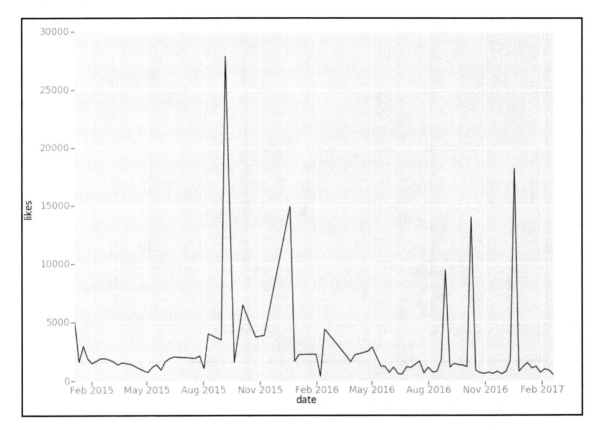

Then, we apply the same method on shares:

```
p = ggplot(dx, aes(x='date', y = 'shares')) + geom_line(
p = p + xlab("Date") + ylab("Number of shares") + ggtitle("Facebok Google
Page")
print(p)
```

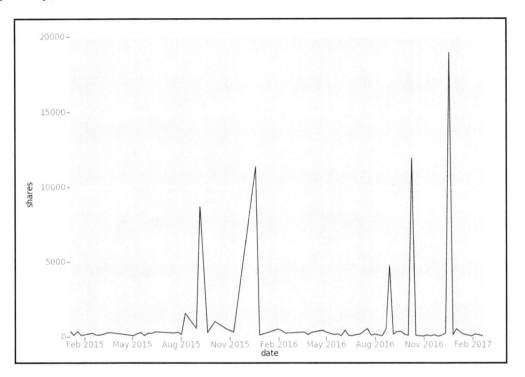

From the two plots, we can see that there are a few peaks that generated the most amount of likes and shares. There's a distinct peak in September 2015 in terms of likes, while there is a big peak during the end of 2016 in terms of shares.

It is interesting to check what is the vocabulary behind the peaks of likes and shares. We will investigate these periods by comparing words used in brand posts and user comments.

We define a function that takes as a parameter a time series of posts, a time series of comments, the name of a column containing keywords, and the criterion of comparison ('shares' or 'likes'):

```
def
max_wordcloud(ts_df_posts,ts_df_comments,columnname,criterium='shares'):
```

Firstly, the function computes an average number of shares/likes per week:

```
mean_week = ts_df_posts.resample('W').mean()
```

Then, it searches for the first day and last day of the global peak on posts time series:

```
start_week = (mean_week[criterium].idxmax() -
datetime.timedelta(days=7)).strftime('%Y-%m-%d')
end_week = mean_week['shares'].idxmax().strftime('%Y-%m-%d')
```

It creates wordclouds with the previously defined function:

```
viz_wordcloud(ts_df_posts[end_week:start_week],columnname)
viz_wordcloud(ts_df_comments[start_week:end_week],columnname)
```

This code allows us to visualize the most popular vocabulary in the defined timeseries that generates the most number of shares and likes.

Maximum shares

As done previously, we examine the brand and the user posts individually for the most popular vocabularies.

Brand posts

The brand posts that generated a lot of shares had content about cardboard, watch, mobility, youth, pride, create, and opportunity among others with varied frequencies, as shown in the following screenshot:

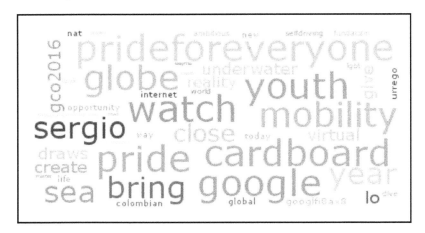

User comments

The users responded to the brand posts with comments having vocabulary containing the words phone, create, support, platform, join, advice, information, service, and camera, as shown in the following screenshot:

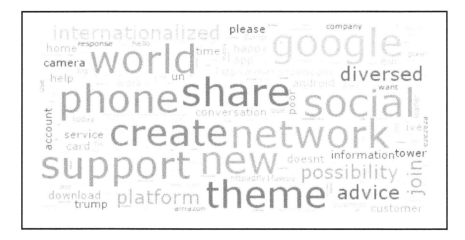

Maximum likes

The next level of engagement is the measure of the number of likes generated by the posts. We will look at this for both brand posts and user comments and visualize the most popular words using wordclouds.

Brand posts

The posts that generated the most amount of likes were about things made by Google, the Google doodle, experience, world, and app, as shown in the following screenshot:

Comments

The users responded to the most liked posts with various vocabularies such as love, world, video, and year among others. As you can see, the most liked posts generated a mix of vocabulary, including spammy content or in different languages, as shown in the following screenshot. As demonstrated, it's possible to dig deeper by analyzing the content, but we will leave that as an exercise for you.

Uncovering emotions

So far in the chapter, we have applied text analysis techniques to extract a lot of information about the Google brand page on Facebook. Now, we'll use some advanced techniques like emotion analysis to get more qualitative about the content. In order to achieve, this we'll be using the Alchemy API, which is now a part of IBM. The Alchemy API has an interesting set of tools that allow you to perform semantic analysis and natural language processing.

How to extract emotions?

We will now have a brief discussion on Emotion Extraction.

Introducing the Alchemy API

Alchemy API became a part of IBM Watson technology, which currently is offered on the Bluemix platform.

The service, called `AlchemyLanguage`, is a collection of text analysis functions that derive semantic information from your content. It can be accessed via API calls and a rich portfolio of methods.

Connecting to the Alchemy API

The authentication to the `AlchemyLanguage` API works by passing an API key as a query parameter in each call.

In order to obtain an API key, you must sign-up for IBMid and create an application.

 You can find the API documentation at the following link: `http://www.ib m.com/watson/developercloud/alchemy-language/api/v1/`

Setting up an application

The following are the steps to set up an application:

1. The web page: `http://www.alchemyapi.com`, redirects to `http://www.ibm.com /watson/alchemy-api.html`
2. Sign up and create an account (IBMid).

3. Finally, you will obtain a verification number via email:

4. Select the Watson API from the menu, select **All products** | **Watson** | **Watson APIs**:

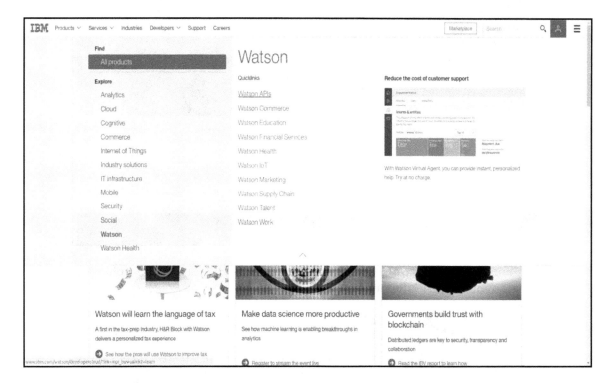

5. You will land on the Bluemix main page.

6. Start Bluemix services. Select the **Start for free on Bluemix** button:

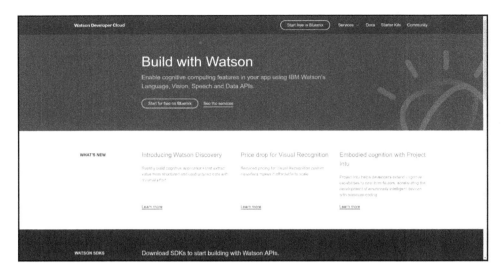

7. **Bluemix configuration**: Create space for your organization and potentially other parameters—just enter a name.

8. You have now reached the IBM Bluemix catalog main page.

9. Select the Alchemy API, from the left-panel menu select **Watson | AlchemyAPI**:

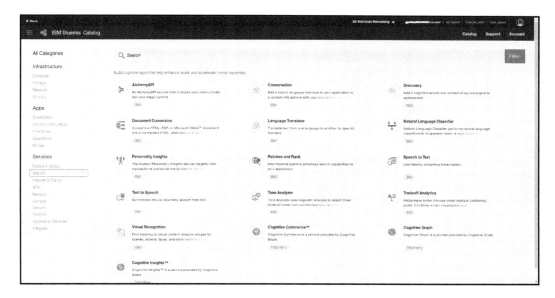

10. Now, you are about to create an application. Just accept defaults and click on **Create**:

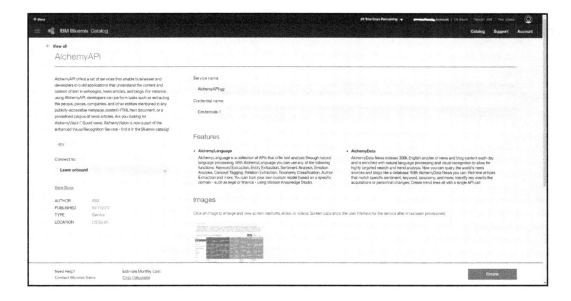

11. Obtain your API key.
12. The application with Alchemy API services is created. Now you can click on **Service Credentials** to get your API key.

Applying Alchemy API

In order to use the Alchemy API we will first create a function that makes the requests to the service:

```
import requests
import json

apikey = "YOUR_KEY"

url = "https://gateway-a.watsonplatform.net/calls/text/TextGetEmotion"

def get_alchemy(apikey,text):
    pms = {'apikey' : apikey, 'outputMode' : 'json', "text" : text}
    result = requests.post(url, data = pms)
    try:
        emotions = json.loads(result.text)['docEmotions']
    except:
        emotions = None
    return(emotions)
```

The free version of the alchemy API is limited to 1000 requests per month. For our analysis, we will take the first 1000 comments:

```
alchemy = df_comments.head(1000)
```

Then, we apply the alchemy API on each message in our dataset using the apply method. We store the results in a column called 'alchemy':

```
alchemy['alchemy'] = alchemy.apply(lambda x:
get_alchemy(apikey,x['message']),axis=1)
```

Emotions are returned in the JSON format, which is stored as a string in the dataframe. We will create a new dataframe containing only the results of emotions predictions:

```
emotions = []

for p in alchemy['alchemy']:
    if not p == None:
        emotions.append(p)

df_emotions = pd.DataFrame(emotions)
```

Then, we convert all the values into a numeric data type:

```
df_emotions = df_emotions.apply(pd.to_numeric, errors='ignore')
```

Next, we compute a mean for each emotion:

```
df_emotions_means = df_emotions.transpose().apply(np.mean,axis=1)
```

In the end, we can visualize the results:

```
df_emotions_means.plot(kind='bar', legend=False)
```

The following histogram shows the distribution of the emotions that we extracted. It is a list of positive and negative emotions:

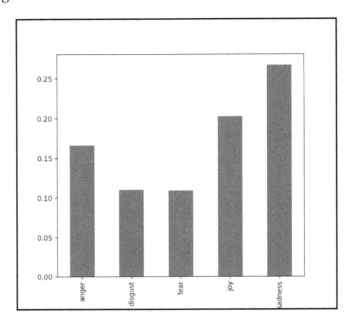

We see that the sadness emotion is the biggest chunk; this could be due to the period of analysis that had lots of negative events in the world. We also see that joy is the next biggest emotion. We will now take a look at some of the example verbatims and see the type of emotion (with the score) it is associated with:

- "Superb!" Joy 0.87
- y sister gave me one for X-mas but I won't use it because it gives Google 24/7 access to listen to you without you knowing it. It's a microphone into your life. Google watches every thing you do already they just put up servers about 5 miles away and they ran fiber optics to the air force base. Google is not a good search engine if you want to be private. Google knows your location all the time just like a cell phone. I won't buy a cell phone that you can't take the sim card out of Sadness 0.66
- You do not build up what is wrong nor encourage someone to do wrong. When they realize it was wrong they will hate u for going along with it the gay lifestyle is destructive. Disgust 0.66
- "Hey Google, do you want feedback on your products or not? I don't see a clear and easy way to do this." Anger 0.26

- "I thought I asked you to take Bartons Pet Boarding House off of your company's list? Now you send me a junk text that you are adding that company to the Review Boosterapp? Even on News Years Day when no one should really be working!!" Fear 0.27

How can brands benefit from it?

Using keywords, hashtags, and nouns phrases, a brand can get a perception of its consumers and fans regarding its content. They can also understand the differences in its own content vis-a-vis its fans. The ability to analyze content on one's Facebook page can help to choose the topics to focus on those that generate more engagement (likes and shares), but also understand the interests of your audience to further adapt your content strategy. This is a very useful technique for marketing departments in companies with a social media strategy and activity.

Summary

Facebook has become the *de facto* place for brands all over the world to communicate about their products, offers, and news. Not at all surprising considering that there are more than a billion users and consumers on the social media. Unlike in traditional media, on Facebook, not just the brand has a voice but also the consumers which in return generates a lot of engagement. The goal of this chapter was to show a glimpse of how to get interesting insights into the activities of Facebook pages of brands without getting lost in all the content. To analyze exhaustively all the content is beyond the scope of this chapter. We chose Google's brand page as an example for the analysis and have demonstrated how to collect, process, and visualize the data from Facebook and measure engagements. Extracting the top keywords, hashtags and noun phrases allowed us to understand the most important content of both the brand and the users. We have also shown how to extract emotions in content of both the brand and the users through the Alchemy API. The results of the analysis showed that *joy* and *sadness* where among the top emotions. The world is a full of people with diverse emotions and so is Social Media!

We hope in this chapter that we have given you early techniques to start analyzing textual content on social media. In the later chapters, we'll show the technique to go beyond keywords, hashtags, and nouns phrases and to automatically create topics of the content by using machine learning. In the next chapter, we will show how to implement sentiment analysis and extracting entities on textual content from Twitter.

4
Analyzing Twitter Using Sentiment Analysis and Entity Recognition

A powerful means of communication that has grown popular in the last decade or so has been microblogging, which is the art of broadcasting short, crisp messages through the internet to a large audience. The leader of the microblogging movement has been Twitter, with millions of tweets (short messages with 140 character text messages with pictures and videos) being sent through its platform by over 300 million monthly active users. Twitter is used across the world by individuals, companies, political parties, celebrities, media, authors, and almost everyone else. The type of messages that are sent varies from mindless chatter to conversational topics to promotional content and news. Unlike traditional media, the popularity of Twitter is due to its brief and instantaneous nature, which allows people to consult or broadcast important pieces of information at a split second at the very moment. Countless breaking and sensational news stories of natural disasters like earthquakes have reached millions of people at the very instant due to the existence of Twitter. A very popular use of Twitter by people is to broadcast their opinion "live" on events they are at or watching such as sports, concerts, television series, or movies. Therefore, Twitter is a great means for those behind these events to gage public perception rapidly and due to the large volume of opinions, exhaustively. To be able to do so, they must apply robust techniques that allow them to gather and store these tweets in large scale and analyze them using relevant techniques.

In this chapter, we have chosen the topic of the football English Premier League, which is one of the most popular football events in the world, to demonstrate the analysis of tweets. We will apply two important semantic algorithms—**Sentiment Analysis** and **Entity Recognition** to understand what the tweets are about (matches, people, players, locations, clubs) and how are the opinions (positive, negative, neutral) being emanated. These are two powerful techniques that can help reveal important information from large amounts of textual data. We will use popular open source modules to show the application of sentiment analysis and entity recognition. Sentiment analysis is an important classification problem in machine learning, so we'll also show you how to implement a sentiment analysis algorithm yourself.

In this chapter, we will cover the following topics:

- Applications of Twitter data
- Sentiment analysis
- Customized sentiment analysis

Scope and process

The project and analysis in the chapter will cover the data gathered from the Twitter feeds through the Twitter API. Working with the API, the user has a selection of different endpoints (functionalities). We will focus on two of the most popular: the streaming and the search endpoints (REST API). The first one gives access to real-time data, showing tweets as they are published (in fact the access is to the sample, not all tweets). The latter allows to query historical tweets (up to about a week), based on several criteria, which is more suitable for a static analysis. The following are the steps to gather the data from the Twitter feeds:

- Getting the data
- Data pull
- Data cleaning

Let us take a look at each one in detail.

Getting the data

The first step to get the data is to set up the Twitter access from its developer platform with two main methods:

- Getting Twitter API keys
- Connecting to the Twitter API:
    - Streaming API
    - REST API (Search endpoint)

Getting Twitter API keys

Firstly, you will need to have a Twitter account and obtain credentials (consumer key, consumer secret, access token, and access secret) on the Twitter developer platform to access the Twitter API, following these steps:

1. Create a Twitter user account.
2. Log in with your Twitter user account at `https://apps.Twitter.com/`.
3. Click **Create New App.**
4. Fill out the form, agree to the terms, and click on **Create your Twitter application.**
5. Go to the next page, click on the **Keys and Access Tokens** tab, and copy your **API key** and **API secret**. Scroll down and click on **Create my access token**, and copy your **Access token**, and **Access token secret**.

Once, we're ready with the Twitter credentials we can move to the next stages of the analysis:

Data extraction

Having all required authorization keys, we can prepare the toolset for data retrieval. The Twitter API gives several ways to extract the data, but we will focus on two main methods:

- Keyword search query to obtain recent, historical tweets
- Streaming facility, to obtain tweets as they are posted

REST API Search endpoint

The search query requires the authorized connection to the search endpoint: `https://api.Twitter.com/1.1/search/tweets.json`

There are many data extraction functionalities of the endpoint, depending on the query format and additional parameters. For our case, we will build the following query:

```
premier league -filter:retweets AND -filter:replies
```

Here:

- `premier league` is a combination of two keywords,
- `-filter:retweets` lets us get rid of all retweets in the extraction results
- `-filter:replies` filters all replies to the tweet often unnecessary for the analysis

It is worth noticing that the query construction contains logical operator `AND` between two `-filter` statements.

Each endpoint has a set of additional parameters, which can help the user to fine tune the results data. We will use:

- `count: 100`: To indicate the number of tweets to be retrieved per one call
- `lang: 'en'`: To filter the language of the tweets for English language only
- `result_type: 'recent'`: To obtain the most recent tweets

All these parameters are optional, but using them we will obtain a much more structured format of data. It saves a lot of work in the phase of data cleaning.

Thus, the full script to call Twitter API and request the data is as follows:

```
import requests
from requests_oauthlib import OAuth1

q = 'premier league -filter:retweets AND -filter:replies'

url = 'https://api.Twitter.com/1.1/search/tweets.json'
### url according to Twitter API

pms = {'q' : q, 'count' : 100, 'lang' : 'en', 'result_type': 'recent'} ###
parameters according to Twitter API

auth = OAuth1(consumer_key, consumer_secret, access_token,
access_token_secret)
```

```
res = requests.get(url, params = pms, auth=auth)
```

If the connection status is OK, we should retrieve a set of documents, which we can convert to json format:

```
tweets = res.json()
```

The documents have similar structure with few main blocks and additional information:

Information about tweet:

```
"_id" : ObjectId("58ee5317b1ffda423e612be2"),    ***** MongoDB id field
"text" : "Arsene Wenger woes continue as fixture reschedule hands
Arsenal five matches in 14 days: Arsenal now face five..
https://t.co/QGyXTwzlhj",
"created_at" : "Wed Apr 12 15:41:21 +0000 2017",
"favorite_count" : NumberInt(0),
"favorited" : false,
"id_str" : "852184875792822272",
"id" : NumberLong(852184875792822272),
"possibly_sensitive" : false,
"in_reply_to_status_id" : null,
"lang" : "en",
"in_reply_to_screen_name" : null,
"in_reply_to_user_id_str" : null,
"in_reply_to_status_id_str" : null,
"retweeted" : false,
"coordinates" : null,
"geo" : null,
"place" : null,
"truncated" : false,
"is_quote_status" : false,
"in_reply_to_user_id" : null,
"source" : "<a href=\"https://www.socialoomph.com\"
rel=\"nofollow\">SocialOomph</a>"
```

Entities attached:

```
"entities" : {
    "symbols" : [

    ],
    "hashtags" : [

    ],
    "user_mentions" : [

    ],
```

```
        "urls" : [
            {
                "expanded_url" : "http://dld.bz/fAZzn",
                "url" : "https://t.co/QGyXTwzlhj",
                "indices" : [
                    NumberInt(113),
                    NumberInt(136)
                ],
                "display_url" : "dld.bz/fAZzn"
            }
        ]
    }
```

Metadata and retweet information:

```
    "metadata" : {
        "iso_language_code" : "en",
        "result_type" : "recent"
    },
    "retweet_count" : NumberInt(0)
```

And finally, information about the tweet's author:

```
    "user" : {
        "profile_background_tile" : false,
        "protected" : false,
        "entities" : {
            "description" : {
                "urls" : [

                ]
            }
        },
        "is_translator" : false,
        "created_at" : "Tue Jan 10 16:09:32 +0000 2017",
        "profile_banner_url" :
"https://pbs.twimg.com/profile_banners/818852281953173506/1484064703",
        "name" : "Football Mania",
        "profile_use_background_image" : false,
        "profile_sidebar_border_color" : "000000",
        "id_str" : "818852281953173506",
        "id" : NumberLong(818852281953173506),
        "followers_count" : NumberInt(2084),
        "notifications" : false,
        "utc_offset" : null,
        "favourites_count" : NumberInt(0),
        "profile_link_color" : "ABB8C2",
        "following" : false,
```

```
    "follow_request_sent" : false,
    "profile_image_url_https" :
    "https://pbs.twimg.com/profile_images/818852991478484995
    /d4NtBzxG_normal.jpg",
    "profile_text_color" : "000000",
    "default_profile_image" : false,
    "time_zone" : null,
    "profile_image_url" :
    "http://pbs.twimg.com/profile_images/818852991478484995
    /d4NtBzxG_normal.jpg",
    "location" : "United Kingdom",
    "has_extended_profile" : false,
    "default_profile" : false,
    "profile_background_image_url_https" :
    "https://abs.twimg.com/images/themes/theme1/bg.png",
    "profile_background_image_url" :
    "http://abs.twimg.com/images/themes/theme1/bg.png",
    "friends_count" : NumberInt(4009),
    "profile_sidebar_fill_color" : "000000",
    "translator_type" : "none",
    "lang" : "en",
    "statuses_count" : NumberInt(31078),
    "profile_background_color" : "000000",
    "screen_name" : "footymania247",
    "description" : "Latest football news from around the
     world,transfers,fixtures,results and much more 18+ only",
    "contributors_enabled" : false,
    "geo_enabled" : false,
    "url" : null,
    "listed_count" : NumberInt(3),
    "is_translation_enabled" : false,
    "verified" : false
  }
```

Loaded JSON becomes a dictionary in Python. Each field can be simply accessed by the following key:

```
tweets['statuses']
```

Nested fields can be accessed using multiple keys and lists by numerical index:

```
tweets['statuses'][0]['text']
```

Rate Limits

After successful connection to the API, we have to prepare our scripts for data retrieval. As the API limits data access (Rate Limits), it is necessary to build an efficient workflow.

Twitter allows you to get up to 100 tweets per one call (thus, we set the parameter count to 100). If we want to retrieve more and we need to remember already downloaded tweets' IDs not to extract the same tweets during next calls. This procedure is commonly called **paging**.

The paging procedure is implemented in the script as follows:

```
pages_counter = 0
number_of_pages = 100

  while pages_counter < number_of_pages:
    pages_counter += 1
    res = requests.get(url, params = pms, auth=auth)
    print("Connection status: %s" % res.reason)
    tweets = res.json()
    ids = [i['id'] for i in tweets['statuses']]
    # collect ids of all tweets to select min(val)
    pms['max_id'] = min(ids) - 1
    # because it would include and then duplicate
    collection.insert_many(tweets['statuses'])
```

The `number_of_pages` variable indicates how many pages we want to retrieve. In combination with the count parameter, we can calculate the theoretical number of tweets count multiply by `number_of_pages`, assuming that for each call the system will find 100 tweets (which is often not the case).

Extracted tweets must be stored, so we should initialize the connection to MongoDB as follows:

```
from pymongo import MongoClient

client = MongoClient('mongodb://localhost:27017/')
db = client[database_name]
collection = db[collection_name]
```

In the previous script, we use the `insert_many` method in order to store all retrieved tweets in the database.

Streaming API

Another method of obtaining information from Twitter is the streaming API. It gives access to Twitter's global stream of data. There are several basic streaming endpoints, each customized to certain use cases. Based on the Twitter documentation:

- **Public streams**: Streams of the public data flowing through Twitter. It is suitable for following specific users or topics, and data mining.
- **User streams**: These are single-user streams, containing roughly all of the data corresponding with a single user's view of Twitter.

In order to connect to the API, we need to use the following endpoint:

```
url = 'https://stream.Twitter.com/1.1/statuses/filter.json'
```

The authorization requires the `oauth` library as follows:

```
from requests_oauthlib import OAuth1

auth = OAuth1(consumer_key, consumer_secret, access_token,
access_token_secret)
```

Finally, we set up the parameters—tracking keywords and the language:

```
pms = {'track' : 'premier league -filter:retweets AND -filter:replies',
'lang': 'en'}
```

The API call should be executed as a POST request with parameters:

```
res = requests.post(url, auth=auth, params = pms, stream = True)

for line in res.iter_lines():
    if line:

        tweet = json.loads(line.decode('utf-8'))

        try:
                mongo.insert(tweet)
        except:
                pass
```

The response comes in a binary format, so we convert it to JSON and save it to the database. This method of getting data may take some time, as tracked tweets are not being posted often. Such workflows enable us to archive a number of queried tweets and prepare a comfortable environment for furthers analysis. However, we have to be aware of the time factor, especially with the Stream API.

Data pull

Having finished with the data retrieval, we can start the preparation of the data structures for further processing. We will load our data into the dataframe model.

Mongo connection object:

```
client = MongoClient('mongodb://localhost:27017/')
db = client['db']
collection = db['collection']

documents = []
for doc in collection.find():
    documents.append(doc)
```

Now, we can create a dataframe object using our `documents` list:

```
df = pd.DataFrame(documents)
```

So, our data structure is in tabular form, where columns indicate the names of the document nodes and the rows represent the data:

	_id.$oid	contributors	coordinates	coordinates.coordinates	coordinates.type	created_at	entities.hashtags	entities.media
0	58ee5316b1ffda423e612ae8	None	NaN	NaN	NaN	Wed Apr 12 16:16:32 +0000 2017	[]	NaN
1	58ee5316b1ffda423e612ae9	None	NaN	NaN	NaN	Wed Apr 12 16:16:10 +0000 2017	[{'text': 'PremierLeague', 'indices': [89, 103]}]	[{'media_url': 'http://pbs.twimg.com/media
2	58ee5316b1ffda423e612aea	None	NaN	NaN	NaN	Wed Apr 12 16:16:10	[{'text': 'PUSB', 'indices': [100,	NaN

Data cleaning

Our goal is to prepare the data in the format which is most appropriate for analysis. It means we need to clean up unnecessary fields and focus only on the relevant parts.

We would like to analyze the sentiments of the tweets that are written by people from their different devices. Therefore, we should get rid of the tweets composed by bots, web pages, automated posting services, and so on. We cannot identify those tweets 100%, but quite a good assumption would be to select tweets posted from physical devices, meaning iPhones, Android phones, desktops, and laptops.

Twitter documents have an interesting feature, because they keep the information about the source of the tweet creation. Whenever someone uses a device to compose a tweet, the information about it is maintained. It can be illustrated by querying our dataframe:

```
df.source
```

As a result, we will get a list of the posting methods:

```
0     <a href="https://ifttt.com" rel="nofollow">IFT...
1     <a href="https://dlvrit.com/" rel="nofollow">d...
2     <a href="http://draldevelopment.uk" rel="nofol...
3     <a href="https://dlvrit.com/" rel="nofollow">d...
4     <a href="https://dlvrit.com/" rel="nofollow">d...
5     <a href="http://rightrelevance.com" rel="nofol...
6     <a href="https://dlvrit.com/" rel="nofollow">d...
7     <a href="http://bufferapp.com" rel="nofollow">...
8     <a href="https://dlvrit.com/" rel="nofollow">d...
9     <a href="http://Twitter.com/download/android" ...
10    <a href="https://about.Twitter.com/products/tw...
11    <a href="https://dlvrit.com/" rel="nofollow">d...
12    <a href="http://www.hootsuite.com" rel="nofoll...
13    <a href="http://www.facebook.com/Twitter" rel=...
14    <a href="https://dlvrit.com/" rel="nofollow">d...
15    <a href="http://www.socialflow.com" rel="nofol...
16    <a href="https://dlvrit.com/" rel="nofollow">d...
17    <a href="https://about.Twitter.com/products/tw...
18    <a href="https://ifttt.com" rel="nofollow">IFT...
19    <a href="https://ifttt.com" rel="nofollow">IFT...
```

We see two issues: first—the information is given in HTML format, second—there are many more posting methods, containing not only devices, but also bots and automated services.

Let's address the issues. In order to clean up the HTML code we will use a library called BeautifulSoup, which is used for web crawling for information. We'll use it here to remove the HTML code from the required information:

```
from bs4 import BeautifulSoup

df['tweet_source'] = df['source'].apply(lambda x:
BeautifulSoup(x).get_text())
```

We have created a new column, tweet_source, where human readable tweet sources are stored:

```
0  IFTTT
1  dlvr.it
2  Coventry City News Twitter
3  dlvr.it
4  dlvr.it
5  RightRelevanceTweetApp
6  dlvr.it
7  Buffer
8  dlvr.it
9  Twitter for Android
10 TweetDeck
11 dlvr.it
12 Hootsuite
13 Facebook
14 dlvr.it
15 SocialFlow
16 dlvr.it
17 TweetDeck
18 IFTTT
19 IFTTT
```

If we scroll down the data, we see the variety of tweet sources. However, we are only interested in devices. The information about devices is very clear—we will find tweet sources like Twitter for iPhone, Twitter for Android, Twitter Web Client, Twitter for BlackBerry, Twitter for Mac, Twitter for Windows, and so on. The names of the devices start with the word "Twitter". We will use this property in addressing our second issue.

We need to create the list of all devices, where the name starts with Twitter:

```
devices =
list(set(df[df['tweet_source'].str.startswith('Twitter')]['tweet_source']))
```

Our devices list looks as follows:

```
['Twitter Lite',
 'Twitter Web Client',
 'Twitter Ads',
 'Twitter for BlackBerry',
 'Twitter for Windows Phone',
 'Twitter for Android Tablets',
 'Twitter for Mac',
 'Twitter for iPad',
 'Twitter for Windows',
 'Twitter for BlackBerry®',
 'Twitter for iPhone',
 'Twitter for Android']
```

Among the names indicating the devices, we have Twitter Advertising Service, which is not needed in our approach. Thus, we must remove it from our list:

```
devices.remove('Twitter Ads')
```

Now, we need to slice our data set by the list:

```
df = df[df['tweet_source'].isin(devices)]
```

Our current dataframe is much smaller, but it contains the tweets composed only on the devices.

When we take a look at our data, mainly the `df.text` column, it is seen that it contains the tweets not only concerning the English Premier League, but also Premier Leagues from other countries. As we want to concentrate on the English Premier League, we must clean the data from other countries. This issue can be addressed by adding "English" in our initial search query, but that could have caused us to lose the relevant tweets that don't have the word "English" attached. We generally prefer to get the maximum data and then clean it rather than specifying too much at the beginning, in order to avoid losing volumes of data.

After identifying the keywords for cleaning, we implement it to our data frame:

```
df =
df[~df['text'].str.contains("Ghana|ghana|jamaica|Jamaica|Ladbrokes|India|Pa
kistan|Ghana Premier League|Vijay|Predictions|Egyptian Premier
League|cricket|Kings|Caribbean Premier League|@cricbuzz|Cricinfo")]
```

The statement means that we want to keep all rows in the `df['text']` column NOT (~) containing the list of keywords. It is worth noticing that the list of keywords is divided by the logical operator OR (indicated by `|`).

After the cleaning process, we have a data frame structure with all tweets referring to the English Premier League, composed using the devices (not bots or automated services).

In order to correctly prepare the textual data, some more extra cleaning is required. Literally, we will remove the stopwords and special characters. The process consists of three steps:

1. Text tokenization.
2. Stopwords removal.
3. Special characters removal.

Tokenization:

```
from nltk.tokenize import TweetTokenizer

df['tokens'] = df['text'].apply(TweetTokenizer().tokenize)

Stopwords:

from nltk.corpus import stopwords

stopwords_vocabulary = stopwords.words('english')
df['stopwords'] = df['tokens'].apply(lambda x: [i for i in x if i.lower()
not in stopwords_vocabulary])
```

Special characters and stopwords removal:

```
import string

punctuations = list(string.punctuation)

df['punctuation'] = df['stopwords'].apply(lambda x: [i for i in x if i not
in punctuations])

df['digits'] = df['punctuation'].apply(lambda x: [i for i in x if i[0] not
in list(string.digits)])

df['final'] = df['digits'].apply(lambda x: [i for i in x if len(i) > 1])
```

Sentiment analysis

Sentiment analysis involves classifying comments or opinions in text into categories such as "positive" or "negative" often with an implicit category of "neutral". A classic sentiment application would be tracking what people think about different topics. Sentiment analysis in data science and machine learning is also called "opinion mining" or in marketing terminology "voice of the customer". It can be a very useful tool to check the affinity to brands, products, or domains. Sentiment analysis is extremely useful in social media monitoring as it allows us to get an overview of the wider public opinion behind specific topics.

Sentiment analysis also has its limitations and is not to be used as a 100% accurate marker.

As natural language can be very ambiguous with multiple connotations, it's hard if not impossible for machines and algorithms to detect them all. Sentiment analysis basically analyses patterns of words in phrases that are more likely to be positive, negative, or neutral, finally, giving a score on each. This approach is quite effective, but not always accurate on informal language.

For example, in the context of coffee, "hot" or "cold" is neutral, but in the context of people "hot" or "cold" can be positive or negative. Another classic example is the word "sick", in the case of people it's a negative concept, but people use it as a positive expression such as for occasions (*it was a sick party and there were tons of cool people!*), and things like skateboard (*it is a sick board and worth every penny of your hard earned cash*). It gets even harder for algorithms to pick up sentiments that contain humor or sarcasm.

Sentiment analysis is essentially a classification problem in machine learning, which is a mathematical model to classify the tweets into certain categories and it relies on labeled datasets. In our case, the categories will be defined as "positive", "negative", and "neutral". A labeled dataset, also called the training dataset, is a sample of data that is manually tagged with the sentiment from human understanding. Based on these labels of the training dataset, the classifier learns the patterns for positive, negative, and neutral content that it applies then to the actual or `test` dataset. The accuracy of the algorithm depends heavily on the size of the labeled dataset. The more examples, the better the pattern recognition, hence, the better the algorithm. Very often the classifiers return the continuous measure instead of discrete ones. It means we get the probability that a tweet belongs to a category:

```
tweet text: { positive: 0.7, neutral: 0.2, negative: 0.1 }
```

For our analysis, we will use a pre-trained model from the NLTK library.

For our sentiment analysis, we chose a sentiment analyzer called **VADER (Valence Aware Dictionary for Sentiment Reasoning)**, which is available with Python's NLTK library as follows:

```
from nltk.sentiment.vader
import SentimentIntensityAnalyzer
```

VADER was designed for analyzing live streams of social media content. The VADER algorithm outputs sentiment scores to four classes of sentiments:

- `neg`: Negative
- `neu`: Neutral
- `pos`: Positive
- `compound`: Compound (that is, aggregated score)

```
from nltk.sentiment.vader import SentimentIntensityAnalyzer

sentiment = SentimentIntensityAnalyzer()

df['sentiment'] = df.text.apply(lambda x:
sentiment.polarity_scores(x)['compound'])
```

After importing the libraries, we need to instantiate the `SentimentIntensityAnalyzer` object. The object has an interesting method, `polarity_scores`, which takes a text as an argument, and returns a sentiment score.

If we call the method with a text argument:

```
sentiment.polarity_scores(text)
```

It returns the dictionary object:

```
{'compound': 0.7003, 'neg': 0.0, 'neu': 0.691, 'pos': 0.309}
```

These are simply the sentiment measures for our text argument. We can focus on specific ones (`'pos'`, `'neg'`, `'neu'`) or refer to the compound value, which is a normalized score of all three categories with a value range between -1 and 1. The normalization function uses alpha (15 by default), which approximates maximum expected value:

$$score_{norm} = \frac{x}{\sqrt{x^2 + \alpha}}$$

$$\alpha = 15$$

In our approach, we have created a new column `['sentiment']` where we calculate the compound measure to all `['text']` rows.

Now, we can plot our results. First, we must count the occurrences of the sentiment categories:

```
pos = len(df[df.sentiment > 0])
neg = len(df[df.sentiment < 0])
neu = len(df[df.sentiment == 0])
```

In the variables we will store the amount of tweets belonging to the categories:

```
y = [pos, neu, neg]  # vector of y-values

plt.title("Sentiment Analysis")
plt.ylabel('Number of tweets')
plt.xticks(range(len(y)), ['positive', 'neutral', 'negative'])
plt.bar(range(len(y)), height=y, width = 0.75, align = 'center', alpha =
0.8)

plt.show()
```

This gives the following result:

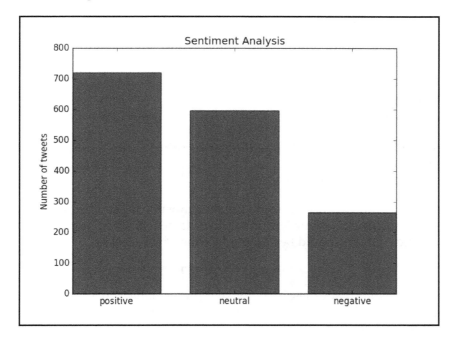

A bar chart like the one in the previous figure is most often a very effective tool for results visualization and interpretation. In general, it shows overall positive affirmation in regard to our topic of the English Premier League. There are more than twice positive tweets than negative and there is a substantial amount of neutral tweets as well.

Customized sentiment analysis

As mentioned earlier, sentiment analysis is the process of identifying and extracting sentiment information related to a specified topic, domain, or entity, from a set of documents. The sentiment is identified using trained sentiment classifiers. Thus, the quality and the type of the training data have a big impact on the classifier's performance. Most pre-trained classifiers (like VADER) are trained on general texts because they are designed to be versatile for use on different topics. Unfortunately, when we need to extract sentiment from a specific textual data (for example, very domain specific) such as a general classifier might not perform very well. That is why, it makes great sense to train our own classifier that will fit specific needs, or alternately, just train a general classifier, but based on customized, verified, and known datasets. In short, the magnitude of adaptation to the domain is what makes the difference between a good sentiment analysis and a better one.

There are many sources of datasets available on the internet free of charge, but in extreme cases, we can also prepare our own.

The preparation of a custom classifier requires two data sets:

- **Training data set**: The data on which the classifier algorithm learns the model parameters
- **Test data set**: This is used to determine the accuracy of the algorithm

There is no rule of thumb for selecting training and testing data set sizes, but there is a broad agreement among practitioners that 60-80% of the total data should be training data, and 40-20% should be testing data, respectively.

As it is a supervised learning task, the data (tweets) must be tagged by output categories. In our case, we want to categorize our texts into three classes: positive, neutral, and negative. Thus, each sentence (tweet) should be assigned to one of the classes:

```
('Kasami vs Palace is the best premier league goal ever by the way', 'pos')
```

In order to create custom-made classifiers for sentiment analysis, we will use the Python `scikit-learn` library. The library features multiple machine learning algorithms, among which, we will find regression, classification, or clustering implementations.

Our first classifier will be a simple sentiment analyzer trained on a small dataset of tweets.

To begin, we will import a few elements from the library:

```
from sklearn.feature_extraction.text import TfidfVectorizer
from sklearn.naive_bayes import MultinomialNB
```

`TfidfVectorizer` is needed for transforming our data into numerical features usable for the model. It means the text will be represented as numerical data. Next, we select the type of the model for our classifier. Naive Bayes is a simple, yet powerful technique, thus very popular in many prototyping cases. Based on Bayes Theorem, it assumes that every feature contributes independently to the probability of each class (positive, neutral, and negative in our case). This machine learning technique is often used for simple classification tasks such as spam or document classification. It is also a very suitable algorithm for our "bag of words" approach to sentiment classification.

In the next step, we import all necessary libraries:

```
from sklearn.metrics import classification_report, confusion_matrix,
accuracy_score
from sklearn.model_selection import cross_val_predict
```

We also need to import several modules for model evaluation. Evaluating the performance of a model is one of the key stages in the model building process. It indicates how successful the predictions of a dataset have been by a trained model.

Labeling the data

As explained in the previous section, we have to manually label a training dataset. We assume that the sentiment is specific to the topic of analysis and that a person who labels the data is able to do it correctly. In order to store the labels, we create a column `label`, which associates a class with a tweet.

The general rule is that the more labeled data the better, but labeling is a costly operation. In order to be efficient we label only observations that are clearly associated with a class. It will help us to get only the best examples of positive, neutral, and negative sentiment. As a result, the algorithm should have a good performance in predicting the most insightful tweets in terms of sentiment, which is the objective. Great...

We create 96 balanced labels, which means that we have around 33% of rows related to each class:

```
classes = ['pos', 'neu', 'neg']

train_data = dataset['final'][0:80]
train_labels = dataset['label'][0:80]

test_data = dataset['final'][80:96]
test_labels = dataset['label'][80:96]

train_data = list(train_data.apply(' '.join))
test_data = list(test_data.apply(' '.join))
```

We merge all the tokens of each tweet and create a list that will be used for vectorization.

Creating the model

Now, we can use the dataset with labeled observations to create a Naive Bayes model:

```
### Create feature vectors

vectorizer = TfidfVectorizer(min_df=5,
                             max_df = 0.8,
                             sublinear_tf=True,
                             use_idf=True)
```

Parameters:

- `min_df` = 5 discards words appearing in less than five documents
- `max_df` = 0.8 discards words appearing in more than 80% of the documents
- `sublinear_tf` = True uses sublinear weighting (scale the term frequency in logarithmic scale)
- `use_idf` = True enables the inverse document frequency

As a result, we obtain, train, and test vectors that can be directly used to train and validate models:

```
train_vectors = vectorizer.fit_transform(train_data)
test_vectors = vectorizer.transform(test_data)
### Perform a logistic regression model, and fit with X and y

nb = MultinomialNB()
nb.fit(train_vectors, train_labels).score(test_vectors, test_labels)
```

Model performance evaluation and cross-validation

Once we finished the training phase, we have to validate the performance and check if the predictions are good enough to keep the model. For this purpose, we will use two techniques:

- Confusion matrix
- K-fold cross-validation

Confusion matrix

A confusion matrix is a technique for summarizing the performance of a classification algorithm. It provides information of what the classification model is getting right and what types of errors it is making. Predictions of the results on a classification problem are usually visualized by the following matrix:

$$Precision = \frac{TP}{TP + FP}$$

For illustration we are using a two-class problem, and we have to select specific outcome from observations and define it as a base case (for example, it rains versus alternative (rejected) no rain). It becomes a reference point for evaluating our model with the test data.

- **True Positive** for correctly predicted values (correct prediction)
- **False Positive** for incorrectly predicted values (incorrect prediction)
- **True Negative** for correctly rejected values (correct prediction)
- **False Negative** for incorrectly rejected values (incorrect prediction)

There are multiple ways to measure the performance of the model. The Key classification accuracy indicator is called precision.

Precision is defined as the proportion of positive predictions to the number of observations that are actually positive. We can express it as follows:

$$Recall = \frac{TP}{TP + FN}$$

Recall tells us what is the proportion of actually positive observations predicted as positive:

$$F1Score = 2 \times \frac{precision \cdot recall}{precision + recall}$$

F1-score combines precision and recall to measure the test accuracy. It can be interpreted as weighted average of precision and recall with its best value at 1 and the worst at 0:

$$F1Score = 2 \times \frac{precision \cdot recall}{precision + recall}$$

Support is the number of observations that are predicted in a particular class.

K-fold cross-validation

The input data is split into K parts where one is reserved for testing, and the other K-1 for training. This process is repeated K times and the evaluation metrics are averaged. This helps in determining how well a model would generalize to new datasets.

In our example, we have labeled 96 observations in three classes (positive, negative, and neutral). We used 80 as a training set and 16 observations (17%) as a test set. Many tweets are ambiguous for sentiment classification even for human beings. Therefore, we would expect the performance in terms of precision of around 80%.

We have split our tests into three parts:

- Training set 83% - Test set 17%
- Cross validation
- Qualitative verbatim evaluation

```
print("Naive Bayes")
print(classification_report(test_labels, nb.predict(test_vectors)))
print(confusion_matrix(test_labels, nb.predict(test_vectors)))
predicted = cross_val_predict(nb, train_vectors, train_labels, cv=10)
print("Cross validation %s" % accuracy_score(train_labels, predicted))
```

The first test showed a precision of 75%, which is acceptable for a dataset with few labels:

Naive Bayes	precision	recall	f1-score	support
negative	0.80	0.50	0.62	8
neutral	1.00	0.20	0.33	5
positive	0.20	0.67	0.31	3
avg / total	0.75	0.44	0.47	16

In terms of k-fold cross-validation, we obtained the results of around 73% of precision:

- **Cross validation = 0.7375**: Thus, the human check of the sentiment of the tweets looks very promising. We have extracted some random verbatims to illustrate the results.
- **Positive**: The success of the Premier League, with its record-breaking takings is impacting in Europe `https://t.co/JDulKICszb`
- **Neutral**: Arsenal and Manchester United home fixtures moved `https://t.co/ky g7H1H6BN`, #saintsfc
- **Negative**: Wenger's future at Arsenal plunged into further uncertainty as Palace profit `https://t.co/gvbbdLH9gi`

As you can see, certain verbatims are too ambiguous for even humans to correctly interpret the sentiment, so a perfect sentiment analysis algorithm is unrealistic. In the cases when we analyze content on a specific topic, such as football in this chapter, creating a custom sentiment analysis algorithm is a good idea. In the case of mixed content, where the topic is not evident, one can use a readily available open source module. However, when building a custom algorithm, it's critical to use validation techniques to be sure of a minimum accuracy.

Named entity recognition

Now, we arrive at another important concept called the **named entity recognition**, which aims to sort textual content into default categories such as the names of persons, organizations, locations, expressions of time, quantities, monetary values, and so on. The process is also known as entity identification, entity chunking, or entity extraction. This is a very powerful technique to understand large chunks of textual content in an automated manner.

Here, we will use an open source module to demonstrate the concept called Stanford **NER** (**named entity recognizer**), which is a widely used and one of the most popular named entity recognition tools. As Stanford NER is implemented in Java, we'll use the NLTK library, which provides an interface of Stanford NER to be used using Python.

The download is a zipped file (mainly consisting of classifiers). After unpacking, we have all needed files for running under Windows or Unix/Linux/macOS, a simple GUI, and the ability to run as a server. It is worth mentioning that Stanford NER requires Java.

Installing NER

Stanford NER requires Java v1.8+ installed on the system:

1. Download Stanford Named Entity Recognizer from the page: `https://nlp.stan ford.edu/software/CRF-NER.shtml#Download`
2. Unpack the zipped file. The classifier can be found in the `/classifiers/` folder.

The use of Stanford NER Tagger is very straightforward. We put the download classifier into an arbitrary directory and indicate this directory in the `StanfordNERTagger` object. Then we invoke a `tag()` method on each tweet to get the results:

```
from nltk.tag import StanfordNERTagger
st =
StanfordNERTagger('path_to_your_folder/english.all.3class.distsim.crf.ser.g
z')
st.tag(sentence.split())
```

We will use three class classifiers `english.all.3class.distsim` that will find three classes of named entities:

- Location
- Person
- Organization

All the words that are not recognized will be labeled as 'O'. We can see an example of tagging in the following list of tuples:

```
[('Is', 'O'),
('this', 'O'),
('like', 'O'),
('when', 'O'),
('Premier', 'ORGANIZATION'),
('League', 'ORGANIZATION'),
('managers', 'O'),
('have', 'O'),
('the', 'O'),
('full', 'O'),
('confidence', 'O'),
('of', 'O'),
('the', 'O'),
('board?', 'O'),
('https:t.coXLcOeLUvpb', 'O')]
```

The classifier found two words that are related to ORGANIZATION: Premier and League. All the other words were tagged as O.

Then, we can iterate through all tweets to extract named entities and store only entities related to three classes:

```
for r in tweets:
    lst_tags = st.tag(r.split())

for tup in lst_tags:
    if(tup[1] != 'O'):
        entities.append(tup)
```

Then, we can create a dataframe with all the results:

```
df_entities = pd.DataFrame(entities)
df_entities.columns = ["word","ner"]
```

And compute the number of occurrences using the Counter module:

```
organizations =
df_entities[df_entities['ner'].str.contains("ORGANIZATION")]
cnt = Counter(organizations['word'])
cnt.most_common(10)
```

Word	Count
League	316
Premier	312
Liverpool	39
Chelsea	36
United	29
Arsenal	25
Manchester	21
Palace	18
Crystal	17
Everton	11

We can notice that the most frequent ORGANIZATION is Premier League expressed by two words. The next places in our ranking correspond to football teams: Liverpool, Chelsea, United, and Arsenal.

We perform the same extraction for PERSON:

Word	Count
Wenger	27
Dybala	21
Chelsea	19
Arsene	15
Mourinho	14
Jorge	11
Sampaoli	11
Alexis	9
Antonio	9
Carragher	9

As we can see, NER classified Chelsea as both ORGANIZATION and PERSON. Some ambiguous words may appear in all classes.

We perform the same extraction for locations:

Word	Count
City	20
Leicester	18
West	14
Ham	10
Europe	6
England	6
Madrid	5
Manchester	5

Spain	4
Brom	4

The words for locations are quite expected, but there is Madrid (which could also be the club Real Madrid) and Spain along with Leicester and Manchester among the locations mentioned. There's always a scope for ambiguity in named entity recognition where words have various meaning such as Manchester being a location is also part of the club named "Manchester United". The essence is to get all the entities tagged and then with a bit of manual cleaning we can get good insight into the content.

Combining NER and sentiment analysis

In order to get insightful information we'll calculate the sentiment for the most frequent entities related to football clubs. We take the three most mentioned clubs and check the mean sentiment for each of them using the `np.mean()` function from numpy as follows:

```
subset = dataset[dataset['tweet'].str.contains('Liverpool')]
avg_sentiment = np.mean(subset['sentiment'])
```

We obtain the following results illustrated by some random verbatim:

- **Liverpool 0.1166:** Milner focused on Liverpool results #SSFootball via @SuperSportTV `https://t.co/CIthkFY5Qs`. Juninho says he is delighted Liverpool forward Philippe Coutinho replaced him as the top-scoring Brazilian in the Premier League. African striker on his love for Liverpool. `https://t.co/Mfk6wXWwhf`

Similarly, applying the other two keywords we get the following results:

- **Chelsea 0.2121:** Melo melo@ChelseaFansUSA: Zouma: One of the best memories I have from my time at Chelsea so far was my first goal in the Premier League.... Would be great to see one of Dybala/ Griezzmann in the premier league next season. Hopefully at Chelsea. "Chelsea coach reveals the advantage Antonio Conte's side have in Premier League title race `https://t.co/pYBV7ZrbNp`.
- **Arsenal 0.0135:** Arsenal face exhausting end to Premier League season with five games in 14 days `https://t.co/SPSxrFD5pW` AW will use as excuse for losses. Arsenal are a damaged club decaying by the day but the solution is obvious `https://t.co/88PYKcKI5Z`. Jamie Carragher absolutely destroys Arsenal "cowards" in extraordinary rant `https://t.co/NHuWc0gBPu`.

This example shows that among the most frequent clubs extracted through the Entity Recognition, we conclude that Liverpool and Chelsea are mentioned in an overall positive context, whereas Arsenal in a negative one. You can always extract the original verbatims to understand precisely the reason.

Summary

Sentiment analysis and entity recognition are two powerful social media analytics techniques to get context around user content. Sports being a sentiment and emotion inciting subject among audiences, for this chapter the dataset we used were tweets using the Twitter API on the English Football Premier League. We used the Twitter REST and Streaming API to collect the data and also applied basic cleaning explained in Chapter 2, *Harnessing Social Data - Connecting, Capturing, and Cleaning*) and new cleaning methods such as device detection from Twitter API metadata. Sentiment Analysis allows us to categorize text into positive, negative, and neutral categories. We also learnt that there are limitations to sentiment analysis with accuracy, especially in ambiguous expressions. We used the **VADER (Valence Aware Dictionary for Sentiment Reasoning**) module from NLTK for sentiment analysis. We also saw that we can build our own sentiment analysis algorithm through machine learning on test and train set datasets. Accuracy of custom sentiment analysis depends heavily on the quality and size of the example or training set. Building and applying our own sentiment analyzer using the Python Scikit Learn library we got an accuracy of around 73%. We applied the cross-validation, confusion matrix, K-Fold, and precision/recall techniques to evaluate the performance of our algorithm.

Entity recognition allows us to categorize textual data into categories such as name, place, organization, and others. This is an efficient method to get a broad understanding on large amounts of social media conversations. We used a Java-based popular entity recognition module, Stanford NER. Using the library on our football dataset allowed us to extract the most frequent clubs, locations, and names being mentioned. We combined Sentiment Analysis and Entity recognition on the chosen dataset by computing sentiments on the entity club detected. Chelsea, Arsenal, and Liverpool being among the most frequent clubs as entities, the application of sentiment analysis on them gave us some insights.

In the next chapter, we will explore data from YouTube to analyze campaigns.

5

Campaigns and Consumer Reaction Analytics on YouTube – Structured and Unstructured

YouTube has changed the way video content is stored, transmitted, and viewed in the world. Yesterday's television is today's YouTube. YouTube has put the ability to publish video content to the world at the fingertips of anyone with an internet connection. The fact that viewing videos on YouTube is free and could be viewed at the convenience of your time generates a humongous amount of traffic. The statistics are staggering:

- 6 out of 10 people prefer online video platforms to live TV
- YouTube is the third most visited site in the world after Google and Facebook
- 300 hours of videos are uploaded on YouTube every hour
- 25 billion hours of video is watched each month

This explains the reason that YouTube was acquired by Google in 2006 for $1.65 billion. One big difference between TV and YouTube is in the ability to measure precisely the impact of video content in terms of traffic and preference. TV content popularity is generally measured using representative sampling metrics and then extrapolating them to understand the number of people that watched a program, while, every view on YouTube videos is recorded and aggregated along with opinions (comments), likes, and dislikes that allow us to understand the impact of video content much more precisely. Most companies today maintain their channels on YouTube the way they have pages on Facebook or Twitter. Like advertising on television, companies put ads and videos of their products and services on YouTube to promote various products or services.

YouTube provides channel and video performance (engagement on views) and audience metrics (demographics) to channel owners, but it is also possible, as a third-party, to analyze, to an extent, the impact of video content by using data from the YouTube API. This has advantages for a media analyst in understanding how different content works and how people react to it. Eventually, it makes an interesting way to be creative using data science.

In this chapter, we will cover the following topics:

- YouTube and campaigns
- Video performance analytics using Pandas
- Video comments analytics using sentiment and emotions
- Combining structured and unstructured data results for measuring campaign effectiveness

Scope and process

In this chapter, we will analyze the YouTube channel of Sony PlayStation, a very popular brand among youth, and rank their published videos in terms of popularity (views, likes, and dislikes) and also go deeper in the analysis by measuring the evolution of sentiment in terms of user comments generated for one particular video and show it on a timeline. It gives a good understanding of the popularity and attitude trends of the viewers.

This approach requires a few steps. The first step to rank videos requires us to extract the statistics, while the second requires us to gather the comments data, clean it, and calculate the sentiment measure. Finally, it will be analyzed in time-series.

This process requires us to gather both structured and unstructured data:

- **Structured data**: The number of views, likes, and dislikes of all videos
- **Unstructured data**: The comments generated for one video

Getting the data

YouTube provides very powerful APIs that can be used for interacting with videos or just getting information about them. The various numbers of APIs, endpoints, and parameters are a good selection of tools for creating applications and for getting informative data for further analysis. To follow the title of the chapter, we will be interested in the data that can bring valuable information about brands or products.

The Google documentation regarding the YouTube API is really large; hence, we will focus only on some parts of it to get started with this API, easily and rapidly. For our objective, we will use the YouTube Data API.

We are going to make authorized HTTP requests to the YouTube API `www.googleapis.com/youtube/v3` for retrieving data.

The endpoint has several resources (methods). For our case, the methods `/videos` and `/commentThreads` will return sufficient amounts of data.

Like other APIs, the YouTube API requires an authorization. Basically, when the user requests some data from YouTube through the API, it first needs to be checked and validated by the platform whether the request sent conforms to the scope of the API.

How to get a YouTube API key

We are going to use the YouTube API v3, which is the latest release of Google to date:

1. First, you need to log in to `https://console.developers.google.com/`.
2. You then need to enable the YouTube Data API shown as follows:

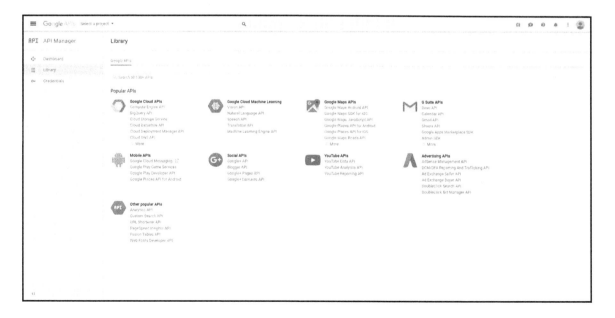

3. Create a project as shown in the following screenshot:

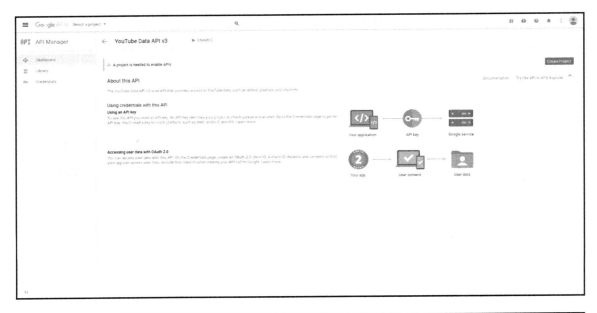

4. Enable the API:

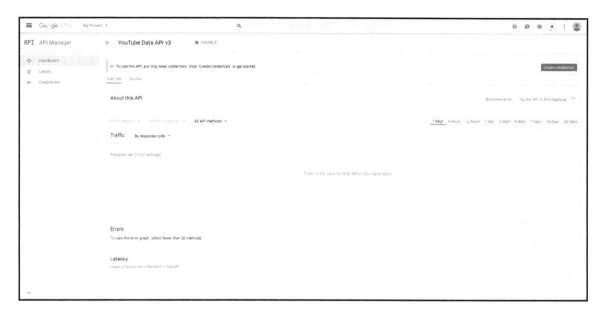

5. Add credentials and create a new key in the **Public API** access area, as shown in the following screenshot:

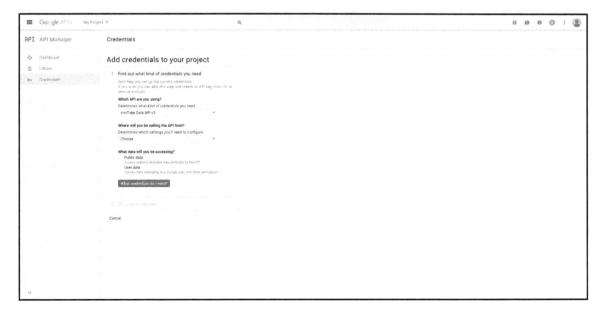

6. Finally, copy your credentials to your application shown as follows:

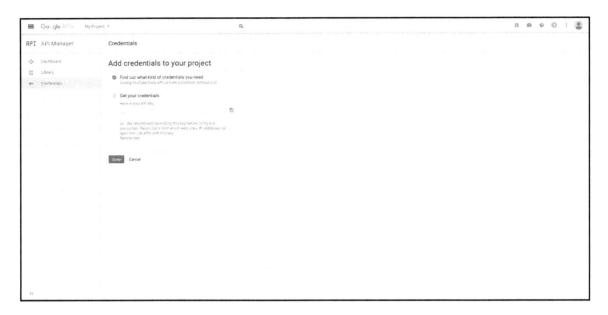

7. The API is now ready to use:

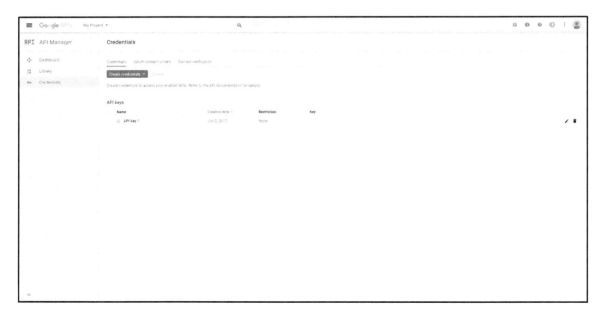

Note that this API key is not only for YouTube, but for many Google services such as Google Maps API, Custom Search API, and so on.

Data pull

We start the analysis by selecting the channel and the video. For the purpose of this chapter we select the Sony PlayStation YouTube channel, as it is one of the most popular brands in the entertainment sector. We find its URL by performing a search on the YouTube search engine and get a result similar to the following:

```
https://www.youtube.com/channel/UC-2Y8dQb0S6DtpxNgAKoJKA
```

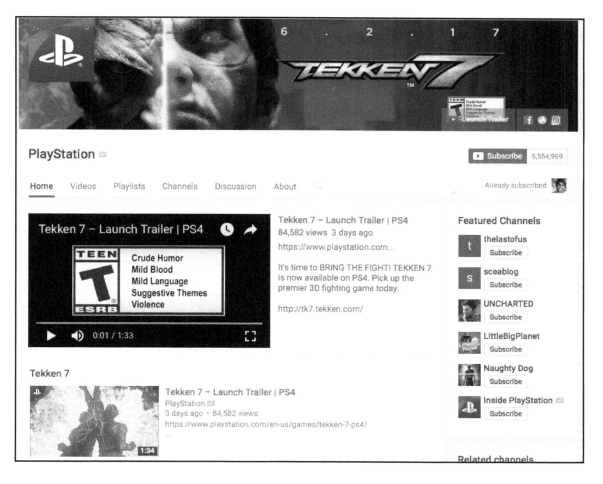

The ID of the channel corresponds to the last element of the URL, which in this case is `UC-2Y8dQb0S6DtpxNgAKoJKA`.

In the first place, we will extract the videos with the most views to understand what kind of videos gather most interest from users. In order to perform this task we have to define two functions:

- `get_channel_videos()`: A function to list all the videos associated with the channel
- `get_statistics()`: A function that collects statistics (number of views, likes, dislikes) for a single video

It is required to split this part in two steps as there is no endpoint that retrieves all the videos for a channel and provides the count of views at the same time.

We define the first function, which returns a JSON object with all the statistics for a `video_id`. Each video consumes one API call, so channels with a high number of them may make substantial amounts of requests. A free version of the YouTube API is limited to 1000 requests per 24 hours:

```
def get_statistics(video_id):
    url = "https://www.googleapis.com/youtube/v3/videos"
    pms = {'key': api_key, 'id': video_id,
'part':'contentDetails,statistics'}
    res = requests.get(url, params = pms)
    data = res.json()
    return(data)
```

The second function uses the YouTube API search endpoint to retrieve all the videos available in a channel. In one query we can retrieve up to 50 results (the `maxResults` field) which are enough to check the most popular ones, but you can get more results by using `nextPageToken` and executing the request again with this parameter.

The endpoint search returns various kinds of results depending on the arguments, which are passed to it. It can be a list of videos by keywords or a playlist related to a user. Our objective is to retrieve all the videos in a channel, so we have to define fields such as `type` and `channelId`:

- `type`: The type of content we are looking for. It might be video, playlist, channel, and so on.
- `key`: API access key.
- `channelId`: The ID of the channel we want to analyze.
- `part`: The type of data we get in response. We can only choose snippet, which returns all basic information such as title, description, and thumbnails. Unfortunately, we cannot obtain any statistics.
- `order`: Field the results are ordered on. We have chosen `viewCount`, but it can be also `likeCount` or `dislikeCount`. By default, the results are ordered by `relevance`.
- `maxResults`: The number of results in a response. It is an integer between 0 and 50.

```
def get_channel_videos(channel_id):

    url = "https://www.googleapis.com/youtube/v3/search"

    pms = {'type': 'video', 'key': api_key, 'channelId': channel_id,
    'part':'snippet', 'order':'viewCount','maxResults':50}

    res = requests.get(url, params = pms)

    data = res.json()

    lst = []

    for video in data['items']:
        video_stats = get_statistics(video['id']['videoId'])

        results_json = {
            'channelTitle' : video['snippet']['channelTitle'],
            'title' : video['snippet']['title'],
            'publishedAt' : video['snippet']['publishedAt'],
            'videoId' : video['id']['videoId'],
            'viewCount' :
video_stats['items'][0]['statistics']['viewCount'],
            'commentCount' : video_stats['items'][0]['statistics']
['commentCount'],
            'likeCount' :
```

```
video_stats['items'][0]['statistics']['likeCount'],
            'dislikeCount' : video_stats['items'][0]['statistics']
            ['dislikeCount'],
    }

    lst.append(results_json)

df = pd.read_json(json.dumps(lst))

return(df)
```

For each item in the top 50 by `viewCount` we execute the `get_statistics` function to get all numerical data. Then we create a list of JSONs with the following fields: `channelTitle`, `title`, `publishedAt`, `videoId`, `viewCount`, `commentCount`, `likeCount`, `dislikeCount`, and then we load it to a dataframe.

As a result we obtain a dataframe with top 50 videos and all relative information shown as follows:

title	viewCount	commentCount	dislikeCount	likeCount	publishedAt	videoId	channelTitle
PlayStation 4	33334786	31407	5559	88340	2013-02-21T01:27:20.000Z	x7QhUL8NUK4	PlayStation
**God of War - E3 2016 Gameplay Trailer	PS4**	17314381	53537	10356	323489	2016-06-14T01:06:31.000Z	CJ_GCPaKywg	PlayStation
Official PlayStation Used Game Instructional Video	16096138	96765	8588	351937	2013-06-11T02:42:20.000Z	kWSIFh8ICaA	PlayStation
**Call of Duty: Infinite Warfare - :60	PS4 Pro**	14755356	791	3542	5621	2016-11-07T20:14:45.000Z	3kdyg3Dfx54	PlayStation
**Final Fantasy VII - E3 2015 Trailer	PS4**	14696915	23285	2769	125509	2015-06-16T01:54:47.000Z	Kznek1uNVsg	PlayStation
**Spider-Man - E3 2016 Trailer	PS4**	13239429	18180	3793	91063	2016-06-14T02:30:27.000Z	3R2uvJqWeVg	PlayStation
Uncharted 4: A Thief's End E3 2014 Trailer (PS4)	10198936	10483	1472	72554	2014-06-10T02:48:57.000Z	y1Rx-Bbht5E	PlayStation

UNCHARTED 4: A Thief's End (5/10/2016) - Story Trailer | PS4	8332330	9286	1305	56589	2016-02-24T20:09:13.000Z	hh5HV4iic1Y	PlayStation
UNCHARTED 4: A Thief's End - E3 2015 Press Conference Demo | PS4	8229800	7792	2033	85785	2015-06-16T02:48:05.000Z	zL46dpNEPPA	PlayStation
Horizon Zero Dawn - E3 2016 Trailer I Only On PS4	7741077	10873	15199	49158	2016-06-06T15:00:30.000Z	u4-FCsiF5x4	PlayStation

Table 1: Top 10 videos on the PlayStation channel.

As we can see in the table, we have successfully extracted the top 10 videos of the Sony PlayStation YouTube channel. These statistics are extremely important for a company to monitor the performance of its channel and most performing videos. We can also determine if the videos with the most views are liked or disliked based on the other statistics in the table. Even though the list of the best videos may not change for a long while, extracting this information regularly allows us to follow the evolution between the best videos. Another interesting use case of this exercise is to gather the top 10 videos of multiple channels to understand the type of content that goes viral or are the best:

Overwatch - Alive Animated Short | PS4	4353806	12140	1371	65768	2016-04-03T19:00:00.000Z	ZyBUMabtslI	PlayStation
The Official PS4 Unboxing Video | PlayStation 4	4145110	8961	3716	47538	2013-11-11T00:43:57.000Z	YQUpg795iBo	PlayStation
HITMAN - E3 2015 Trailer | PS4	3718831	5169	914	44768	2015-06-16T01:38:23.000Z	LVqxMCZ3u6k	PlayStation
Official Batman: Arkham Knight Gameplay Trailer - "Evening The Odds"	3585089	3507	525	28413	2014-05-21T13:00:05.000Z	dxa34RatmSc	PlayStation
Introducing the PlayStation®Move	3553396	9350	1383	7402	2010-03-11T23:45:04.000Z	s9ybHddDMgM	PlayStation

Table 2: Ranking between 31-35

To go beyond the top 10, we perform some iteration to get some more videos in the list. For the next part of the analysis we'll choose an interesting video that has less than 10,000 comments, which is the daily limit for the Google Data API, beyond which it's paid, and also with an older publication date to have a longer timeline of analysis. Therefore, we will use The Official PS4 Unboxing Video | PlayStation 4. This video is popular—more than 4.1 million views and 8962 comments. The volume of comments allows us to prepare sufficient dataset for our analysis.

The first task is to obtain the video ID. When we search the video on the YouTube page (`https://www.youtube.com/`), and click it to play, the id is shown in the browser's URL tab as follows: `https://www.youtube.com/watch?v=YQUpg795iBo`

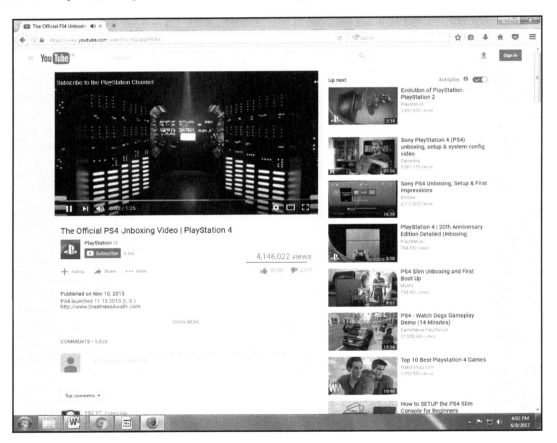

Here, `YQUpg795iBo` is the ID. It would be one of our parameters to retrieve data from the API.

Next, we need to build the script to get information about the video. As usual, the requests library will be used to call the API:

```
import requests

url = 'https://www.googleapis.com/youtube/v3/videos'
pms = {'part': 'snippet, statistics', 'id' : 'YQUpg795iBo', 'key': 'xxx'}
res = requests.get(url, params = pms)
data = res.json()
```

The call requires the ID of the video, and the filter parameters part. Snippet and statistics attributes will return the general information about the video (title, description, tags, and channel information among others) and the statistics. The statistics will be in the following structure:

```
'statistics': { 'commentCount': '8962',
                'dislikeCount': '3713',
               'favoriteCount': '0',
                'likeCount': '47479',
                'viewCount': '4140155'
              }
```

It is worth noting that there are multiple other filter attributes for the part parameter (see the YouTube API documentation https://developers.google.com/youtube/).

The data we retrieved is quite informative; however, we will go further by gathering the comments on the video, which is necessary for our analysis. This task requires another call to the API:

```
url = 'https://www.googleapis.com/youtube/v3/commentThreads'

full_data = []                  # return list
page = ''                       # initialization of paging

while True:

pms = {'part': 'snippet', 'videoId' : 'YQUpg795iBo', 'maxResults' : 50,
'key': 'xxx', 'pageToken': page}
   res = requests.get(url, params = pms)
   print("Connection status: %s" % res)       # check the status of the
connection
   data = res.json()
   full_data.extend(data['items'])
   print("Just downloaded: %s, Total: %s" % (len(data['items']),
len(full_data)))

   try:
```

```
        page = data['nextPageToken']
    except:
            break
```

The call returns the video's comments, but the number of comments we get is limited by the `maxResults` parameter. Acceptable values are 1 to 100, inclusive. In order to simplify the process, we will gather only top-level comments (threads) without replies.

If a video has a large amount of interactions, it is necessary to use paging to get all the comments.

In general, every time someone is calling the API for a large amount of information, in order to keep servers balanced, the system will automatically paginate the requested items. Information about pagination is provided in the `nextPageToken` key in returned json objects. The key contains information about the next token, which should be submitted as a `pageToken` parameter in the next API call. It is applied in the `while loop`, where such a parameter is submitted to pms, and the loop is broken while the `nextPageToken` is not existing (end of data).

Data processing

Now that the data is extracted, it's time to process it and prepare for the final analysis.

The `full_data` variable will contain a list of items, where a single item looks as follows:

```
{'etag': '"m2yskBQFythfE4irbTIeOgYYfBU/XgRZI3UhbKRFQZGd-n-2OCOKR8A"',
 'id': 'z13jynay3seygpvzy04cef5r2tm5ihh4d0k',
 'kind': 'youtube#commentThread',
 'snippet': {'canReply': False,
  'isPublic': True,
  'topLevelComment': {'etag':
  '"m2yskBQFythfE4irbTIeOgYYfBU/jW3EfLcy4MnIFrtFloQEjokBPXU"',
   'id': 'z13jynay3seygpvzy04cef5r2tm5ihh4d0k',
   'kind': 'youtube#comment',
   'snippet': {'authorChannelId': {'value': 'UCuJkT4Bsd1qiIQoI8Rbf_hg'},
   'authorChannelUrl':
'http://www.youtube.com/channel/UCuJkT4Bsd1qiIQoI8Rbf_hg',
   'authorDisplayName': 'Vince / FCB',
   'authorProfileImageUrl': 'https://yt3.ggpht.com/-9DZP7TJ0J-
   4/AAAAAAAAAAI/AAAAAAAAAAA/dvUasDtmZFw/s28-c-k-no-mo-rj-
c0xffffff/photo.jpg',
   'canRate': False,
   'likeCount': 0,
   'publishedAt': '2017-05-06T17:52:51.000Z',
```

```
'textDisplay': 'i don't like this',
'textOriginal': "i don't like this",
'updatedAt': '2017-05-06T17:52:51.000Z',
'videoId': 'YQUpg795iBo',
'viewerRating': 'none'}},
'totalReplyCount': 0,
'videoId': 'YQUpg795iBo'}}
```

We will focus on the `snippet` object, where we can find `textOriginal` and `publishedAt` values.

The dataframe structures are very efficient ways to store and process data. Thus, we will add relevant information to such structures as shown in the following code snippet:

```
import pandas as pd

df = pd.DataFrame()

df['comments'] = [k['snippet']['topLevelComment']['snippet']['textDisplay']
for k in full_data]
df['date'] = [k['snippet']['topLevelComment']['snippet']['publishedAt'] for
k in full_data]
```

In our analysis, we are going to look at the comments as a function of time. For that purpose, we will use time series functionality of data frames. It requires us to set the dataframe index as a `datetime` object shown as follows:

```
df = df.set_index(['date'])            # sets index
df.index = pd.to_datetime(df.index)    # converts to datetime object
```

The dataframe has two columns: date and comments, which contain the data gathered from the YouTube API:

```
date comments
2013-11-11 00:49:49 Greatness Awaits. :)
2013-11-11 00:49:48 HNNNNNNGH!!! My body isn't ready! PS4 the ...
2013-11-11 00:49:41 Epic
2013-11-11 00:49:35 Quite possibly the coolest unboxing video ever.
2013-11-11 00:47:36 GREATNESS HAS ARRIVED
2013-11-11 00:47:01 I thought they said they were leaving this to ...
2013-11-11 00:46:56 simmbaaa
2013-11-11 00:46:37 cant leave fingerprints or else hes going to jail
2013-11-11 00:46:05 4th!!!!
2013-11-11 00:45:10 WOOT WOOT
```

The comments are in the form as they were extracted from YouTube. Therefore, they contain many characters, punctuation, emojis, and other elements that create noise in sentiment analysis. Before we calculate sentiment analysis on each comment as explained in previous chapters, we should process the text to remove all such elements. The text processing workflow for this case consists of the following steps:

- Tokenization
- Conversion to lowercase
- Stopwords removal
- Punctuation removal
- Removal of words shorter than two characters

We implement all the steps in a single function and then apply them on the whole dataset.

The language processing tasks are well handled by the NLTK library:

```
from nltk import word_tokenize
from nltk.corpus import stopwords
import string

def clean(text):
    tokens = word_tokenize(text.strip())
    clean = [i.lower() for i in tokens]
    clean = [i for i in clean if i not in stopwords.words('english')]
    clean = [i.strip(''.join(punctuations)) for i in clean if i not in
list(string.punctuation)]
    clean = [i for i in clean if len(i) > 1]

    return " ".join(clean)
```

Such a method of cleaning provides good enough results for the kind of analysis we perform in this chapter. As an example, the function will process the post:

Greatness needs to stop awaiting and get here already! 5 more days!

Into:

greatness needs stop awaiting get already days

Now, we can apply the function to our dataset:

```
df['clean_comments'] = df['comment'].apply(clean)
return(" ".join(clean))
```

We have now created a new column with clean comments, on which we will calculate sentiment.

The sentiment will be calculated using the NLTK Vader classifier:

```
from nltk.sentiment.vader import SentimentIntensityAnalyzer

sentiment = SentimentIntensityAnalyzer()
df['sentiment'] = df['clean_comments'].apply(lambda txt:
sentiment.polarity_scores(txt)['compound'])
```

The new column contains compound sentiment for each comment, where values closer to +1 describe positive attitude and values closer to -1 negative, respectively.

Now we have completed all the data preparation that will allow us to compute the results for the analysis for the channel and the video for sentiment perception over time. We have seen that each time that the data extracted from the Social Media APIs requires a sufficient amount of data processing and preparation for attaining the objectives set. In this case, we needed to add a feature regarding the sentiment analysis. This could differ for different objectives.

Data analysis

As the data is ready, we can start our analysis. We'll explore time-series analysis for analyzing our dataset using the features that we have extracted. Our goal is to answer the following questions:

- How does sentiment evolve over time? Are there any peaks?
- What are the periods when users comment more?
- What is the day of week when users put the most positive comments?
- What is the day of week when they comment most actively?

In order to answer these questions, we need to work on data in time. Pandas dataframe structures have many interesting properties for time series handling. In previous steps, we have changed the index in our data frame by setting it to the `datetime` object. We can now use it to resample our data according to the time frame.

Sentiment analysis in time

Firstly, we'll compute the average sentiment score per month:

```
df['sentiment'].resample('M').mean()
```

The argument of the `resample()` method indicates time window. We could also use other periods, for example:

- **B**: Business day
- **D**: Calendar day
- **W**: Weekly
- **Q**: Quarter end
- **A**: Year end

There are many other possible ways to resample timeseries data. It can be found in the Pandas library documentation: `http://pandas.pydata.org/pandas-docs/stable/timeseries.html#offset-aliases`.

Then, we use `matplotlib` to plot the average monthly sentiment as follows:

```
import matplotlib.pyplot as plt
import matplotlib
matplotlib.style.use('ggplot')

df['sentiment'].resample('M').mean().plot(title = "Sentiment over Time", lw =2, ylim = (-1,1))

plt.axhline(0, color='k', lw = 2)
plt.xlabel('Date')
plt.ylabel('Sentiment score')

plt.show()
```

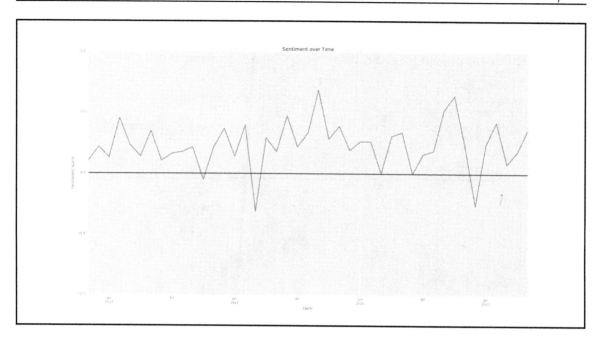

The chart illustrates the evolution of the sentiment for the video analyzed. The global sentiment for the video seems to be positive and appreciated. However, there are moments when the curve has gone to the negative side. To understand precisely the reasons for a positive or a negative peak, we can always look at the exact comments corresponding to the time; however, this is beyond the scope of this chapter. We can always use the verbatim extraction methods provided in the previous chapters to complete this analysis. We will leave this as an exercise for readers.

Sentiment by weekday

We use a similar approach for sentiment to keep the results comparable:

```
dx = df[df.index > '2013-11-18']
ax = dx.groupby(dx.index.weekday)['sentiment'].mean().plot(kind = 'bar',
title = 'Average sentiment by day of week')
ax.set_xticklabels(['Monday', 'Tuesday', 'Wednesday', 'Thursday', 'Friday',
'Saturday', 'Sunday'])
plt.show()
```

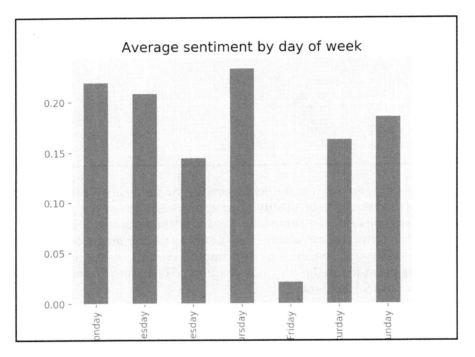

The analysis by the day of the week shows an interesting trend. While the maximum number of comments is on Friday, the most positive sentiment is on Thursday. Based on these two extreme days, we notice a correlation between the number of comments and its sentiment saying that the lesser number of comments implies more positive attitude. This is, of course, a rule that cannot be generalized and the contents should be verified by studying the verbatims on these days.

This approach is an interesting way to do trend analysis on video content combining quantitative (comment counts) and qualitative (sentiment) metrics.

Comments in time

Secondly, it is interesting to know the periods when users comment most actively on the video.

We use a similar approach to plot the number of comments on a chart:

```
df['sentiment'].resample('M').count().plot()

plt.axhline(0, color='k', lw = 2)
plt.xlabel('Date')
plt.ylabel('Number of comments')

plt.show()
```

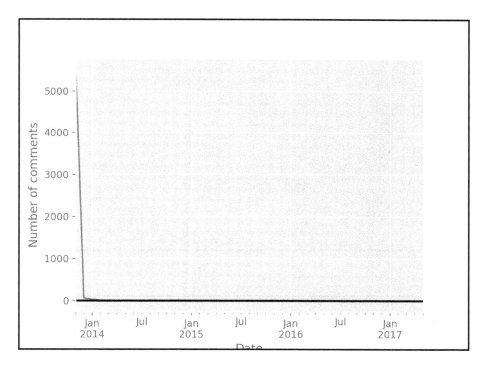

We can see that the majority of comments were published within the first few days after publication. It means that this is the most crucial period for a brand to capture the attention of its target audience.

Then, we can check what happens after this period by analyzing comments from the second week onwards:

```
dx = df[df.index > '2013-11-18']
dx['sentiment'].resample('M').count().plot()

plt.axhline(0, color='k', lw = 2)
plt.xlabel('Date')
plt.ylabel('Number of comments')
plt.show()
```

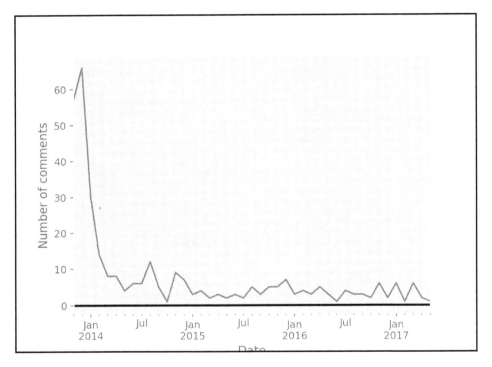

Analyzing from the second week onwards allows us to reduce the cannibalizing effect of the most popular week eliminating the trends of the successive weeks and days. We can see certain peaks and dips in the graph, but overall there is a decreasing trend. It's always interesting to make time-series analysis on different dimensions. If the period is sufficiently long, we can visualize the trends in years, months, and also weeks. To go further in our analysis, we will check the trends of a week in terms of the days of the week.

Number of comments by weekday

In order to remove the bias of the first week, which we have seen previously, we will subset that dataframe to get only the data that appears after 2013-11-15:

```
dx = df[df.index > '2013-11-15']

ax = dx.groupby(dx.index.weekday)['comments'].count().plot(kind = 'bar',
title = 'Number of comments per day')

ax.set_xticklabels(['Monday', 'Tuesday', 'Wednesday', 'Thursday', 'Friday',
'Saturday', 'Sunday'])

plt.show()
```

Then we print a bar chart that shows the number of comments per day:

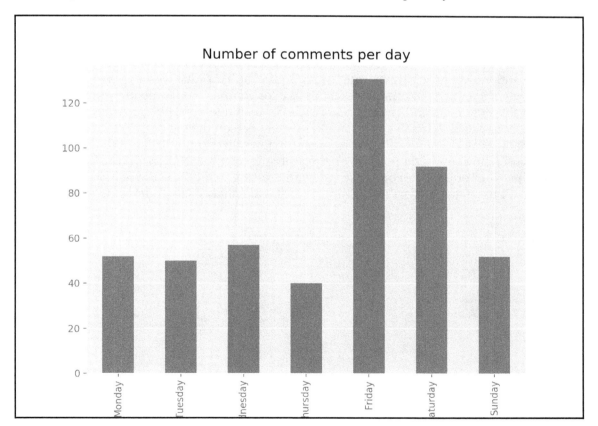

The result of the visualization shows us that the video we chose has a stable rate of engagement with respect to the days of weeks, though the weekend days of Friday and Saturday gather the most engagement. This phenomenon could be explained by the fact that the audience of this video of Sony PlayStation has more time to check out and give opinions on videos at the weekend. It could be an interesting exercise to make the same analysis of more videos of the channel and see if the trend can be generalized for the whole channel. Such insights on time-series are great inputs for marketing teams of companies that need to prioritize the publication of content and interaction with its audience. If certain days of the week generate more activity from the audience, it's efficient to reserve those days to interact and exchange with your audience. This phenomenon could be different for the individual audiences of each social media asset (YouTube, Twitter, Facebook, Instagram, and others).

Summary

YouTube has emerged as the most preferred platform for video viewing, going ahead of television. This popularity has resulted in astronomical amounts of video hours being uploaded and viewed every hour. Due to its popularity, YouTube was acquired by Google in 2006. Since then, it has become a de facto place for companies to upload promotional videos for its consumers and fans. The significant advantage YouTube provides over TV is in the ability to precisely analyze the impact of the video on the viewers. We do this through data accessed by its API like, number of views, likes, and dislikes. YouTube also allows its users to express their views on the videos by commenting displayed under the videos. This piece of information is extremely interesting to measure the response of video audience. All the data on users is a goldmine for media analysts to understand user behavior.

In this chapter, we accessed all publicly available data using the Google Data API. We chose the Sony PlayStation official YouTube channel to perform the data analytics process of registering and connecting to the Google Data API and thereafter, gathering, processing, and analyzing the data. For the analysis we ranked the videos of the channel in the order of their views, likes, and dislikes. We went deeper in the analysis by analyzing the user comments of a very popular video of the channel and computing the sentiment over time. The results of the time-series sentiment analysis of the comments were overall positive with some variations in the intensity and both positive and negative peaks present. We left the extraction of the comments for the peaks as an exercise for the readers. We also observed that for our case that the launch of the video generated most engagement in terms of opinions, which indicates that it is the right time for the brand to capitalize on its audience. Lastly, we also saw that the volume of engagement and the sentiment generated can vary on different days of the week.

In the upcoming chapter, we will change explore trends on a totally different type of platform, GitHub, the collaborative social coding, platform to discover the most popular technology in the world of programming.

6
The Next Great Technology – Trends Mining on GitHub

Those who love to code, love GitHub. GitHub has taken the widely used version controlling approach to coding to the highest possible level by implementing social network features to the world of programming. No wonder GitHub is also thought of as Social Coding. We thought a book on Social Network analysis would not be complete without a use case on data from GitHub. GitHub allows you to create code repositories and provides multiple collaborative features, bug tracking, feature requests, task managements, and wikis. GitHub has about 20 million users and 57 million code repositories (source: Wikipedia). These kind of statistics easily demonstrate that this is the most representative platform of programmers. It's also a platform for several open source projects that have contributed greatly to the world of software development. Programming technology is evolving at such a fast pace, especially due to the open source movement, and we have to be able to keep a track of emerging technologies. Assuming that the latest programming tools and technologies are being used with GitHub, analyzing GitHub could help us detect the most popular technologies. The popularity of repositories on GitHub is assessed through the number of commits it receives from its community. We will use the GitHub API in this chapter to gather data around repositories with the most number of commits and then discover the most popular technology within them. For all we know, the results that we get may reveal the next great innovations.

In this chapter we will cover the following topics:

- Introduction to GitHub
- GitHub API manipulation
- Trend discovery
- Trend analysis in time
- Clustering to detect most interesting and relevant projects in trends

Scope and process

GitHub API allows us to get information about public code repositories submitted by users. It covers lots of open-source, educational and personal projects. Our focus is to find the trending technologies and programming languages of last few months, and compare with repositories from past years. We will collect all the meta information about the repositories,

- **Name**: The name of the repository
- **Description**: A description of the repository
- **Watchers**: People following the repository and getting notified about its activity
- **Forks**: Users cloning the repository to their own accounts
- **Open issues**: Issues submitted about the repository

We will use this data, a combination of qualitative and quantitative information, to identify the most recent trends and weak signals. The process can be represented by the steps shown in the following figure:

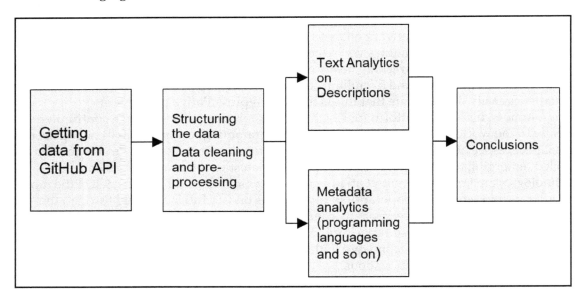

Getting the data

Before using the API, we need to set the authorization. The API gives you access to all publicly available data, but some endpoints need user permission. You can create a new token with some specific scope access using the application settings. The scope depends on your application's needs, such as accessing user email, updating user profile, and so on.

Password authorization is only needed in some cases, like access by user authorized applications. In that case, you need to provide your username or email, and your password.

All API access is over HTTPS, and accessed from the `https://api.github.com/` domain. All data is sent and received as JSON.

Rate Limits

The GitHub Search API is designed to help to find specific items (repository, users, and so on). The rate limit policy allows up to 1,000 results for each search. For requests using basic authentication, OAuth, or client ID and secret, you can make up to 30 requests per minute. For unauthenticated requests, the rate limit allows you to make up to 10 requests per minute.

Connection to GitHub

GitHub offers a search endpoint which returns all the repositories matching a query. As we go along, in different steps of the analysis we will change the value of the variable q (query). In the first part, we will retrieve all the repositories created since January 1, 2017 and then we will compare the results with previous years.

Firstly, we initialize an empty list `results` which stores all data about repositories. Secondly, we build get requests with parameters required by the API. We can only get 100 results per request, so we have to use a pagination technique to build a complete dataset.

```
results = []

q = "created:>2017-01-01"

def search_repo_paging(q):

url = 'https://api.github.com/search/repositories'
params = {'q' : q, 'sort' : 'forks', 'order': 'desc', 'per_page' : 100}
while True:
```

```
res = requests.get(url,params = params)
result = res.json()
results extend(result['items'])
params = {}

try:
        url = res.links['next']['url']
except:
        break
```

In the first request we have to pass all the parameters to the `GET` method in our request. Then, we make a new request for every next page, which can be found in `res.links['next']['url']`. `res.links` contains a full link to the resources including all the other parameters. That is why we empty the `params` dictionary.

The operation is repeated until there is no next page key in `res.links` dictionary.

For other datasets we modify the search query in such a way that we retrieve repositories from previous years. For example to get the data from 2015 we define the following query:

```
q = "created:2015-01-01..2015-12-31"
```

In order to find proper repositories, the API provides a wide range of query parameters. It is possible to search for repositories with high precision using the system of qualifiers.

Starting with main search parameters q, we have following options:

- `sort`: Set to forks as we are interested in finding the repositories having the largest number of forks (you can also sort by number of stars or update time)
- `order`: Set to descending order
- `per_page`: Set to the maximum amount of returned repositories

Naturally, the search parameter q can contain multiple combinations of qualifiers.

Data pull

The amount of data we collect through GitHub API is such that it fits in memory. We can deal with it directly in a pandas dataframe. If more data is required, we would recommend storing it in a database, such as MongoDB.

We use JSON tools to convert the results into a clean JSON and to create a dataframe.

```
from pandas.io.json import json_normalize
import json
import pandas as pd
import bson.json_util as json_util

sanitized = json.loads(json_util.dumps(results))
normalized = json_normalize(sanitized)
df = pd.DataFrame(normalized)
```

The dataframe `df` contains columns related to all the results returned by GitHub API. We can list them by typing the following:

```
df.columns
```

```
Index(['archive_url', 'assignees_url', 'blobs_url', 'branches_url',
       'clone_url', 'collaborators_url', 'comments_url', 'commits_url',
       'compare_url', 'contents_url', 'contributors_url', 'default_branch',
       'deployments_url', 'description', 'downloads_url', 'events_url',
       'fork',
       'forks', 'forks_count', 'forks_url', 'full_name', 'git_commits_url',
       'git_refs_url', 'git_tags_url', 'git_url', 'has_downloads',
       'has_issues', 'has_pages', 'has_projects', 'has_wiki', 'homepage',
       'hooks_url', 'html_url', 'id', 'issue_comment_url',
       'issue_events_url',
       'issues_url', 'keys_url', 'labels_url', 'language', 'languages_url',
       'merges_url', 'milestones_url', 'mirror_url', 'name',
       'notifications_url', 'open_issues', 'open_issues_count',
       'owner.avatar_url', 'owner.events_url', 'owner.followers_url',
       'owner.following_url', 'owner.gists_url', 'owner.gravatar_id',
       'owner.html_url', 'owner.id', 'owner.login',
       'owner.organizations_url',
       'owner.received_events_url', 'owner.repos_url', 'owner.site_admin',
       'owner.starred_url', 'owner.subscriptions_url', 'owner.type',
       'owner.url', 'private', 'pulls_url', 'pushed_at', 'releases_url',
       'score', 'size', 'ssh_url', 'stargazers_count', 'stargazers_url',
       'statuses_url', 'subscribers_url', 'subscription_url', 'svn_url',
       'tags_url', 'teams_url', 'trees_url', 'updated_at', 'url',
       'watchers',
       'watchers_count', 'year'],
      dtype='object')
```

Then, we select a subset of variables which will be used for further analysis. Our choice is based on the meaning of each of them. We skip all the technical variables related to URLs, owner information, or ID. The remaining columns contain information which is very likely to help us identify new technology trends:

- `description`: A user description of a repository
- `watchers_count`: The number of watchers
- `size`: The size of repository in kilobytes
- `forks_count`: The number of forks
- `open_issues_count`: The number of open issues
- `language`: The programming language the repository is written in

We have selected `watchers_count` as the criterion to measure the popularity of repositories. This number indicates how many people are interested in the project. However, we may also use `forks_count` which gives us slightly different information about the popularity. The latter represents the number of people who actually worked with the code, so it is related to a different group.

Data processing

In the previous step we structured the raw data which is now ready for further analysis. Our objective is to analyze two types of data:

- Textual data in description
- Numerical data in other variables

Each of them requires a different pre-processing technique. Let's take a look at each type in detail.

Textual data

For the first kind, we have to create a new variable which contains a cleaned string. We will do it in three steps which have already been presented in previous chapters:

- Selecting English descriptions
- Tokenization
- Stopwords removal

As we work only on English data, we should remove all the descriptions which are written in other languages. The main reason to do so is that each language requires a different processing and analysis flow. If we left descriptions in Russian or Chinese, we would have very noisy data which we would not be able to interpret. As a consequence, we can say that we are analyzing trends in the English-speaking world.

Firstly, we remove all the empty strings in the description column.

```
df = df.dropna(subset=['description'])
```

In order to remove non-English descriptions we have to first detect what language is used in each text. For this purpose we use a library called `langdetect` which is based on the Google language detection project (`https://github.com/shuyo/language-detection`).

```
from langdetect import detect

df['lang'] = df.apply(lambda x: detect(x['description']),axis=1)
```

We create a new column which contains all the predictions. We see different languages, such as `en` (English), `zh-cn` (Chinese), `vi` (Vietnamese), or `ca` (Catalan).

```
df['lang']

0           en
1           en
2           en
3           en
4           en
5        zh-cn
```

In our dataset `en` represents 78.7% of all the repositories. We will now select only those repositories with a description in English:

```
df = df[df['lang'] == 'en']
```

In the next step, we will create a new clean column with pre-processed textual data. We execute the following code to perform tokenization and remove stopwords:

```
import nltk
from nltk import word_tokenize
from nltk.corpus import stopwords

def clean(text = '', stopwords = []):

#tokenize
    tokens = word_tokenize(text.strip())
#lowercase
```

```
    clean = [i.lower() for i in tokens]

#remove stopwords
    clean = [i for i in clean if i not in stopwords]

#remove punctuation
    punctuations = list(string.punctuation)
    clean = [i.strip(''.join(punctuations)) for i in clean if i not in
    punctuations]

    return " ".join(clean)

df['clean'] = df['description'].apply(str) #make sure description is a
string
df['clean'] = df['clean'].apply(lambda x: clean(text = x, stopwords =
stopwords.words('english')))
```

Finally, we obtain a clean column which contains cleaned English descriptions, ready for analysis:

```
df['clean'].head(5)

0                     roadmap becoming web developer 2017
1     base repository imad v2 course application ple...
2             decrypted content eqgrp-auction-file.tar.xz
3              shadow brokers  lost translation  leak
4     learn design large-scale systems prep system d...
```

Numerical data

For numerical data, we will check statistically both what the distribution of values is and whether there are any missing values:

```
df[['watchers_count','size','forks_count','open_issues']].describe()
```

NA	watchers_count	size	forks_count	open_issues
count	787.000000	7.870000e+02	787.000000	787.000000
mean	696.656925	2.079364e+04	129.127065	13.270648
std	1652.487989	2.056537e+05	208.778257	30.909030
min	0.000000	0.000000e+00	33.000000	0.000000
25%	0.000000	3.250000e+01	58.000000	0.000000

50%	124.000000	4.540000e+02	76.000000	3.000000
75%	656.500000	6.859000e+03	99.000000	12.000000
max	20792.000000	5.657792e+06	2589.000000	458.000000

We see that there are no missing values in all four variables: `watchers_count`, `size`, `forks_count`, and `open issues`. The `watchers_count` varies from 0 to 20,792 while the minimum number of forks is 33 and goes up to 2,589. The first quartile of repositories has no open issues while top 25% have more than 12. It is worth noticing that, in our dataset, there is a repository which has 458 open issues.

Data analysis

We have seen so far that the GitHub API provides interesting sets of information about the code repositories and metadata around the activity of its users around these repositories. In the following sections, we will analyze this data to find out which are the most popular repositories through the analysis of its descriptions and then drilling down to the watchers, forks, and issues submitted on the emerging technologies. Since, technology is evolving so rapidly, this approach could help us to stay on top of the latest trending technologies.

In order to find out what are the trending technologies, we will perform the analysis in a few steps:

- Detect the most trending topics/technologies based on descriptions
- Identify the most popular programming languages globally
- Find out what programming languages are used for the top technologies
- What are the differences between technologies in terms of repository size, open issues, number of forks, and watchers
- See what are the most popular projects and top technology in 2017

Top technologies

First of all, we will use text analytics techniques to identify what are the most popular phrases related to technologies in repositories from 2017. Our analysis will be focused on the most frequent bigrams.

We import a `nltk.collocation` module which implements n-gram search tools:

```
import nltk
from nltk.collocations import *
```

Then, we convert the clean description column into a list of tokens:

```
list_documents = df['clean'].apply(lambda x: x.split()).tolist()
```

As we perform an analysis on documents, we will use the method `from_documents` instead of a default one `from_words`. The difference between these two methods lies in the input data format. The one used in our case takes as argument a list of tokens and searches for n-grams document-wise instead of corpus-wise. It protects against detecting bi-grams composed of the last word of one document and the first one of another one:

```
bigram_measures = nltk.collocations.BigramAssocMeasures()
bigram_finder = BigramCollocationFinder.from_documents(list_documents)
```

We take into account only bi-grams which appear at least three times in our document set:

```
bigram_finder.apply_freq_filter(3)
```

We can use different association measures to find the best bi-grams, such as raw frequency, pmi, student t, or chi sq. We will mostly be interested in the raw frequency measure, which is the simplest and most convenient indicator in our case.

We get top 20 bigrams according to `raw_freq` measure:

```
bigrams = bigram_finder.nbest(bigram_measures.raw_freq,20)
```

We can also obtain their scores by applying the `score_ngrams` method:

```
scores = bigram_finder.score_ngrams(bigram_measures.raw_freq)
```

All the other measures are implemented as methods of `BigramCollocationFinder`. To try them, you can replace `raw_freq` by, respectively, `pmi`, `student_t`, and `chi_sq`.

However, to create a visualization we will need the actual number of occurrences instead of scores. We create a list by using the `ngram_fd.items()` method and we sort it in descending order.

```
ngram = list(bigram_finder.ngram_fd.items())
ngram.sort(key=lambda item: item[-1], reverse=True)
```

It returns a dictionary of tuples which contain an embedded tuple and its frequency. We transform it into a simple list of tuples where we join bigram tokens:

```
frequency = [(" ".join(k), v) for k,v in ngram]
```

For simplicity reasons we put the frequency list into a dataframe:

```
df=pd.DataFrame(frequency)
```

And then, we plot the top 20 technologies in a bar chart:

```
import matplotlib.pyplot as plt
plt.style.use('ggplot')

df.set_index([0], inplace = True)
df.sort_values(by = [1], ascending = False).head(20).plot(kind = 'barh')

plt.title('Trending Technologies')
plt.ylabel('Technology')
plt.xlabel('Popularity')
plt.legend().set_visible(False)

plt.axvline(x=14, color='b', label='Average', linestyle='--', linewidth=3)
for custom in [0, 10, 14]:
    plt.text(14.2, custom, "Neural Networks", fontsize = 12, va = 'center',
bbox = dict(boxstyle='square', fc='white', ec='none'))

plt.show()
```

We've added an additional line which helps us to aggregate all technologies related to neural networks. It is done manually by selecting elements by indices, (0,10,14) in this case. This operation might be useful for interpretation.

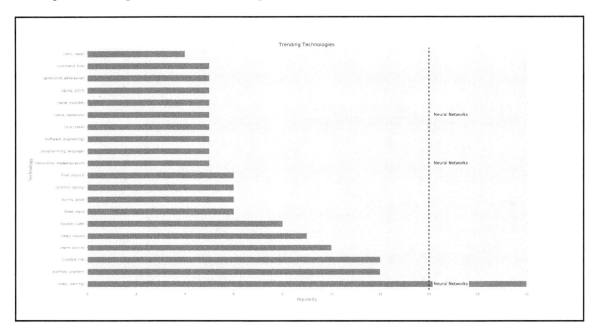

The preceding analysis provides us with an interesting set of the most popular technologies on GitHub. It includes topics for software engineering, programming languages, and artificial intelligence. An important thing to be noted is that technology around neural networks emerges more than once, notably, deep learning, TensorFlow, and other specific projects. This is not surprising, since neural networks, which are an important component in the field of artificial intelligence, have been spoken about and practiced heavily in the last few years. So, if you're an aspiring programmer interested in AI and machine learning, this is a field to dive into!

Programming languages

The next step in our analysis is the comparison of popularity between different programming languages. It will be based on samples of the top 1,000 most popular repositories by year.

Firstly, we get the data for last three years:

```
queries = ["created:>2017-01-01", "created:2015-01-01..2015-12-31",
"created:2016-01-01..2016-12-31"]
```

We reuse the `search_repo_paging` function to collect the data from the GitHub API and we concatenate the results to a new dataframe.

```
df = pd.DataFrame()

for query in queries:

    data = search_repo_paging(query)
    data = pd.io.json.json_normalize(data)
    df = pd.concat([df, data])
```

We convert the dataframe to a time series based on the `create_at`column.

```
df['created_at'] = df['created_at'].apply(pd.to_datetime)
df = df.set_index(['created_at'])
```

Then, we use aggregation method `groupby` which restructures the data by language and year, and we count the number of occurrences by language:

```
dx = pd.DataFrame(df.groupby(['language',
df.index.year])['language'].count())
```

We represent the results on a bar chart:

```
fig, ax = plt.subplots()

dx.unstack().plot(kind='bar', title = 'Programming Languages per Year', ax
= ax)

ax.legend(['2015', '2016', '2017'], title = 'Year')

plt.show()
```

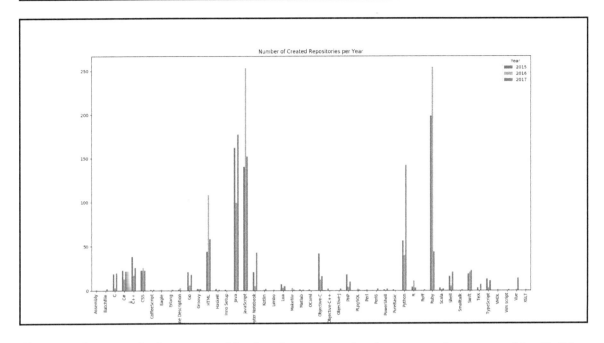

The preceding graph shows a multitude of programming languages from assembly, C, C#, Java, web, and mobile languages, to modern ones like Python, Ruby, and Scala. Comparing over the three years, we see some interesting trends. We notice HTML, which is the bedrock of all web development, has remained very stable over the last three years. This is not something that will not be replaced in a hurry. Once very popular, Ruby now has a decrease in popularity. The popularity of Python, also our language of choice for this book, is going up. Finally, the cross-device programming language, Swift, initially created by Apple but now open source, is getting extremely popular over time. It could be interesting to see in the next few years, if these trends change or hold true for long.

Programming languages used in top technologies

Now we know what are the top programming languages and technologies quoted in repositories description. In this section we will try to combine this information and find out what are the main programming languages for each technology.

We select four technologies from previous section and print corresponding programming languages. We look up the column containing cleaned repository description and create a set of the languages related to the technology. Using a set will assure that we have unique values.

```
technologies_list = ['software engineering', 'deep learning', 'open
source', 'exercise practice']

for tech in technologies_list:
    print(tech)
    print(set(df[df['clean'].str.contains(tech)]['language']))


software engineering
{'HTML', 'Java'}

deep learning
{'Jupyter Notebook', None, 'Python'}

open source
{None, 'PHP', 'Java', 'TypeScript', 'Go', 'JavaScript', 'Ruby', 'C++'}

exercise practice
{'CSS', 'JavaScript', 'HTML'}
```

Following the text analysis of the descriptions of the top technologies and then extracting the programming languages for them we notice the following:

- We get None as one of the results as certain technologies are developed with multiple programming languages.
- Deep learning, which is from a distance the most popular, uses Python (including Jupyter Notebooks) as its main programming language. It could be linked to TensorFlow, a popular Neural Network module released by Google which is heavily used in Python.
- Open source, which is among the most popular repositories, is associated with almost every programming language, and it's quite interesting to know that open-source is so diverse and popular.
- We also notice that people learn and practice several web-related technologies. It's probably an easy and interesting way to start before picking more complex ones.
- Finally, Java is the obvious choice for software engineering projects, along with HTML which is indispensable for engineering web pages.

Top repositories by technology

We know now which are the most quoted technologies and which are the most used programming languages. In the next step, we will try to understand what kind of repositories are the most watched in every category.

We select four main technologies which are quite different one from another:

```
technologies_list = ['software engineering', 'deep learning', 'open
source', 'exercise practice']
```

We sort the data by the number of watchers:

```
result = df.sort_values(by='watchers_count', ascending=False)
```

Then, we print the top five repositories for each technology using its name and description. The subsetting is done on the `clean` column to be sure that we use the same data as in technology extraction:

```
for tech in technologies_list:
    subset = result[result['clean'].str.contains(tech)].head(5)
    print(tech)
    for i,line in subset.iterrows():
        print(line['name'])
        print(line['description'])
        print('\n')
```

We obtain the following results for each technology:

```
software engineering
========
codeu_project_2017
codeu is a program created by google to develop the skills of future
software engineers. this project is a playground for those looking to
develop their coding and software engineering skills.

3354-git
assignment 1 of software engineering class

CS362W17Section-001
cs 362 (section 001, i.e., on-campus cs 362) software engineering ii
winter 2017 (aburas, ali ali)

INT2208-2-2017
software engineering course 2017
```

The top repositories for software engineering gives us mainly courses. This is probably not a trend, but it goes to show that GitHub is the platform of choice for these courses teaching software engineering.

```
deep learning
========
pytorch-tutorial
pytorch tutorial for deep learning researchers


DeepLearningForNLPInPytorch
an ipython notebook tutorial on deep learning for natural language
processing, including structure prediction.

deep-learning
repo for the deep learning nanodegree foundations program.

DeepLearningProjectWorkflow
machine learning workflow, from andrew ng's lecture at deep learning summer
school 2016

lectures-labs
slides and jupyter notebooks for the deep learning lectures at m2 data
science université paris saclay
```

The repositories around deep learning are a mix of advanced deep learning projects, and also a lot of learning material for picking up, like that from well-known deep learning expert Andrew Ng. Good news for aspiring deep learning enthusiasts, as there is an amazing amount of learning material out there.

```
open source
========
postal
a fully featured open source mail delivery platform for incoming & outgoing
e-mail

AirSim
open source simulator based on unreal engine for autonomous vehicles from
microsoft ai & research

commento
a lightweight, open source, tracking-free comment engine alternative to
disqus

code.mil
an experiment in open source
```

```
earthenterprise
google earth enterprise - open source
```

A diverse set of projects that we get through open-source, including the Google Earth Enterprise and AirSim for autonomous vehicles from Microsoft AI and Research.

```
exercise practice
========
lab-css-spotify-clone
a css exercise to practice positioning and layout

lab-javascript-memory-game
an exercise to practice jquery and understand how to separate logic and
user interactions

lab-jquery-pizza-builder
an exercise to practice jquery events and dom manipulation

lab-javascript-koans
a very zen exercise to practice javascript

lab-javascript-vikings
a javascript exercise to practice object oriented programming
```

The exercise practice section is dominated by modules related to Javascript and CSS.

Comparison of technologies in terms of forks, open issues, size, and watchers count

In the next step, we will focus on the two most important technologies: deep learning and open source to see what are the patterns in terms of numerical data.

Firstly, we compare the overall statistics. For this purpose we will compute mean, minimum, and maximum value for each variable:

```
df.groupby('technology')['forks', 'watchers', 'size', 'open_issues'].mean()

                   forks      watchers          size   open_issues
technology
deep learning  128.388889    329.222222  33976.611111           3.0
open source    160.700000   1403.100000  55267.100000          58.7


df.groupby('technology')['forks', 'watchers', 'size', 'open_issues'].min()
```

```
                forks   watchers   size   open_issues
technology
deep learning     52        41       2           0
open source       52         7      79           1
```

```
df.groupby('technology')['forks', 'watchers', 'size', 'open_issues'].max()
```

```
                forks   watchers      size   open_issues
technology
deep learning     756       1719    229058            17
open source       470       6534    305343           318
```

Analyzing the numerical data, we see that even though deep learning is very popular in terms of forks, open source repositories are the most engaging by watchers and issues submitted. A conclusion that could be derived is that there is a lot of curiosity around deep learning, and, as a result, many people are forking them to discover more. However, it's open source projects that people are really engaged in improving and working with. This trend could evolve in the next few years as people get more and more comfortable with deep learning and start submitting issues and following on in detail.

Then, we will check the differences in variables distribution to check if there are some patterns. We will represent each pair of variables on a scatterplot. As we have four variables to analyze will plot six different plots (all combinations between four variables).

Forks versus open issues

In the first comparison, we pick forks and open issues and we show them on a chart.

```
x = df['forks']
y = df['open_issues']
```

We create a plot where forks will be shown on x axis and open issues on y axis. The colors indicate technologies:

- `red`: Deep learning
- `blue`: Open source

We will follow the same color code in the next examples:

```
fig, ax = plt.subplots()
colors = dict(zip(set(df['technology']), ['red', 'blue']))
ax.scatter(x=x, y=y, c=df['technology'].apply(lambda x: colors[x]), s =
200, alpha = 0.5)
```

There are two additional parameters that we use to obtain prettier results:

- `alpha`: Transparency level of dots
- `s`: Size of dots

We add plot descriptions such as title, *x* axis label and *y* axis label:

```
ax.set(title='Deep Learning and Open Source Technologies', xlabel='Number
of forks', ylabel='Number of open issues')
```

Then, we show the chart.

```
plt.show()
```

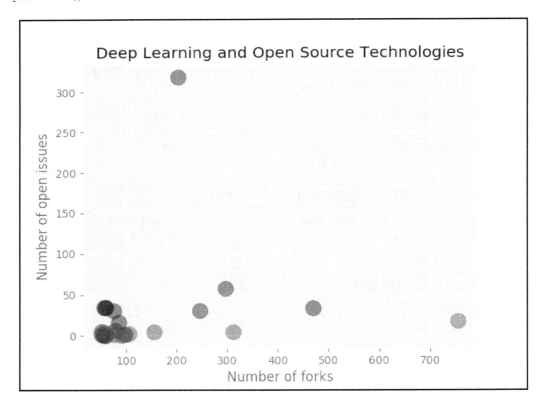

Forks versus size

We use the same logic to create a chart for the next two variables: `forks` and `size`.

```
x = df['forks']
y = df['size']
```

The only change we do in the code is a change in descriptions:

```
ax.set(title='Deep Learning and Open Source Technologies', xlabel='Number
of forks', ylabel='Repos size')
```

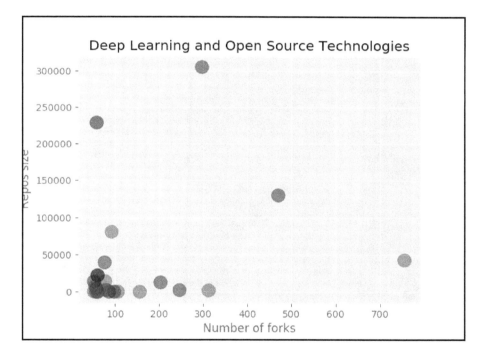

The preceding scatterplot confirms that there's no correlation between the number of forks and open issues. Deep learning has much fewer open issues, globally. Users following open source are more active in submitting issues, regardless of whether they fork the repositories or not.

Forks versus watchers

We use the same logic to create a chart for next two variables: `forks` and `size`.

```
x = df['watchers']
y = df['forks']
ax.set(title='Deep Learning and Open Source Technologies', xlabel='Number
of watchers', ylabel='Number of forks')
```

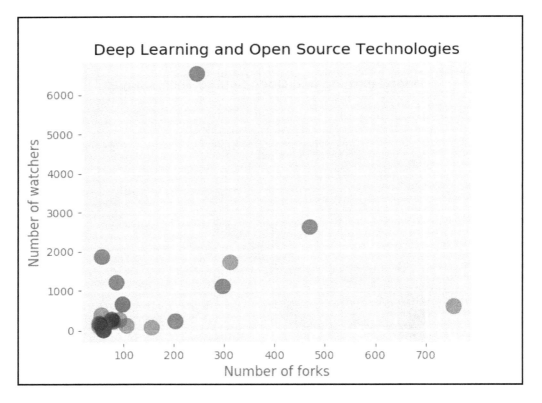

Again, there's no correlation between forks and watchers in the case of deep learning and open source. Certain open source repositories have high number of watchers compared to deep learning.

Open issues versus Size

Subsequently, we check the correlation between open issues and repository size for deep learning and open-source.

```
x = df['open_issues']
y = df['size']
ax.set(title='Deep Learning and Open Source Technologies', xlabel='Number
of open issues', ylabel='Repos size')
```

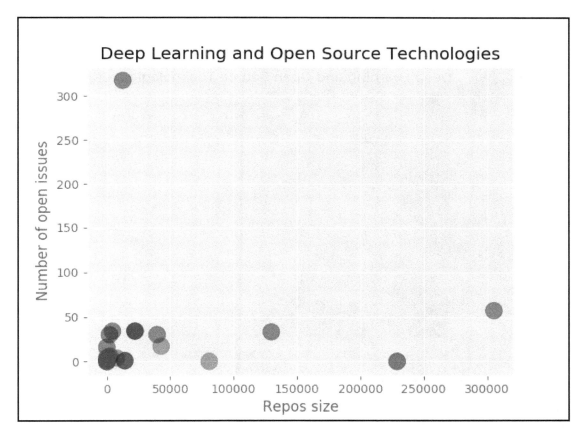

In the distribution between Size and Open Issues, we observe that both deep learning and open-source projects are a mix of large sized projects and smaller projects. However, there isn't a correlation between size of project and the open issues submitted as we see that the project with the most issues submitted is one of the smaller sized ones.

Open issues versus Watchers

Intuitively, we might think that if there are more watchers, there will be more open issues in the repository. Let's check our hypothesis by checking the distribution of these two variables:

```
x = df['open_issues']
y = df['watchers']

ax.set(title='Deep Learning and Open Source Technologies', xlabel='Number
of open issues', ylabel='Number of watchers')
```

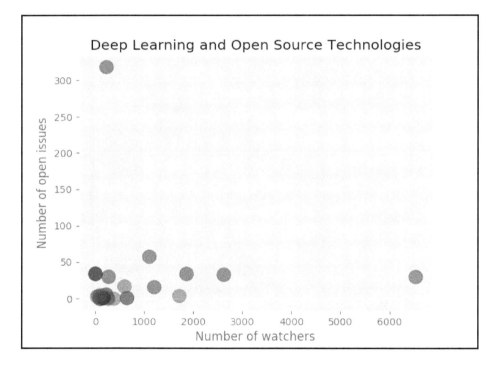

Comparing the number of watchers and open issues for the two projects, we see a bunch of repositories clustered with less than 1,000 watchers and 50 open issues. There's a lot more variation in the two metrics for the open source repos than those for deep learning.

Size versus watchers

Finally, we want to check if there is a relationship between the size and the number of watchers:

```
x = df['size']
y = df['watchers']

ax.set(title='Deep Learning and Open Source Technologies', xlabel='Repos
size', ylabel='Number of watchers')
```

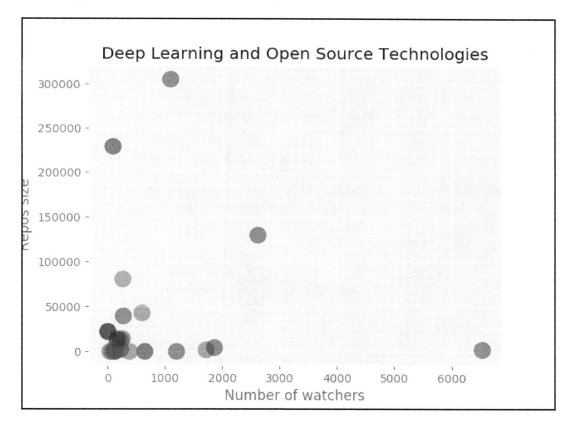

In the final scatterplot, we complete the visualizations for all the combinations of dimensions for the numerical metrics provided by the GitHub API. Here again we don't find correlations between the number of watchers and repos size.

Summary

In recent years, GitHub has emerged as the most well-known coding platform. With 20 million users and 57 million repositories, it's the most extensively used version control system. The social networking features provided by the platform for code repositories is also termed Social Coding. The API provided by GitHub allows you to perform an interesting analysis on data. Using the GitHub API, we used a combination of textual descriptions and other numerical data to figure out the latest trending technologies. The numerical data we extracted included watchers, open issues, forks, and repository size. Text analytics of the description using bi-grams gave an interesting list of technologies that are the most popular, mainly Artificial Intelligence technologies like deep learning and TensorFlow, and also a mix of open source projects and various diverse repositories related to software engineering. Analysis of the programming languages for these repositories showed us that Python and SWIFT have been growing in popularity in the last few years. Finally, we tried to find correlations using scatterplots between the numerical variables (size, forks, open issues, and watchers). The conclusion was that the variables are not really correlated and vary from project to project.

In the next chapter, we will explore the exciting world of online forums, a rich and engaged source of conversations on all kinds of topics. The goal of the chapter will be to apply topic modeling, an advanced machine learning technique to summarize and extract topics automatically from huge amounts of textual conversations data.

7
Scraping and Extracting Conversational Topics on Internet Forums

In the last few chapters, we have explored several social networks to analyze the data that we gathered through their APIs. However, there is another world, the world of internet forums or message boards, which most often do not have APIs. Even though they are public, internet forums differ significantly from social networks, as their users are mostly anonymous. This is unlike social networks, where, more often than not, users make their identities available. The anonymous nature of these platforms leads to free and fearless topical discussions on almost every subject on Earth. Technology, health, religion, politics, social activism, markets and industries, and movies are just a few of the threads or topics on which millions of people engage in deep discussions on online forums. Unlike Twitter, which has a limitation on the number of characters on each tweet, forums have no such limits. Therefore, online forums are a better alternate source of information than social networks about people and for companies and their consumers. Many companies are analyzing discussions on forums about their products, categories, and promotions to gather invaluable insights about their business. The lack of APIs to collect this conversation data means that we need to create crawlers or spiders that can parse the data from the pages of the forums and structure the conversational data. The art of crawling internet data could be used for almost every content on web pages that doesn't prohibit us from doing so. Google and other search engines crawl billions of web pages on the Internet to effectively rank them on search engine results. We shall use similar techniques using Python modules to gather data from online forums. Gathering data from online forums is one task, but making sense out of it is quite another.

Since the textual content from forums is rich and topical, we need sophisticated techniques to understand them. We shall use a generative statistical modeling technique called a **Latent Dirichlet Algorithm**, part of a family of algorithms known as **Topic Modeling**, to extract topics from the textual data. This is by far one of the most powerful text mining techniques that can be used by data scientists.

Scope and process

The process of topic modelling that we will present in this chapter consists of three steps:

1. Data crawling.
2. Data pre-processing.
3. Topic modelling and interpretation.

Each step represents a logical data analysis flow, which will finally lead us to different clusters of topics.

First, we will try to find out what the main topics are:

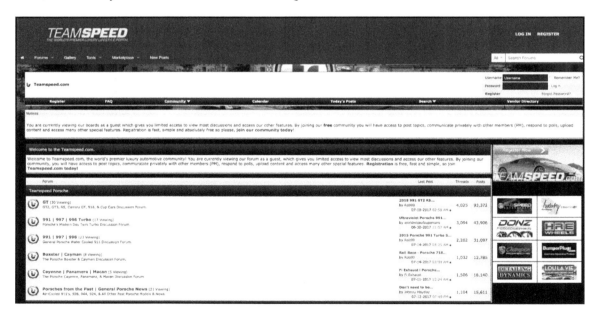

Getting the data

Forums do not provide programmatic interfaces (APIs) to capture data. However, you can connect to the website as a user to see all the conversations and collect data. The process of data extraction automatically from websites is called 'web scraping'.

Introduction to scraping

Since the beginning of the web, web scraping has been the main challenge for anyone who wanted to exploit the richness of information available on the Internet. In the very beginning, very few APIs were available and people used to copy the content of websites by just using copy-paste schema. Then, some programmatic tools were created to follow links (**crawling**) and extract the content from web pages (**scraping**). The information was structured by using text patterns (regex) or **DOM** (**Document Object Model**) parsing methods. More recently, the development of semantic analysis tools and artificial intelligence enabled alternative approaches, which are much more efficient and closer to human understanding and interpretation of website content. Search engines, especially Google, have been leaders in web scraping, as they go about crawling the entire web to index content from web pages and make it available through its search engine for the entire world. However, nowadays scraping is an essential component of many applications of unstructured web content for natural language processing and other requirements.

We can summarize these techniques into six main groups, even though there exist some other targeted approaches:

- Human extraction
- Text patterns
- DOM parsing
- Semantic annotation
- Computer vision

In our analysis of forum conversations, we will focus on DOM parsing techniques as it is a very relevant approach for semi-structured data. Semantic annotation and computer vision techniques are very advanced concepts and are beyond the scope of this book.

Scrapy framework

This is an open source and collaborative framework for extracting data from websites. To be clear, scrapy is not a library, it is a framework that provides many functionalities, such as managing requests, preserving user sessions, following redirects, and handling output pipelines. It is fast, simple and extensible, which makes scrapy one of the most useful toolkits for scraping to a data scientist.

There are many other data scraping services available, but usually they are all paid services. Scrapy is one of the most robust and simple open source frameworks in the Python market today.

How it works

A scraping framework has two main independent components. The spider crawls the site and the pipeline processes the scraped data, as shown in this diagram:

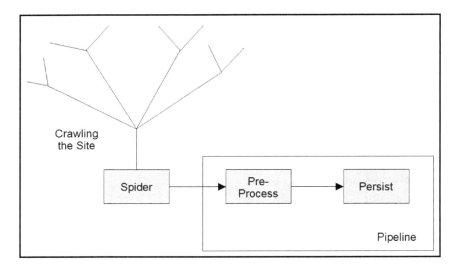

These two components are independent because the spider is dependent on the format and structure of the website whereas the pipeline is dependent on the structure of the persisted data.

The spider works as follows: it takes a URL as the entry point (for example, the landing page), extracts all the links present on the page, and crawls to the next page. On the next page, the spider will repeat the crawling process until it reaches a predefined level of depth. On a forum, usually the depth of pages is between three and five due to the standard structure such as **Topics | Conversations | Threads**, which means the spider usually has to travel three to five levels of depth to actually reach the conversational data.

The data pipeline process handles the post-crawled data. It is in charge of validations, cleaning, normalization, and finally persisting data for further analysis. The usual steps in the pipeline are to verify that the required fields are present in the data points and that the structure of the data is coherent (for example, the email actually resembles an email and such, because websites can change the structure of their information, so we must make sure that we are not storing flawed data).

Another very handy feature of Scrapy is that it records the history of all the URLs already scraped, which means that we can restart spiders and not have to recrawl all the URLs that have already been treated.

Related tools

Usually, Scrapy comes with all the tools required to create the scraper and, when parsing, the HTML to target the right elements using xpath expressions or simple tag class or ID selectors. But there exists a tool that is worth mentioning here because it is one of the simplest HTML/XML parsers, called BeautifulSoup.

To install it, do the following:

```
$TODO add$
```

We will use the following document in our examples:

```
html_doc = """
<html><head><title>The Dormouse's story</title></head>
<body>
<p class="title"><b>The Dormouse's story</b></p>
<p class="story">Once upon a time there were three little sisters; and
their names were
<a href="http://example.com/elsie" class="sister" id="link1">Elsie</a>,
<a href="http://example.com/lacie" class="sister" id="link2">Lacie</a> and
<a href="http://example.com/tillie" class="sister" id="link3">Tillie</a>;
and they lived at the bottom of a well.</p>
<p class="story">...</p>
"""
```

To extract information from an HTML document using BeautifulSoup is as simple as:

- Extracting the `title` of the document:

```
soup.title
# <title>The Dormouse's story</title>
```

- Extracting the `title` as string:

```
soup.title.string
# u'The Dormouse's story'
```

- Extracting the parent element of the `title` element:

```
soup.title.parent.name
# u'head'
```

- Extracting all first p element:

```
soup.p
# <p class="title"><b>The Dormouse's story</b></p>
```

- Extracting the class name of the first p element:

```
soup.p['class']
# u'title'
```

- Extracting all the a elements:

```
soup.find_all('a')
# [<a class="sister" href="http://example.com/elsie"
id="link1">Elsie</a>,# <a class="sister"
href="http://example.com/lacie" id="link2">Lacie</a>,# <a
class="sister" href="http://example.com/tillie"
id="link3">Tillie</a>]
```

- Extracting the element with ID `link3`:

```
soup.find(id="link3")
# <a class="sister" href="http://example.com/tillie"
id="link3">Tillie</a>
```

Using BeautifulSoup (or XPath) gives us full control of what information we want to extract from the HTML/XML documents.

Creating a project

Let's first create a project called `tutorial`:

```
mkdir tutorial
cd tutorial
scrapy startproject tutorial
```

Now that the project is set up, we can generate a spider for the forum `teamspeed`:

```
scrapy genspider teamspeedteamspeed.com
```

Finally the project is set up and the first basic spider is created; in the next chapter, you will will complete the spider.

Creating spiders

Although a full tutorial for the Scrapy framework is beyond the scope of the chapter, we will show you how to create a simple and efficient spider.

The first important thing to understand about Scrapy is the project structure.

```
tutorial/
    scrapy.cfg          # deploy configuration file

    tutorial/           # project's Python module, you'll import your code from here
        __init__.py

        items.py        # project items definition file

        pipelines.py    # project pipelines file

        settings.py     # project settings file

        spiders/        # a directory where you'll later put your spiders
            __init__.py
```

Source: https://doc.scrapy.org/en/latest/intro/tutorial.html

Directories `tutorial` will be replaced by your project name. In the first level, we store Scrapy configuration file. All the options are given by default. Usually, for simple scraping, there is no need to change the parameters. In the second level, we find `items.py`, `pipelines.py`, and `settings.py`. `Items.py` defines the type of elements we want to collect from the websites while `pipelines.py` helps us to define the sequences of operations when a spider is launched. In `settings.py`, we can define very useful things such as headers sent to the website or download delay time. Finally, we have a directory called spiders where we put the classes implementing our spiders.

Teamspeed forum spider

Before writing the code for our spider, we have to understand what are we going to use Scrapy for.

First of all, we want to visit all the forums on the Teamspeed website, which we will call categories.

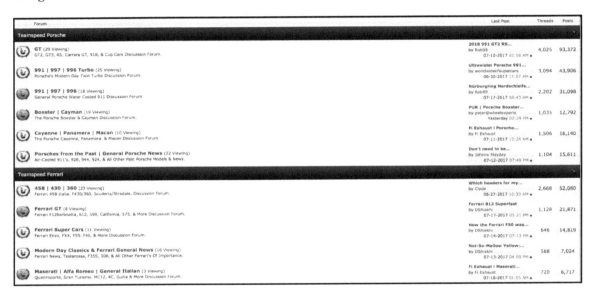

Then, get all the threads for each forum (called **subject**).

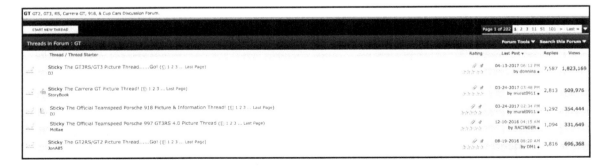

Finally, we extract post content in each thread:

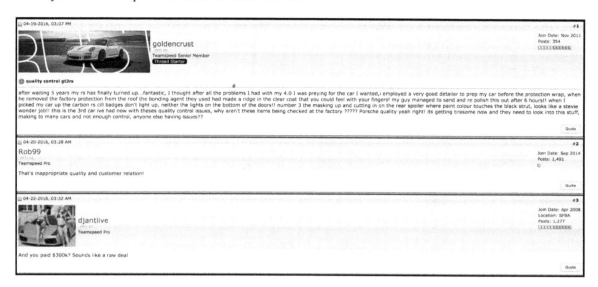

This means that we will need three methods to scan each level of the website's tree structure.

We can now create a file called `spider_teamspeed.py` under the `spiders` directory.

Inside the Python file, we import all the needed libraries: `pymongo` (database connection), `BeautifulSoup` (data scraping), `datetime` (date and time management), `logging` (logging tool), `scrapy` (crawling framework), `json` (JSON helpers module), `time` (manage waiting time), and the `re` (regex operations) module:

```
from pymongo import MongoClient
from bs4 import BeautifulSoup
import datetime
import logging
import scrapy
import json
import time
import re
```

Then, we create a Scrapy spider, `ForumTeamSpeedSpider`, and give it a name: `forum_teamspeed`. We have to define a domain name associated with our forum to allow only the links that belong to it. We also initialize a MongoClient with credentials for our database. The data will be stored in the `forum_teamspeed` collection:

```
class ForumTeamSpeedSpider(scrapy.Spider):
    name = "forum_teamspeed"
    allowed_domains = ['teamspeed.com']
    def __init__(self):
        self.client = MongoClient('DB_IP', 'DB_PORT')
        self.mongo_db = self.client['DB_NAME'].forum_teamspeed
```

 When you work in production mode, it is recommended to use pipelines to save the data in MongoDB (`https://doc.scrapy.org/en/latest/topics/item-pipeline.html`).

We might also need several helper methods to perform some operations.

We define a method, `foreach`, which will apply a function to all the elements of an iterable. The aim of this method is to simulate the same behavior as apply in pandas dataframes:

```
def foreach(self,fn, args):
    for x in args:
        fn(x)
```

The method `get_messages` returns a list of DOM elements containing all posts. In order to find the elements and their attributes, we may use Google Chrome and Mozilla Firefox inspector. You simply select the element you want to scrap and then you right-click and open code inspector. It will directly indicate the div element that points to the content, as shown in this example:

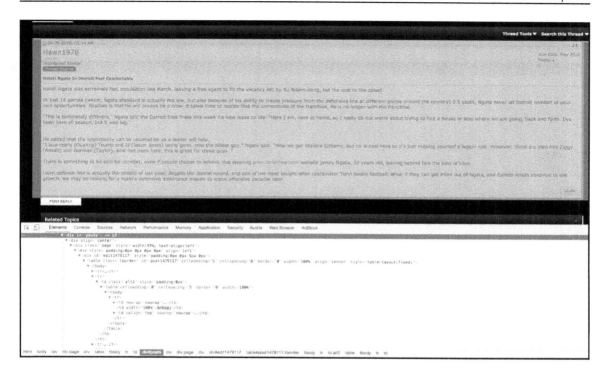

Then, we use the BeautifulSoup object soup to select the elements:

```
def get_messages(self,soup):
  msgs = soup.select('div[id=posts]')
  return msgs
```

We use a similar approach to extract post content, username and date from a single post (soup object `msg`):

```
def get_info(self,msg, subject, subject_url):
```

The content of the post is included in `div` tags that contain the word `message` in their ID, such as `post-message-1929`. We will use regex to find all elements that match this condition in a single post:

```
#post
regex = re.compile('.*message.*')
post = msg.find('div',id=regex).text.strip()
```

The extraction of the username is straightforward, because it is defined by a specific class, bigusername:

```
#username
try:
  username = msg.find('a', class_ = 'bigusername').text.strip()
except Exception as e:
  logging.warning('Username not found on page {}'.format(url))
  return
```

However, the date appears in the second element of class normal, so we have to subset results:

```
#date
try:
  date = msg.find_all('div', class_ = 'normal')[1].text.strip()
except Exception as e:
  logging.debug('Date not found on page {}'.format(url))
  date = None
```

Finally, we create an JSON structure called item, which is then inserted into MongoDB:

```
item = { 'forum': 'forum_teamspeed', 'subject': subject.strip(), \
  'post': post, 'username': username, 'date': date, 'subject_url': \
  subject_url.strip() }
self.mongo_db.insert_one(item)
```

The next helper method, parse_post, executes the get_messages method on the complete page source and then applies get_info on each element returned by get_messages:

```
def parse_posts(self, res, meta):
  soup = BeautifulSoup(res.text, 'html.parser')
  messages = self.get_messages(soup)
  infos = self.foreach(lambda x: get_info(x, meta['subject'],
  meta['subject_url'], res.url), messages)
```

Then, we go to the core part of the spider. The start_requests method uses the initial URL list (a single URL in our case) to create a request and invoke the get_categories method in callback:

```
def start_requests(self):
  """ Start function for crawling """
  urls = ['https://teamspeed.com/forums/']
  for url in urls:
    yield scrapy.Request(url = url, callback = self.get_categories)
```

The `get_categories` method will crawl through all the categories. It will extract URLs from `<tbody>` elements which contain `forumbit` in their IDs and then invoke a `get_subject` method in callback:

```
def get_categories(self, res):
    """ Crawl over the categories."""
    domain = 'https://teamspeed.com/forums/'
    urls = {(path.extract(), cat.extract()) for path, cat in
zip(res.xpath('//tbody[contains(@id,"forumbit")]/tr/td[2]/div/a/@href'),
        res.xpath('//tbody[contains(@id,"forumbit")]
        /tr/td[2]/div/a/strong/text()'))}
    for url in urls:
        yield scrapy.Request(url = url[0], callback = self.get_subject,
        meta = {'rec': True, 'cat': url[1], 'dont_redirect': True})
```

The `get_subject` method finds all the threads in a category, taking into account the pagination:

```
def get_subject(self, res):
    """ Crawl over the subjects """
```

We get the total number of pages in a category which is stored under the following xpath:

```
nb_pages =
int(res.xpath('//div[@class="pagenav"]/table/tr/td[@class="vbmenu_control"]
/text()').extract()[0].split("of")[1].strip().replace(",",""))
```

We build a new URL based on the URL parts from the category URL:

```
next_links = []
url_parts = res.url.split('/')
new_url = "https://" + url_parts[2] + "/" + url_parts[3] + "/"
+ url_parts[4] + "/index"
```

We add a page number to this URL and execute a loop to get a list of thread list URLs:

```
for i in range(0,nb_pages):
    next_links.append(new_url + str(i) + '.html')
```

We extract the single-thread urls from thread list pages:

```
domain = 'https://teamspeed.com/forums/'
urls = [(path.extract(), subject.extract()) for path, subject in
zip(res.xpath('//tbody[contains(@id,"threadbit")]/tr/td[3]/div[1]/a/@href')
,
res.xpath('//tbody[contains(@id,"threadbit")]/tr/td[3]/div[1]/a/text()'))]
```

Then, we iterate through single-thread pages to extract all the posts:

```
for url in urls:
  yield scrapy.Request(url = url[0], callback=self.get_posts,
  dont_filter = False, meta = {'subject': url[1], 'subject_url':
  url[0],'rec': True, 'dont_redirect': True})
```

Next, we go to each link from thread list:

```
for next_link in next_links:
  yield scrapy.Request(next_link, callback = self.get_subject,
  dont_filter = False, meta = {'domain': domain})
```

Finally, we parse every page that contains posts with our helper method, `parse_posts`. We also collect all the links for posts that have multiple pages (pagination):

```
def get_posts(self, res):
  """ Crawl over the posts"""
  domain = 'https://teamspeed.com/forums/'
  next_links = []
  try:
    nb_pages =
    int(res.xpath('//div[@class="pagenav"]/table//tr/td
    [@class="vbmenu_control"]/text()').extract()[0].split("of")
    [1].strip().replace(",",""))
    url_parts = res.url.split('/')
    new_url = "https://" + url_parts[2] + "/" + url_parts[3] + "/" +
    url_parts[4] + ".html"
    for i in range(0,nb_pages):
      next_links.append(new_url + str(i) + '.html')
    except:
      nb_pages = 1
    self.parse_posts(res, res.meta)
    for next_link in next_links:
      yield scrapy.Request(next_link, callback = self.get_posts,
      dont_filter = False, meta = {'domain': domain})
```

We can now launch the crawler with the following command:

```
scrapy crawl forum_teamspeed
```

The logging results start appearing in your console. A crawl might take few minutes or even a few days depending on the size of the website.

Data pull and pre-processing

Once the crawling is finished, we have all the data in the MongoDB database. We can now query the database to put all the posts into a pandas dataframe:

```
import pandas as pd

from pymongo import MongoClient

client = MongoClient('HOST:PORT')
db = client.teamspeed
collection = db.forum_teamspeed

dataset = []
for element in collection.find():
  dataset.append(element)
df = pd.DataFrame(dataset)
```

At this stage, we will also create a new column called `full_verbatim`, where we concatenate the subject (thread title) and post content:

```
df['full_verbatim'] = df.apply(lambda x: x['subject'] + " " +
x['post'],axis=1)
```

There exists a direct link between thread title and post, so the textual data included in both variables might be insightful with respect to a single thought of the forum user. It will help us to capture the broader and contextual meaning of the ideas expressed in forum posts.

Data cleaning

Thereafter, as seen in the earlier chapters, we need to clean and structure the data pulled from the last section using the following methodology:

- Removing extra whitespaces
- Removing html tags
- Removing URLs
- Removing punctuations
- Word standardization
- Splitting of attached words
- Lowercase conversion

- Stopword removal
- Tokenization

```
import re, itertools
import nltk
from nltk.corpus import stopwords
def data_cleaning(verbatim):
  verbatim = verbatim.strip() #remove whitespaces
  verbatim = re.sub(r'<[^<]+?>', ' ', verbatim) #remove html tags
  verbatim = re.sub(r'https?:\/\/.*[\r\n]*', ' ', verbatim,
flags=re.MULTILINE)
  #remove urls
  verbatim = re.sub(r'[^\w\s]',' ',verbatim) #remove ponctuation
  verbatim = ''.join(''.join(s)[:2] for _, s in
itertools.groupby(verbatim))
  #Standardize words
  verbatim = ' '.join(re.findall('[A-Z][^A-Z]*', verbatim)) #Split attached
words
  verbatim = verbatim.lower() #Lowercase
  verbatim = ' '.join([word for word in verbatim.split() if word not in
  (stopwords.words('english'))]) #Stopwords
  tokens = nltk.word_tokenize(verbatim) #Tokenize
  return(tokens)
df['cleaned'] = df.apply(lambda x:
data_cleaning(x['full_verbatim']),axis=1)
```

The results of these operations are stored in the `dataframe df['cleaned']`.

Part-of-speech extraction

In our further analysis, we will only work on certain parts of speech that provide the most information about conversation topics. We'll now apply the power NLP technique of **part of speech (pos)** extraction using the framework of The Penn Treebank tagset is represented as follows with a tag code and description:

Number	Tag	Description
1.	CC	Coordinating conjunction
2.	CD	Cardinal number
3.	DT	Determiner
4.	EX	Existential *there*
5.	FW	Foreign word

6.	IN	Preposition or subordinating conjunction
7.	JJ	Adjective
8.	JJR	Adjective, comparative
9.	JJS	Adjective, superlative
10.	LS	List item marker
11.	MD	Modal
12.	NN	Noun, singular or mass
13.	NNS	Noun, plural
14.	NNP	Proper noun, singular
15.	NNPS	Proper noun, plural
16.	PDT	Predeterminer
17.	POS	Possessive ending
18.	PRP	Personal pronoun
19.	PRP$	Possessive pronoun
20.	RB	Adverb
21.	RBR	Adverb, comparative
22.	RBS	Adverb, superlative
23.	RP	Particle
24.	SYM	Symbol
25.	TO	*to*
26.	UH	Interjection
27.	VB	Verb, base form
28.	VBD	Verb, past tense
29.	VBG	Verb, gerund or present participle
30.	VBN	Verb, past participle
31.	VBP	Verb, non-3rd person singular present
32.	VBZ	Verb, 3rd person singular present

33.	WDT	Wh-determiner
34.	WP	Wh-pronoun
35.	WP$	Possessive wh-pronoun
36.	WRB	Wh-adverb

The following methods allow us to extract the `pos` from the textual data collected:

```
def pos_extraction(tokens):
    pos_tokens = nltk.pos_tag(tokens)
    return(pos_tokens)
```

We will also create a function that will subset only the tokens that are related to the `pos` of our choice:

```
def select_pos(pos_tokens,lst_pos):
    subset = [pos_token[0] for pos_token in pos_tokens for pos in lst_pos
    if pos_token[1].startswith(pos)]
    return(subset)
```

We apply `pos_extraction` on the whole dataset:

```
df['pos'] = df.apply(lambda x: pos_extraction(x['cleaned']),axis=1)
```

Then, we select only nouns (`NN`) and adjectives (`JJ`), which will be used for topic modelling:

```
df['cleaned_nn_jj'] = df.apply(lambda x:
select_pos(x['pos'],['NN','JJ']),axis=1)
```

Each part of speech provides a different kind of information. You can choose the POS which are most likely to answer your question. In our case, we will use nouns and adjectives only to understand what people talk about in a domain of sports cars. As we are not interested in any activities, we will simply omit verbs.

Data analysis

Introduction to topic models

As per Wikipedia, a topic model is defined as follows :

> *"In machine learning and natural language processing, a topic model is a type of statistical model for discovering the abstract "topics" that occur in a collection of documents. Topic modeling is a frequently used text-mining tool for discovery of hidden semantic structures in a text body."*

Topic models are essentially iterative algorithms that work with document feature matrices, to use overlapping features to group documents together. Features could simply be all the words in a sentence, or selected features such as nouns or named entities, and so on. To explain in a simplistic manner, we imagine that we have a corpus of documents of mixed subjects and we use words as features to represent a document. If we had to analyse these documents using topic models, and the topic model would group words like **"team"**, **"match"**, **"game"**, and **"score"** in a single topic (as these word frequently appear together) which we would name as a **SPORT** topic, while words like **"attorney"**, **"case"**, **"law"**, and **"crime"** in another topic that we would name as a **LEGAL** topic. This example shows that the documents that we used for topic models were essentially containing two topics, **SPORT** and **LEGAL**, as you can see in the following illustration:

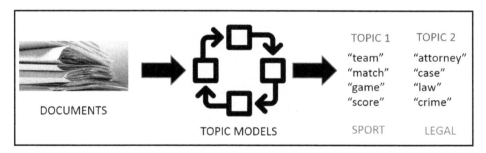

The preceding example is very simplistic one to understand the concept of how to discover the topics in a number of given unknown documents. In practice, the process could be very complex.

Two of the best known topic models are **Latent Semantic Analysis (LSA)** and **Latent Dirichlet Allocation (LDA)**. To go deep into the mathematical explanations and comparisons of the two is beyond the scope of this book, however, we will use LDA in this chapter, as it is proven to be better suited for clustering with high dimensionality and more accurate in identifying topics than LSA. The latter, of course, is faster to implement.

Latent Dirichlet Allocation

LDA is a generative probabilistic model of a corpus. The fundamental idea is that documents are a mixture of random latent topics, where a topic is characterized by a distribution over words.

The generative process of LDA can be illustrated as follows:

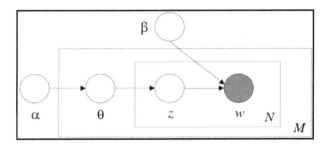

1. Choose $N \sim Poisson(\xi)$
2. Choose $\theta \sim Dir(\alpha)$
3. For each of the N words w_n:
   (a) Choose a topic $z_n \sim Multinomial(\theta)$
   (b) Choose a word w_n from $p(w_n|z_n, \beta)$, a multinomial probability conditioned on the topic z_n

$$[\beta]_{k \times V} \quad \beta_{ij} = p(w^j = 1|z^i = 1)$$

To simplify, the algorithm assumes a Poisson and Dirichlet distribution on the model and then constitutes the members of each cluster by maximizing the probability of a new word being in the cluster given the current members.

The Dirichlet equation, where a k-dimensional Dirichlet random variable θ can take values in the (k-1)-simplex, has the following probability density on this simplex:

$$(1) \quad p(\theta|\alpha) = \frac{\Gamma(\sum_{i=1}^{k} \alpha_i)}{\prod_{i=1}^{k} \Gamma(\alpha_i)} \theta_1^{\alpha_1-1} \cdots \theta_k^{\alpha_k-1}$$

Now that we've learnt the theoretical concepts of topic models and latent Dirichlet allocation, we shall apply it using Python on our conversational dataset to make sense out of it. The exercise will help us to understand the practical workings of LDA in order to understand huge amounts of textual data.

Applying LDA to forum conversations

In this section we will build a topic analysis class based on the `lda` library. As usual, we first import all the needed libraries:

```
import sys
import numpy as np
import lda
import json
import pandas as pd
from collections import Counter, OrderedDict
import nltk
from nltk.corpus import stopwords
from itertools import *
from sklearn.feature_extraction.text import CountVectorizer
```

Then, we create a `topic_analysis` class with 5 class properties: `dataframe`, `vocab`, `model`, `vectorizer`, and `topics`:

For datasets that exceed your RAM capacities, you should use a distributed computing approach.

```
class topic_analysis(object):
    """
    A class to extract topics and associate all the verbatims with a specific
```

```
topics
Input: dataframe, column_name with cleaned verbatims
Output: verbatims & topic & weights, top keywords
"""
dataframe = None
vocab = None
model = None
vectorizer = None
topics = []
```

In the object constructor, we add our dataframe to the object property `dataframe`:

```
def __init__(self,dataframe):
    self.dataframe = dataframe
```

We create a method called `compute_lda_model()`, which performs all the steps of topic modelling. It takes as an argument a list of verbatims and number of topics:

```
def compute_lda_model(self,learning_set_lda,n_topics=10):
    """ Method to compute LDA model """
```

We create a `CountVectorizer` object (from the `scikit-learn` library), which will convert a list of verbatims into a bag-of-words array. We use the following parameters by default:

- `analyzer`: "word" so as to create an array of words,
- `tokenizer`: None
- `preprocessor`: None
- `stop_words`: None, because our dataset has been already pre-processed
- `max_features`: 5000 to avoid creating huge arrays with irrelevant keywords

```
vectorizer = CountVectorizer(analyzer = "word", \
tokenizer = None, \
preprocessor = None, \
stop_words = None, \
max_features = 5000)
```

The method `fit_transform()` fits the model, learns the vocabulary from our dataset, and creates a feature vector. The latter part causes the difference between `fit()` and `fit_transform()`:

```
train_data_features = vectorizer.fit_transform(learning_set_lda)
self.vectorizer = vectorizer
train_data_features = train_data_features.toarray()
```

Chapter 7

We get the vocabulary and put it into the object property to make it accessible for further analysis:

```
self.vocab = vectorizer.get_feature_names()
```

Then, we can train the model with our array of features:

```
X = train_data_features
```

We use 10,000 iterations by default, but you can optimize the number by checking whether the log likelihood values do change significantly after a certain number of iterations:

```
model = lda.LDA(n_topics, n_iter=10000, random_state=1)
model.fit(X)
return(model)
```

Now, we have a method that computes the LDA model and we want to get the results:

```
def get_results(self,dataframe,column_name,n_topics):
  self.topics = []
  weights = []
```

We compute the LDA model using the previously defined method:

```
model = self.compute_lda_model(self.dataframe[column_name],n_topics)
self.model = model
```

For each verbatim, we add the topic with the highest score to the dataframe:

```
doc_topic = model.doc_topic_
topics = []
scores = []

for i in doc_topic:
  topics.append(i.argmax())
  scores.append(i.max())

self.dataframe['Topic_id'] = topics
self.dataframe['Score'] = scores
```

Then, we save the top 50 words and their weights in `topics` property:

```
topic_word = model.topic_word_ #get the labels (words)
n_top_words = 50

#####Store results in topics
for i, topic_dist in enumerate(topic_word):
  #Get the topic
  topic_words = np.array(self.vocab)[np.argsort(topic_dist)]
```

```
[:-n_top_words:-1]
weights = ' '.join(topic_dist[np.argsort(topic_dist)]
[:-n_top_words:-1].astype('str'))
words = ' '.join(topic_words)
self.topics.append((i,words,weights))
```

In order to learn the LDA model, we have to define the number of topics in advance. There is no single solution to select the optimal number. One statistical approach is to test the model with different numbers of topics and select the one that maximizes the log likelihood. This is the approach that we are going to show in the next part.

We instantiate a list of log likelihoods:

```
loglikelihoods = []
```

Then we calculate the log likelihood for models with `nb_topics` between 10 and 50 using a step of 10 topics. The upper and lower bounds values are again an arbitrary choice. We should have a range as wide as possible, but at the same time we should be able to make interpretations of so many topics and have enough computational power to perform the calculation in a reasonable amount of time:

```
for i in range(10,50,10):
    model_lda = topic_analysis()
    model_lda.get_results(df,'cleaned_nn_jj',i)
    loglikelihoods.append((i,model_lda.model.loglikelihood()))
```

Once the results are ready, we select the maximum log likelihood value; it outputs the optimal number of topics, 20:

```
element = max(enumerate(loglikelihoods), key=lambda x: x[1])
print("Optimal number of topics : {}
({})".format(element[1][0],element[1][1]))
```

We rebuild our model and get the following results:

```
model_lda = topic_analysis()
model_lda.get_results(validation,'cleaned_nn_jj',element)

model_lda.topics
```

Topic Id	Top keywords	Top keywords	Top keywords	Top keywords	Top keywords	Top keywords	Top keywords	Top keywords	Top keywords	Top keywords
0	watch	steel	case	time	watches	black	dial	new	call	hours
1	race	car	track	series	team	cars	mans	time	cup	world
2	new	audi	car	engine	model	mercedes	production	coupe	series	version
3	engine	new	performance	system	power	high	speed	car	rear	front

4	turbo	stock	performance	kit	car	engine	factory	suspension	power	exhaust
5	tube	video	aston	martin	corvette	car	nissan	ford	bugatti	pagani
6	team	race	year	season	formula	laren	grand	prix	red	teams
7	carbon	black	front	fiber	interior	rear	wheels	edition	car	side
8	ferrari	tube	maserati	italia	car	spider	scuderia	f430	california	video
9	porsche	turbo	carrera	new	panamera	cayenne	spyder	cayman	boxster	tube
10	wheels	black	wheel	series	finish	vellano	mercedes	new	matte	front
11	phone	email	new	camera	available	order	sale	free	apple	system
12	car	paint	detail	wheel	correction	wheels	wash	cleaner	film	clear
13	exhaust	system	sound	tube	performance	armytrix	valvetronic	mode	power	titanium
14	pics	car	cars	day	event	photos	pictures	great	guys	new
15	car	drive	time	way	much	cars	road	good	little	first
16	lamborghini	gallardo	aventador	game	boat	super	superleggera	p560	league	tube
17	month	base	rate	residual	lease	audi	vehicle	eligible	com	compare
18	car	anyone	good	new	guys	thanks	time	something	miles	people
19	new	cars	car	world	company	year	design	years	brand	laren

In this table, we see the results of our topic modeling using LDA. The rows are the topics and the columns have those words associated with those topics in descending order of their weights. Later we'll visualize the weights using histograms and analyze a few selected topics. Analyzing all the 20 topics is beyond the scope of this chapter.

Even though we have used an optimization algorithm to define the number of topics, it can also be defined by the user on the granularity of information that one is interested in. This can be a highly iterative process with a rule of thumb: not to have too few or too many topics. The reason is that too few topics would result in singular topic with many other topics within it, and too many topics would give unnecessarily duplicate topics.

In the next step, we might need to print the top words for each topic and show a sample of verbatims for each of them. For this purpose, we create a function, `print_topics()`, which takes as an argument the `lda` model object:

```
def print_topics(model_lda):
```

We get the topics and the dataframe:

```
topics = model_lda.topics
dataframe = model_lda.dataframe
```

For each topic, we build a bar chart and save it as a `.png` file:

```
for topic in topics:
  labels = topic[1].split(" ")
  dx = [float(x) for x in topic[2].split(" ")]

  fig, ax = plt.subplots()
  ind = range(0,len(labels))

  width = 0.25

  ax.bar(ind,dx ,width, color='b')
  ax.set_xticks(np.arange(len(ind)) + width/2)
  ax.set_xticklabels(labels,rotation=90)

  plt.tight_layout()
  #plt.show() #Optional

  plt.savefig('topic' + str(topic[0]) + '.png', dpi=300)

  subset = dataframe[dataframe['Topic_id']==topic[0]]
```

Then, we create a sample of 10 verbatims and print it in the console:

```
print("Topic " + str(topic[0]) + ":\n\n\n")
for i,row in subset.sample(10).iterrows():
  print(row['full_verbatim'] + "\n")
```

This function will lead us to topic interpretation in the next section:

Topic interpretation

Here, we'll go deeper into the analysis by trying to interpret the meaning of each topic that we have discovered in the earlier steps. The way to interpret the topics is to analyse by linking the higher and lower weighted words and extracting examples of verbatims for the individual topic. This is quite a time-consuming process but the results are the most qualitative as it gives context to the results of the algorithm. An important aspect to keep in mind is that not all the topics will be interesting or making sense, so we need to identify those which are interesting to the subject we are working on. In our case, we are looking for topics which have discussion around car usage, maintenance, brands, and so on. We are not so interested in topics that are full of promotional context and also those that are spammy.

After going through the words and verbatims of the 20 topics that we have generated, we have chosen the following that seem interesting to us, though it could differ from other perspectives:

To interpret the topics, we'll plot histograms of the word weights and extract a few verbatims for each topic as examples.

Topic 1 : Racing and motor-sports

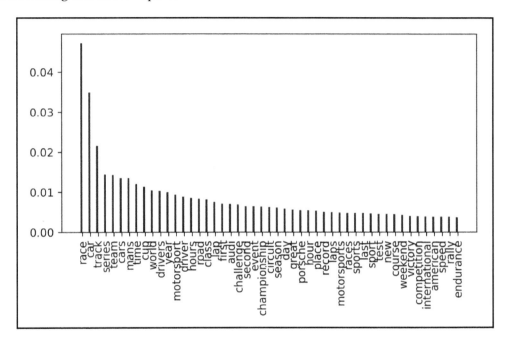

Topic 1 : Racing and motor-sports

In this topic the words with the strongest weight are "race", "car", "track", "series", and "team".

Looking at these words, it seems to be a discussion on car racing and other sub topics based on it, such as teams, drivers, motorsport, and so on.

A few verbatims that are linked to this topic:

"Wright Motorsport 1-2-3-4 1-2-3-4. That's not something you see very often.

Wright preps some good cars, as evidenced by last weekend's events!

Congratulations to Wright, as well as all of their drivers. First time winner Sean Johnston, who won on Friday, as well as Madison Snow, who won Saturday's event."

"TPC Racing Returns to Victory Lane at CTMP TPC Racing / Porsche of Towson Back On Top in Canada

For rounds seven and eight of the IMSA GT3 Cup Challenge Series by Yokohama, the TPC Racing / Porsche of Towson / Merkle team was at the Canadian Tire Motorsport Park. The team went into rounds seven and eight leading the team and drivers' championship in the Gold Class as well, first and second in the Masters Class standings. ......"

"Supercars: Gumpert Apollo | Nat Geo Supercars: Gumpert Apollo

The Gumpert Apollo Enraged is a race car than a million dollars that can be used legally on the streets. It is one of the fastest cars in the world and one of the most exclusive."

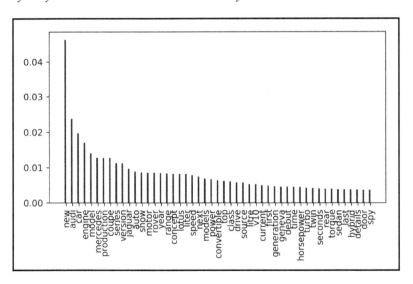

Topic 2 : High-end models and brands

The second topic has main words such as "new", "audi", "car", "engine", "model", and "mercedes". It seems to be a discussions on new cars from different brands and their features.

The sample verbatims are as follows:

"Lamborghini Gallardo LP560-4 on Video!! It has been some time since we first saw the Lamborghini Gallardo LP560-4 unveiled at a preview evening the day before the Geneva Motor Show, but in that time the interest in the the Italian Marque's latest creation has not wavered. So we are hardly going to pass up an opportunity to see the monster beating down the track giving us the orchestral symphony coming from the 5.2-liter V10 engine found in the mid-engined supercar. The engine which will also make its way over to the Audi R8 V10 is mated to 6-speed transmission passing the 560hp of power to all four wheels which uses a 4WD Viscous Traction system. 0-100km/h is achieved in 3.7 seconds (although some claim it to be 3.5 seconds) with 200km/h reached after 11.8 seconds, top speed lies at 325km/h. Base price is set at $201,000 in the US with sales to commence this summer. YouTube - OFFICIAL VIDEO: Lamborghini Gallardo LP560-4"

"New Porsche Macan Reported to Debut at LA Auto Show New Porsche Macan Reported to Debut at LA Auto Show

The long awaited smaller SUV from Porsche is said to debut this November at the LA Auto Show, with a spring 2014 release date, according to UK magazine AutoExpress.

The new Porsche will be based on the same underpinnings as the Audi Q5, but will be much lighter due to a more extensive use of aluminium components. AutoExpress goes on to note this could save roughly 130kg over its Q5 sibling."

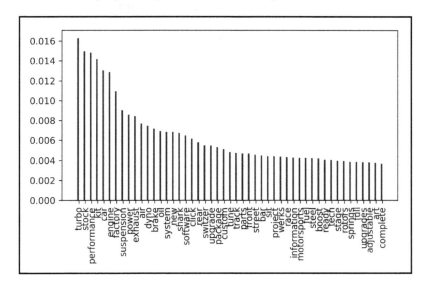

Topic 4 : Engine and performance

"Turbo", "stock", "performance, "car", "engine", and "factory" are the strongest words of this topic, which indicates that there are more technical discussions that are driving the topic. Users are discussing the engine and performance aspects of certain cars and models and also asking for or giving advice to help each other.

We can see this in the following verbatims:

"....Sportec SP750 Porsche 997 GT2 Porsche enthusiasts will undoubtedly count the 997-generation 911 GT2 as one of the most extreme supercars ever to roll out of Stuttgart - right up there with the 959 and the Carrera GT. But where there's speed, there's always room for more speed, and the Swiss aren't about to stay neutral on this matter...."

"Hi all,

I need some advise. Recently I started tracking my car and am running the stock suspension and stock Michelin tires. Tires are about toast so I am thinking of getting some cup tires unless any of you have a better recommendation. Currently I have upgraded my exhaust, headers, I/C and ecu. So I have plenty of power but, would like to utilize that power by being on the gas earlier coming out of corners. I need better grip for this.

My questions:

Will Bilstein PSS10 Coil overs work with PASM?

If I just do new springs and sway bars will this be as good as the Bilsteins?

What is the difference between H&R and Bilsteins? Better recommendations?

What tires have any of you used and what is recommended?

At this point I do not have a trailer for my car so I drive to the track. The tracks are 70 to 200 miles away. I hope to get a trailer soon, but, not sure when.

Thanks for reading my post."

"Coolant leaking? Could be your coolant expansion tank... It's pretty early for the 997 cars to be experiencing this problem, but with the same coolant expansion tank, it's a matter of time before 997 owners will see the same problem. "

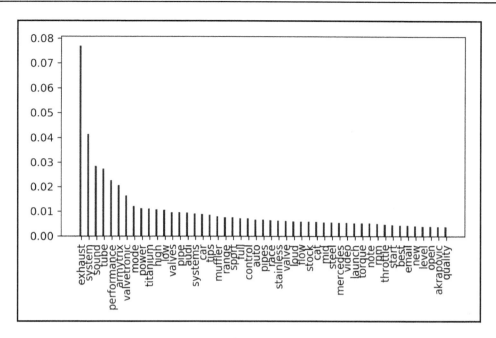

Topic 13 : Car features and performance

This topic too seems to be rich in technical discussions but more focused on specific aspects such as "exhaust", "system", "tube", and "performance", which have the biggest weights.

Looking at the verbatims:

"Ford Mondeo ST220 in our shop for "one-off" exhaust system. Hello.

Couple weeks ago, the Ford Mondeo ST220 arrived our shop.

For those who doesn't know about this car, this is sports model of the Ford Mondeo for European market.

This car sports Duratec 3.0 V6(225hp) with manual tranny.

This car actually had SuperSprint exhaust system, but the customer wanted get full Kreissieg exhaust system. ..."

"After having my RS from new & having now covered 22000 miles in her I decided she was due an upgrade (I have done other small items - spacers, seat inserts etc but nothing BIG).

I previously had snarkys bypass fitted & this was an amazing mod for the money but I decided I wanted more. I looked to upgrading the exhaust & suspension, so naturally I went straight to Akrapovic, purchased at a fantastic price through Revolution247 over here.

It took two weeks to arrive but they system is simply a work of art as I am sure you all know.

The car feel great with the system on, the weight loss & power gains is EASILY noticeable throughout the whole rev-range & general driving of the car, though you should note MASSIVE torque loss is present low in the rev range, so low though (under 2k rpm) this is almost irrelevant. ...."

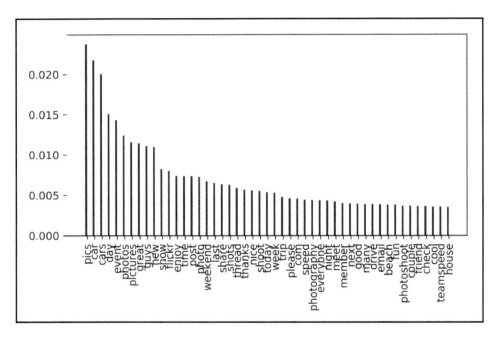

Topic 14 : Experience sharing through pictures

The last topic chosen has words with peak weights such as "pics", "car", "day", "event", and "photos". Often users on online forums like to share pictures of things of their interest and here it seems to be the same case. The verbatims corresponding to this topic also confirm that excited users are sharing pictures and information with their community on the thread:

"New BMW Teaser: X1 in white and on the beach A week from tomorrow, BMW will officially present the X1 during an event at the Leipzig plant in Germany, but we expect the press release and photos to go out a few days prior to that."

"Cars from Paris... I am in Paris last week and take some pics of the cars I have seen..Like Koeningsegg(Special one),SLR with Brabus wheels,Pink SV, murci, 599's, SLS's, F430's(scudi,spider,coupe),LP570-4 Superleggera,LP560-4, M5 with great sounding Eissenmann exhaust, DBS, Vintage Vespa's and parking skills on streets..

I have seen TDF Blue 458 with full cuicuo interior..Daymmm...Its amazing..In real life its better than pics....."

"Lambo's St. Morritz I found this on Classic driver.com. Great article, and lot's of cool pictures. I know that some were posted before, but these are more pictures. Never hurts to see more of these pics. Lamborghini St. Moritz 2010 - Classic Driver - MAGAZINE - events"

At the end, we would like to mention that it's important to detect spammy topics that don't have any substantial discussion but more of promotional posts, quite like those you receive in your emails. One such topic is Topic 17.

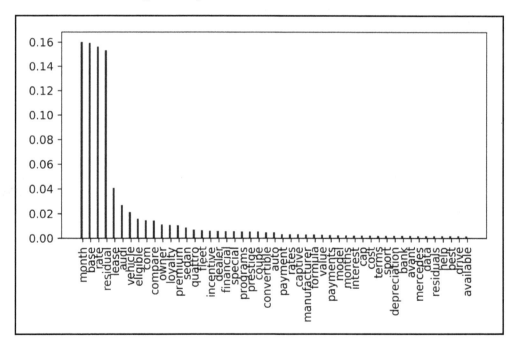

In this topic, we see the most important words as "month", "base", "rate", and "lease", among others. Analysing some of the verbatims, we can recognise that this is promotional content around leasing programs, which doesn't give us any insights into user interest in cars.

"Audi Auto Lease Programs - September 2010 Audi Auto Lease Programs - Effective September 2010 These lease rates and residuals are provided courtesy of LeaseCompare.com by dealer partners and are NOT for redistribution. This information is to help you evaluate different lease offers from your Audi dealer and an independent leasing company....."

"BMW Auto Lease Programs - March 2009 BMW Auto Lease Programs - Effective March 2009 These lease programs are provided courtesy of LeaseCompare.com by dealer partners and are NOT for redistribution. Follow these 3 steps for the best lease deal! 1) Use the data listed below each vehicle model, and the Lease Formula at the bottom of this page, to calculate a manufacturer (captive) lease payment. 2) Compare special Bank Lease programs by clicking on the vehicle model name to see instant lease payments. 3) You've done your homework, now choose the best lease and start driving your car! NOTE: Choosing a lease program, captive or bank, with the lowest money factor and a realistic residual value will provide you with the best overall leasing option...."

"Swap A Lease / Lease Takeover Has anyone had luck with swap a lease (getting out of a lease) websites before? Thinking to get out of a '11 MBZ E350 lease and weighing my options...

Thanks guys."

Going through all the topics and their verbatims in detail is beyond the scope of the book, but we hope that you have got a reasonable idea of applying topic models and qualitatively interpreting the topics that are most interesting verses those that are less interesting or spammy. This is a great way to establish the relevance of web content on the information that you're looking for and separate the noise from the surface.

Summary

Conventional social media such as Facebook and Twitter with user-generated content are an interesting way to analyze information about individuals and organizations. The APIs of these platforms are useful to gather and analyse a lot of this data emanating from these platforms. on the other hand, online forums without structured freely available APIs provide a great sources of topical discussions. The main difference is mostly the anonymous nature of the forums, which encourages individuals to have long and deep discussions on various topics (technology, politics, culture, and so on), unlike on other social media where one is often identified through pseudonyms and actual identifiers. These millions of rich conversations on Internet forums have become extremely interesting for companies to learn about the trends of their consumers.

To harness conversational data, we explored the techniques to create crawlers using the Scrappy framework. After extraction and storage of this data, we used parts-of-speech tagging to better understand the data. Finally, we learned about Topic Models and the Latent Dirichlet Allocation algorithm; they allow us to analyse huge amounts of textual content and organize them into topics. Topic Models essentially are machine learning algorithms that detect groups of words that occur together in multiple documents and classify them into topics. We scraped and gathered data from a popular online car forum using the crawler we created. Thereafter, we used the python LDA module to optimize and explore the topics in the discussions in the car forum. The optimal number of topics for our dataset was 20, and we extracted verbatims for a few of them to understand the conversations in more depth.

In the next chapter, we will learn about a totally different social media site that has grown immensely popular, Pinterest; and we will introduce you to more advanced crawling features and the concepts of graph theory and network analysis.

8
Demystifying Pinterest through Network Analysis of Users Interests

So far in the preceding chapters, we have explored various social media platforms such as Facebook, Twitter, and YouTube. These have had an incredible impact on billions of people and millions of companies, in connecting and sharing messages, posts, microblogs and video content. We have seen techniques for capturing, storing, and analyzing the content on these platforms. However, in 2009 a new platform was launched, Pinterest, with a different aim and format. Pinterest is a next generation digital form of the physical pinboards that people have used over the years. With those physical pinboards, one would gather and organize various pieces of paper, content, and information from sources such as newspapers, magazines, and one's own creations. Pinboards have been used for both work and hobbies. Pinterest is a new generation pinboard where one can collect interesting pieces of digital content from all over the internet and *pin* them on one's personal boards. Unlike physical pinboards, anyone on the platform can actually follow and *repin* this content on their own boards. Founder and CEO of Pinterest, Ben Silberman, summarized Pinterest as a *catalog of ideas*. This format makes it different from social networks which are more communication platforms to share news, thoughts, and information, whereas, Pinterest is a platform with curated content highlighting the interests and ideas of individuals. As of April 2017, there are over 170 million active users on Pinterest, which proves a growing interest for users to organize and share their ideas. This nature of curated ideas of users makes it an interesting network of communities with similar ideas and interests. In this chapter, we will explore the use of the Pinterest API, and also other advanced data collecting techniques to gain deeper knowledge in order to gather content from Pinterest and then build a graph of content and users to identify similar communities.

We will introduce you to the graph and network analyses and also use the text analysis techniques that we've learned in previous chapters to better understand and analyze the content associated with the pins of individual users.

Scope and process

In this chapter, we will guide you through the following steps:

1. Getting all your pins via Pinterest API.
2. Extracting bigrams and their relationships.
3. Creating and analyzing a simple graph to understand these relationships.
4. Scraping Pinterest API results.
5. Extracting bigrams, and building a user relationship graph.
6. Creating and analyzing a graph to find influencers and community structure.

Getting the data

In this section, we will work on two types of data:

- Your own pins extracted through Pinterest API
- Scraped search results

Pinterest API

Pinterest uses a RESTful API that lets you access the platform data. The data comes in the form of boards, pins, followers, and more. In order to interact with the API it is necessary to use OAUTH which allows both read and write permissions.

Communication with the API requires an access token. The access token can be obtained by creating an application on a user's Pinterest account. After creating an application, we need to go through a few steps to get all the access privileges.

Step 1 - creating an application and obtaining app ID and app secret

The first task is to create an application to communicate with the API:

1. Log in to your Pinterest account.
2. Go to apps at `https://developers.pinterest.com/apps/`.
3. Agree to the terms and policy and click on **Create app**.
4. Choose a name and create the app.

Pinterest has clear rules and policies in terms of using its API. Before connecting to the service it is recommended you read the *Developer guidelines* at (`https://policy.pinterest.com/en/developer-guidelines`) where you can find cases explaining how to use the API.

After registering the application, we can go to its page.

The application page gives us two important codes: `AppID` and `Appsecret`. We will use them later to obtain an access token.

It is also important to set the redirect **Uniform Resource Identifier** or **URI**. The redirect URI is the callback entry point of the application. In other words, the redirect URI is the location where the user will be redirected after successfully logging into the application. In our case, the redirect URI will return the codes necessary for further authorization.

The URI must be the secured protocol HTTPS. It might look like: `https://mysite.com/`.

Step 2 - getting your authorization code (access code)

To get an access code, we need to go to `https://api.pinterest.com/oauth/` and obtain the code, which will be returned with a redirect URI. We can do it using Python's `requests` library.

When calling the authorization service, we must submit some parameters:

```
response_type - takes the value 'code'
redirect_uri - our previously defined URI
client_id -  our App ID
scope - list of permission scopes
state - any value we can define (used for security reasons)

import requests
```

```
url = 'https://api.pinterest.com/oauth/'

params = {
    'response_type' : 'code',
    'redirect_uri' : 'https://mysite.com/',
    'client_id' : 'CLIENT_ID',
    'scope' : 'read_public,write_public',
    'state' : '145ABc'
    }

response = requests.get(url, params = params)
```

The response object contains several pieces of information, but we are especially interested in the `response.url` value.

`response.url` returns the HTTP link to be pasted to our browser. When we paste it, the app will ask us to confirm the permission and we get our code in the browser's address bar as follows: `https://mysite.com/?state=145ABc&code=xxxxxxxxxxx`

Now we have the access code, which will be used in the next step.

Step 3 - exchanging the access code for an access token

After you get your access code, you can request an access token. We will use a previously obtained access code and the application data: App ID and App secret.

```
url = 'https://api.pinterest.com/v1/oauth/token'

code = 'CODE'
app_id = 'APP_ID'
app_secret = 'APP_SECRET'

params = {
    'grant_type' : 'authorization_code',
    'client_id' : app_id,
    'client_secret' : app_secret,
    'code' : code
    }
```

In this case, we have to make a POST request:

```
response = requests.post(url, params = params)
```

If we inspect the `response.text` variable, we can find our access token:

```
{"access_token": "xxxxxxxx", "token_type": "bearer", "scope":
["read_public", "write_public", "read_private", "write_private",
"read_write_all"]}
```

Once we have the access token we can make calls to the API and obtain the requested data.

Step 4 - testing the connection

Once we have successfully obtained the access token, we can make a test request to check if everything works correctly. To do this, we will use a simple endpoint returning the information about the authorized user.

```
url = 'https://api.pinterest.com/v1/me'
params = {'access_token': 'xxx'}

response = requests.get(url = url, params = params)

print(response, response.reason)
print(response.json())
```

The first print command should display the connection status. If the connection is working correctly, we get the following:

```
<Response [200]> OK
```

The next print command will display the authorized user's details, shown as follows:

```
{'data': {'first_name': NAME,
  'id': 'YOUR_ID',
  'last_name': LASTNAME',
  'url': 'https://www.pinterest.com/USERNAME/'}}
```

By default, all fetch requests return the first 25 items in the list. However, the maximum number of items returnable at one call is 100. It can be set with `limit` parameter.

The problem of items to be fetched can be addressed via pagination. The object returned after the API call contains the cursor and next value. The best way to get the next page is to use the `next URL` given at the end of the response.

Like many other API services, Pinterest also limits the number of calls. You are allowed to make 1000 calls per hour for each unique user token.

All API responses return a header that gives you an update about rate limiting:

```
url = 'https://api.pinterest.com/v1/me'
response = requests.get(url = url, params = {'access_token': 'xxx'})

response.headers
```

The `response.headers` value might look like this:

```
{'Access-Control-Allow-Origin': '*', 'X-Content-Type-Options': 'nosniff',
'Content-Length': '129', 'Connection': 'keep-alive', 'Cache-Control':
'private', 'Pinterest-Generated-By': 'devplatform-devapi-prod-0a01af8e',
'X-Pinterest-RID': '339128364818', 'Date': 'Wed, 07 Jun 2017 12:33:43 GMT',
'Content-Type': 'application/json', 'Age': '0', 'Pinterest-Version':
'c0f3f7d', 'X-Ratelimit-Limit': '1000', 'X-Ratelimit-Remaining': '998'}
```

`X-Ratelimit-Remaining` indicates the limit remaining.

Getting Pinterest API data

The Pinterest API has the following three main endpoints:

- **Users**: Users endpoint provides a convenient way to get information about an authenticated user. It also allows you to search for boards or pins for the user.
- **Boards**: Boards endpoint allows you to work with authenticated users' boards. It also provides the ability to fetch the boards and pins of any other user.
- **Pins**: The Pins endpoint, besides providing a way to manage your own pins, allows you to fetch pins, boards, and the pins on a board for any user.

We create a function `pinterest_paging()` which will help us to deal with pagination. It will return a list with JSON elements as a result:

```
import requests

### Pinterest API connection with paging
def pinterest_paging(url = '', params = ''):

    data = []
```

```
response = requests.get(url = url, params = params)
response = response.json()

data.extend(response['data'])

while response['page']['next'] != None:

    response = requests.get(url = response['page']['next'])

    response = response.json()

    data.extend(response['data'])

return data
```

Then, we create a code which will execute the `pinterest_paging()` function and convert a list of JSONs into a pandas dataframe.

```
import pandas as pd
from pandas.io.json import json_normalize

access_token = 'YOUR_ACCESS_TOKEN'
```

In the Pinterest API, we can define the fields that we want to retrieve. For the purposes of analysis we will select: ID, board, note, and counts (the full list of available fields is available in the API documentation at `https://developers.pinterest.com/docs/api/overview`).

```
fields = 'id, board, note, counts'
```

We use `/v1/me/pins/` endpoint to get all pins associated with our own Pinterest account:

```
pin_data = pinterest_paging(url = 'https://api.pinterest.com/v1/me/pins/',
params = {'access_token': access_token, 'fields': fields})
```

Then, we convert it to a dataframe.

```
pins = pd.io.json.json_normalize(pin_data)
```

Finally, we obtain a dataframe with the following columns:

- `board.id`: Board ID
- `board.name`: Board name
- `board.url`: Board URL link
- `counts.comments`: Number of comments
- `counts.saves`: Number of saves
- `id`: Pin ID
- `note`: Description

It is interesting to see the boards and how many pins are linked to them. We can use the pandas functionality `groupby()` to print the count of pins for each board as follows:

```
pins.groupby('board.name')['board.name'].count()
```

```
board.name
Data Science      34
Luxury brands     53
Tech              18
```

We can see that in our account we have three boards: `Data Science`, `Luxury brands`, and `Tech` and we've got 105 pins in total (`34` for data science board, `53` for luxury brands, and `18` for tech).

Scraping Pinterest search results

The Pinterest API data collection possibilities are limited to the user's own pins and relationships. However, we can extract more data through web scraping techniques, but usually such an approach has its own limitations due to scalability, maintenance, and complexity issues. You should also consider the platform's Terms and Policy before deciding to build a product based on this data collection technique. For the purposes of this chapter, we will demonstrate how to analyze scrapped data in graph structures and identify groups of related topics.

Building a scraper with Selenium

First of all, we have to decide what kind of data we are going to scrape. In our case, the most interesting information are keyword-based search results which return a list of pins with their titles, descriptions, and usernames. We will try to see the users which are closest to each other in terms of similar interests. In order to start building the scraper we have to analyze the search results first.

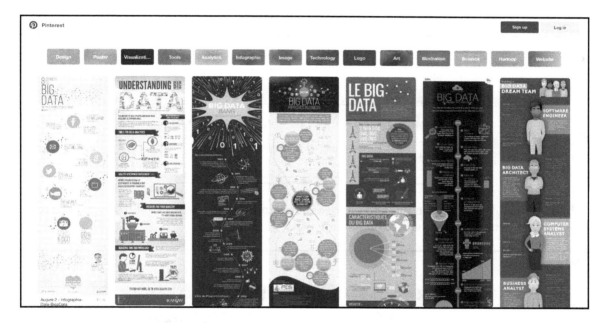

We can see that the endpoint for the search is: `https://www.pinterest.com/search/pins/`. It already contains the search query under the q parameter.

Then, we can use Google Chrome or Mozilla Firefox inspector to check what the DOM structure of the document is in order to find the elements link with the information we are looking for. The DOM structure represents a tree of all the HTML elements with their attributes.

An example of a DOM structure is shown in the following diagram:

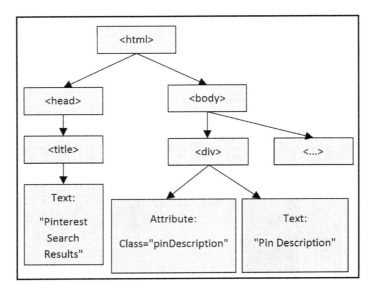

When you right-click on the Pin and choose **inspector**, you are redirected to the part of the page source related to the highlighted element.

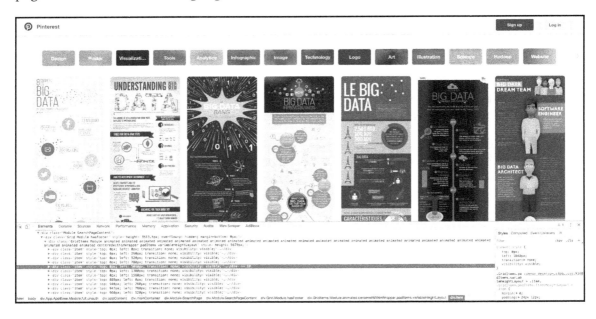

By analyzing the HTML of the website we can see that each Pin is wrapped in a `<div>` element of class `pinWrapper`. Then we notice that the fields we are interested in are given in the following fields under `<div class="pinWrapper">`:

- **Pin ID**: `<div class="pinHolder">`
- **Title**: `<h3 class="richPinGridTitle>`
- **Description**: `<p class="pinDescription">`
- **Username**: `<div class="creditName">`
- **Image source**: `<img src>` under `<div class="pinHolder">`

However, we notice that only 11 pins are visible in the code. The next set of pins appears only if we scroll down the page. It means that the content is generated dynamically, so we will not be able to scrape it using get requests. For this purpose we will use a Selenium library which can simulate user behavior in the browser.

Selenium is a software testing framework available in many programming languages. It is used to define and simulate user behaviour and test if the software output is as expected. However, it is very often used to create bots that perform user actions in the same way as humans. We will use this approach to collect search results.

In our case, we will simulate the action of scrolling down a page in a browser using the Google Chrome webdriver. A webdriver is an instance of a browser which is run and controlled through Python code.

Firstly, we import all necessary libraries: `BeautifulSoup` to parse and scrape HTML code, `time` to manage the delay between actions, and `selenium` to create web browser instances.

```
from bs4 import BeautifulSoup
import time
from selenium import webdriver
```

We create a function which extracts all elements from a `soup` object (parsed DOM structure). As arguments, it takes `soup` object and the query term that we used to perform the search on Pinterest and returns a list of tuples:

```
def get_pins(soup,query_term):
```

We search for all pins, which are stored in `<div class="pinWrapper">`:

```
pins = soup.findAll('div', {"class":"pinWrapper"})

all_pins = []
```

For each Pin, we extract all the elements that we listed previously:

```
for pin in pins:
        pinId = str(pin.find('div', {"class":"pinHolder"}).a['href'])

        pin_title = ""

        if(pin.find('h3', {"class":"richPinGridTitle"})!=None):
            pin_title = str(pin.find('h3',
            {"class":"richPinGridTitle"}).getText())

        pin_description = ""
        if (pin.find('p',{'class':'pinDescription'})!=None):
            pin_description = str(pin.find('p',
            {'class':'pinDescription'}).getText().encode('utf-8').strip())

        pin_user = ""
        if (pin.find('div',{'class':'creditName'})!=None):
            pin_user = str(pin.find('div',
            {'class':'creditName'}).getText().encode('utf-8').strip())

        pin_img = str(pin.find('div', {"class":"pinHolder"}).img['src'])
    all_pins.append((pinId,pin_title.strip(),pin_description.strip(),pin_user,p
in_img,query_term))

    return(all_pins)
```

Secondly, we create a function which will perform actions and collect the data. It only takes query terms as an argument:

```
def query_pinterest(query_term):
```

We define the URL of Pinterest search results containing the q argument, which stands for query.

```
url = 'https://www.pinterest.com/search/pins/?q='
```

We replace spaces in query terms by + in order to build a request URL:

```
query_term = query_term.replace(' ','+')
```

We build the request url.

```
url = url + query_term
```

Then we create an instance of Chrome WebDriver. It is worth noticing that the structure of the Pinterest website is built using the ReactJS technique, which dynamically outputs the content of the website. We have to maximize the window of our WebDriver to have the same DOM structure as presented before. We will add argument `--kiosk` to open the driver in fullscreen mode.

```
options = webdriver.ChromeOptions()
options.add_argument("--kiosk")
```

In the next step, we have to download the Chrome driver from `https://sites.google.com/a/chromium.org/chromedriver/downloads` and pass the path to the driver in an `executable_path` argument:

```
driver =
webdriver.Chrome(chrome_options=options,executable_path="/PATH_TO_CHROME_DR
IVER/chromedriver")
```

Now we are able to see the search results in our instance of WebDriver, but if we try to scroll, we notice that, without being logged in, scrolling stops after a few refreshes. We will implement the login feature of our bot next.

We go to the login page:

```
driver.get("https://www.pinterest.com/login/")
```

We simulate human behavior and we wait for five seconds until the page has rendered. It might be a shorter time period and you can set it up empirically or by checking when the page has completely rendered.

```
time.sleep(5)
```

In the following step, we get the email and password fields, fill them with our credentials, and click programmatically on **Login** (the `submit` button).

```
username = driver.find_element_by_name("id")
password = driver.find_element_by_name("password")
username.send_keys("EMAIL")
password.send_keys("PASSWORD")
login_attempt = driver.find_element_by_xpath("//*[@type='submit']")
login_attempt.submit()
```

We initialize a list where we store the results and wait 10 seconds until we are fully redirected to the home page after login; then we go to our URL with the search results. Here again we wait 14 seconds until the results are generated. The time values are purely arbitrary, so you can change them:

```
all_pins = []

time.sleep(10)
driver.get(url)
time.sleep(10)
```

Now, we go to the main part of the script. We will try to scroll 100 times to get new search results. You can define this number in many ways:

- Empirical arbitrary value (the following case)
- Stop when there is no change in data (you've scrolled all the results)
- Stop when the processing time is exceeded
- Stop when the memory needed to store the results is too high

The choice depends on your use case. We will stick to the simplest one and define the number of required scrolls as 100:

```
for i in range(0,100):
```

We scroll the page:

```
driver.execute_script("window.scrollTo(0, document.body.scrollHeight);")
```

We wait five seconds and then we the parse page source with BeautifulSoup:

```
time.sleep(5)
html_page = driver.page_source

soup = BeautifulSoup(html_page)
```

We extract the data we previously defined with function get_pins, we wait four seconds, close the driver, and output the results:

```
all_pins = all_pins + get_pins(soup,query_term)
time.sleep(4)

driver.close()
return(all_pins)
```

The whole process can be executed with a single command:

```
pins = query_pinterest('fashion')
```

Scraping time constraints

The main disadvantage of such an approach is the time needed to extract the information. If we take into consideration only the time spent waiting, we have to wait for 529 seconds to scroll a page 100 times. Then, we have to add processing time which will take another few seconds.

As a result, we will get up to 1,100 pins meaning we get around 11 pins per one page scroll (this value might differ for pins of different sizes). Even if we reduce the time dedicated to waiting it will still be difficult to scale this approach to get hundreds of thousands of pins. However, the purpose of this analysis is to get some targeted insight for personal use (a constraint of web scraping), and we'll still obtain a sufficient amount of data to perform our study.

Data pull and pre-processing

In the previous step, we obtained two DataFrames:

- Our own pins through the Pinterest API
- Search results from the scraping tool

Now we will create different graph structures to analyze the relationships between users and topics.

Pinterest API data

One may wonder how we can build a relevant graph structure from a user's own pins. Intuitively, the only information which may be used to build a network is a board name. However, we can extract much more interesting relationships from the Description and Title and build a graph with them.

For this purpose we will extract bigrams, which will be considered as topics, and we will check how strong the links between these bigrams are.

Bigram extraction

Firstly, we use the code presented in previous chapters to find the most relevant bigrams in our dataset.

We import all the necessary libraries:

```
import nltk
from nltk.collocations import *
from nltk.corpus import stopwords
import re
```

We define a function which will perform data cleaning and pre-processing tasks:

- Remove whitespace characters at the beginning and the end of verbatim
- Remove URLs
- Remove punctuations
- Convert to lowercase
- Tokenize the text
- Remove English stopwords

Finally, it will return a list of tokens:

```
def preprocess(text):

    #1)Basic cleaning
    text = text.strip()
    text = re.sub(r'https?:\/\/.*[\r\n]*', '',text, flags=re.MULTILINE)
    text = re.sub(r'[^\w\s]',' ',text)
    text = text.lower()

    #2) Tokenize single comment:
    tokens = nltk.word_tokenize(text)


    #3) stopwords removal
    stopwords_list = stopwords.words('english')
    tokens = [token for token in tokens if token not in stopwords_list]

    return(tokens)
```

Then, we apply the function on our dataset and obtain a `clean` column:

```
pins['clean'] = pins['note'].apply(lambda x: preprocess(x))
```

We use the cleaned column to extract the most frequent bigrams document-wise. For this purpose, we convert the column to a list:

```
list_documents = pins['clean'].tolist()
```

Then, we use `nltk.collocations.BigramAssocMeasures()` on our list of documents to extract the bigrams as follows:

```
bigram_measures = nltk.collocations.BigramAssocMeasures()
bigram_finder = BigramCollocationFinder.from_documents(list_documents)
```

We apply a frequency filter equal to two to be sure that a bigram appears at least twice in our dataset to increase the probability of a relationship with other bigrams. This step is optional and depends on the size of the dataset:

```
bigram_finder.apply_freq_filter(2)
```

As an output, we want to obtain a list of tuples (bigram and its frequency) in our document list. We will also limit the results to the top 20 bigrams:

```
bigrams = bigram_finder.nbest(bigram_measures.raw_freq,20)
freqs = bigram_finder.score_ngrams(bigram_measures.raw_freq)
```

By default, `BigramCollocationFinder()` uses scores instead of raw frequencies. In order to obtain the data we are interested in, we have to get `ngram_fd.items()`, which represents the raw frequency values and then sorts the bigrams in descending order:

```
ngram = list(bigram_finder.ngram_fd.items())
ngram.sort(key=lambda item: item[-1], reverse=True)
```

Finally, we obtain a list of tuples that we need for further analysis:

```
frequency = [(" ".join(k), v) for k,v in ngram]
```

We can now print the list of the 20 most frequent bigrams in our pins descriptions:

```
print(frequency)

('data science', 14),
('big data', 7),
('virtual reality', 4),
('machine learning', 4),
('science central', 4),
('data scientist', 4),
('data analysis', 4),
('autres gadgets', 3),
('analytics data', 3),
('iphone 7', 2),
```

```
('zoom lens', 2),
('aston martin', 2),
('brilliant luxury', 2),
('cote montres', 2),
('automne hiver', 2),
('printemps 2017', 2),
('haute couture', 2),
('louis vuitton', 2),
('learning algorithms', 2),
('algorithms data', 2)
```

We notice that our dataset contains pins about data science, tech gadgets, and luxury products.

Building a graph

In the next step, we will build a graph of the most frequent bigrams. To build the graph, we need to know what it means.

The graph originates from the basic mathematical graph theory, where a graph is essentially a group of objects, called nodes or vertices, where certain pairs of nodes are related to each other. Diagrammatically, a graph is represented as follows, where the dots represent a **Node** and the relationship by the lines is known as an **Edge**.

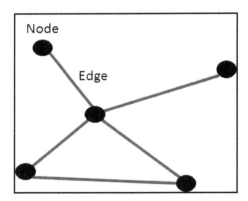

Now, coming back to Pinterest, the relationship between concepts is defined as a co-occurrence in a Pin description. It means that if data science appears together with machine learning in a Pin description, they are linked to each other.

We import two additional libraries: `numpy` and `networkx` as well as `matplotlib` to create visualizations:

```
import numpy as np
import networkx as nx
import matplotlib.pyplot as plt
```

Then, we have to convert our data structure to obtain a matrix of co-occurrences of bigrams, so columns and rows will both represent bigrams.

We create a variable column that contains a list of bigram strings:

```
columns = [t[0] for t in frequency]
```

In the next transformation, we create a column `clean_join` which contains a string of merged tokens (instead of a list of tokens):

```
pins['clean_join'] = pins['clean'].apply(lambda x: " ".join(x))
```

Then, for each bigram, we create a column which will contain a Boolean variable if this bigram exists in a cleaned Pin description (`clean_join` column):

```
for column in columns:
    pins[column] = pins['clean_join'].str.lower().str.contains(column)]
```

We convert the Boolean variable into integers.

```
df_asint = pins[columns].astype(int)
```

We create a co-occurrences matrix by matrix multiplication to obtain the required data structure presented with the following code:

```
cooccurrences = df_asint.T.dot(df_asint)
```

The required data structure is presented with the following table:

...	data science	machine learning	...
data science	0	1	...
machine learning	1	0	...
...	...	...	...

We convert the dataframe into a numpy matrix and fill the diagonal values with zeros to remove loop edges (a node linked to itself):

```
cooccurrences = cooccurrences.values

np.fill_diagonal(cooccurrences, 0)
```

Now, we can create a graph G from our numpy matrix:

```
G = nx.from_numpy_matrix(cooccurrences)
```

However, at this stage, our graph will contain many nodes which are not connected to any other node. In our analysis, we will only focus on connected components as this is the most interesting information we are looking for. To get nodes which are connected, we use a `networkx` module, `node_connected_component`. Once we obtain a list of connected nodes, we create a subgraph with these elements:

```
connected = list(nx.node_connected_component(G, (len(cooccurrences)-1)))
G = G.subgraph(connected)
```

Our graph structure is ready, so we can now visualize it. We will use the `matplotlib` library along with the `networkx` methods.

There are multiple layout generation algorithms that can be used to find the most readable visualization. Networkx offers six layouts:

- `circular_layout`
- `random_layout`
- `shell_layout`
- `spring_layout`
- `spectral_layout`
- `fruchterman_reingold_layout`

You can test all of them to see which one best fits your data. In our example we have chosen `fruchterman_reingold_layout`.

```
pos=nx.fruchterman_reingold_layout(G) # positions for all nodes
```

In the following code lines we define styles for nodes and edges. You can find the complete documentation at: `https://networkx.github.io/documentation/networkx-1.10/refere nce/drawing.html`.

```
# nodes
nx.draw_networkx_nodes(G,pos,node_size=500,alpha=0.3,node_color='blue')

# edges in undirected graph
nx.draw_networkx_edges(G,pos,width=2,alpha=0.2)

labels = dict([(i,df_asint.columns[i]) for i in connected])
nx.draw_networkx_labels(G,pos,labels,font_size=12)

nx.draw_networkx_edges(G,pos,edgelist=esmall,width=6,alpha=0.5,edge_color='
b',style='dashed')

# labels
#nx.draw_networkx_labels(G,pos,font_size=14,font_family='sans-serif')

plt.axis('off')
```

Once the layout and styles are ready we can save the graph as a `.png` file and at the same time display it in Python:

```
plt.savefig("topics_graph.png") # save as png
plt.show() # display
```

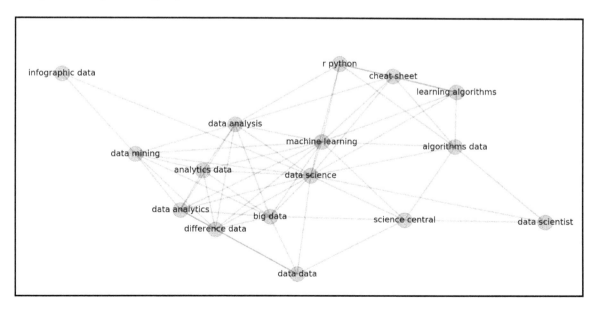

We obtained a graph of our own chosen topics. We can see that the pins are centered on topics such as machine learning, data science, data analysis, or big data. The interesting aspect of the preceding graph is that data science is at the center with connections to machine learning, big data, algorithms, analytics, and data scientist. These are all relevant components of data science. A simple story to create here would be that a data scientist practices data science, using machine learning on big data technologies and implements machine learning for various algorithms! We can even see that machine learning is connected to a node with R and Python, two of the most essential programming languages to implement machine learning. Science central is linked to a popular data science journal called Data Science Central (we recommend you visit it at `http://www.datasciencecentra l.com/`). Even with data scraping limitations on Pinterest we get such valuable information around the topic. Imagine all the knowledge that could be discovered if we explored different topics! In the following sections we will explore the features of these relationships in the graph and also explore the similarities between users pinning content on our chosen topics.

Pinterest search results data

In this second part of the chapter we'll deal with the data that we scraped from the Pinterest search results, which we will use to find insights about the community. The goal of this part of the analysis is different from the previous section, so we have to structure the data with respect to the defined objectives. In this example, we will use the topic to find relationships between users. This means that if both users create Pins with "fashion week" in its description, then they are linked by this topic.

Bigram extraction

Firstly, as in the previous example, we have to extract all the topics (defined as bigrams) from our dataset. We use exactly the functions from the bigram extraction section and then we obtain the following results:

```
print(frequency)

('fashion week', 64),
```

```
('street style', 50),
('automne hiver', 44),
('haute couture', 29),
('printemps 2017', 28),
('style fashion', 22),
('week printemps', 20),
('comment porter', 20),
('hiver 2016', 20),
('summer outfits', 18),
('ons porter', 15),
('tendances mode', 15),
('prêt porter', 15),
('garde robe', 14),
('street looks', 14),
('printemps 2016', 13),
('2016 2017', 13),
('sweat shirt', 13),
('looks fashion', 12),
('pinterest 30', 12),
('porter jean', 12),
('printemps 2014', 12),
('week automne', 12),
('outfit ideas', 12),
('30 looks', 11),
('plus beaux', 11),
('hiver 2017', 11)
```

The results differ a lot from our own Pins, because this time we extracted Pins by a search query `fashion`.

The bigrams found on the fashion topic include events such as the fashion week, autumn week, and styles, such as street style, street look, 30 looks, and high end fashion of haute couture, among others. We also see `Printemp`, which is a famous French fashion brand, emerge among the bi-grams. Since, our Pinterest is configured in French, a few French words, such as hiver (winter), prêt porter (ready to wear), plus beaux (most beautiful), tendance mode (trend and fashion), and garde robe (wardrobe), are also present. No complaints, as France is famous for fashion and the results are super relevant.

Building a graph

In this section, we will follow a similar logic to create our graph, but we will engineer the nodes and edges differently to obtain the relationship that we are looking for.

We create a list of topics which will be used to build the links:

```
columns = [t[0] for t in frequency]
```

Then, we create a list of usernames that are stored as an index in our dataframe:

```
usernames = users.index.tolist()
```

We merge lists of cleaned tokens into a string:

```
users['clean_join'] = users['clean'].apply(lambda x: " ".join(x))
```

For each topic, we create a Boolean variable to check if a topic was expressed by a user and we store this information in a topic column:

```
for column in columns:
    users[column] = users['clean_join'].str.lower().str.contains(column)
```

Then, we subset the topic column:

```
users = users[columns]
```

Finally, we transpose the dataframe to have users as columns and topics as rows:

```
users = users.transpose()
```

This transformation helps us to build a matrix where users are linked by topics, similar to previous example of our own Pins:

```
df_asint = users[usernames].astype(int)
cooccurrence = df_asint.T.dot(df_asint)
cooccurrence = cooccurrence.values

np.fill_diagonal(coocc, 0)
```

...	user 1	user 2	...
user 1	0	1	...
user 2	1	0	...
...	...	...	...

Then, we build and visualize the graph as in the first example:

```
#####graph

G=nx.from_numpy_matrix(cooccurrence)
```

```
connected = list(node_connected_component(G, (len(cooccurrence)-1)))
G = G.subgraph(connected)

pos=nx.fruchterman_reingold_layout(G) # positions for all nodes

# nodes
nx.draw_networkx_nodes(G,pos,node_size=50,alpha=0.3,node_color='blue')

# edges
nx.draw_networkx_edges(G,pos,width=1,alpha=0.2)

labels = dict([(i,df_asint.columns[i]) for i in connected])
nx.draw_networkx_labels(G,pos,labels,font_size=5)

nx.draw_networkx_edges(G,pos,edgelist=esmall,width=6,alpha=0.5,edge_color='
b',style='dashed')

# labels
#nx.draw_networkx_labels(G,pos,font_size=14,font_family='sans-serif')

plt.axis('off')
plt.savefig("users_graph.png") # save as png
plt.show() # display
```

We obtain the following graph as the result:

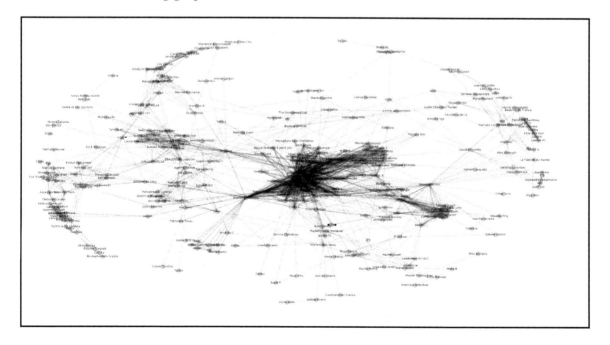

The second example represents many more nodes compared to the first. Interestingly a dense section of connected nodes are at the center with lots of connections all over. We also notice that there are some communities that group together different topics. We will analyze the communities programmatically in the next part of this chapter.

Data analysis

Once we've captured and structured the two kinds of data on Pinterest, we want to use them to find answer, to three main topics:

- Understand what are the most important topics in our own Pins
- Find influencers on a topic in the search results
- Find communities on a topic in the search results

Understanding relationships between our own topics

The aim of this part of the analysis is to answer a few questions about the topics that we are interested in on Pinterest:

- What are the most important topics (central or main topic) by direct connections?
- What are the topics which are most connected with others?
- What are the topic hubs? Or how important is the topic in terms of connecting other topics?
- What are the most important topics (central or main topic) by indirect connections?

To answer the preceding questions we are going to use a concept in graph theory and network analysis called **centrality**.

Centrality is essentially metrics that allow you to identify the most important vertices or nodes within a graph structure. Centrality is an offshoot of the research work in social network analysis but today is used for multiple purposes, such as in internet infrastructure networks, transportation networks, and the spreading of diseases. Basically, whenever a problem can be examined in graph networks and there's a need to identify the important nodes, centrality can be applied. Going into the mathematical depths of centrality theory is beyond the scope of the book, but we'll understand it from an intuitive and basic mathematical point of view, before applying it, using Python, to see it at work.

For a given graph $G := (V, E)$, where V is the set of nodes or vertices and E is the set of edges, there are four main centrality measures which will help us to answer these questions. The graphs can be of one of two types: a directed graph (where the edges point in a certain direction: towards or out of the node), and an undirected graph (edges do not point in any direction). In this chapter, we are going to work only with undirected graphs because this is relevant to our problem statements.

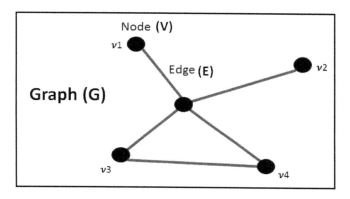

- **Degree centrality**: This is the easiest to measure using the rule that the node with the most number of connections is the most important. The measure can be made more specific by using the notion of indegree (edges directed towards the node) and outdegree (edges directed out of the node).
- Mathematically, the degree centrality of a node (v) can be represented as follows, where $deg(v)$ is the number of edges to or from the node or vertex, v:

$$C_D(v) = \deg(v)$$

- **Closeness centrality**: Intuitively, closeness tries to measure the node closest to all the other nodes in a connected graph. Mathematically, it's the average length of the shortest path between the node in question and all the other nodes. Hence, the more central the node is, the closer it is to all the other nodes in the graph. Mathematically, it looks like the following, where, $d(y,x)$ is the distance between node x and y:

$$C(x) = \frac{1}{\sum_y d(y, x)}$$

- **Betweeness centrality**: This was inspired by social network analysis to measure the control of people in communication between other people in the social network. Essentially, it counts the number of times a node is present in the shortest path between two other nodes:

$$C_B(v) = \sum_{s \neq v \neq t \in V} \frac{\sigma_{st}(v)}{\sigma_{st}}$$

Here σ_{st} is total number of shortest paths from node s to node t and $\sigma_{st}(v)$ is the number of those paths that pass through v

- **Eigenvector centrality**: This is another very important centrality measure that computes the influence of a node in the network. For example, the Google page rank is a variation of eigenvector centrality. It works on scores (number of connections to that node) of nodes, and assumes that connections to highly scored nodes are more influential than those to the lowly scored ones:

$$x_v = \frac{1}{\lambda} \sum_{t \in M(v)} x_t = \frac{1}{\lambda} \sum_{t \in G} a_{v,t} x_t$$

Here, $M(v)$ is a set of the neighbors of v and λ a constant. With a small rearrangement this can be rewritten in vector notation as the eigenvector equation:

$$\mathbf{Ax} = \lambda \mathbf{x}$$

Now we'll link the measures to each of our respective questions regarding the fashion topic on Pinterest:

- **Degree**: What are the most important topics (central or main topic) by direct connections?
- **Closeness**: What are the topics which are most connected with others?
- **Betweenness**: What are the topic hubs? Or how important is the topic in terms of connecting other topics?
- **Eigenvector**: What are the most important topics (central or main topic) by indirect connections (number of connections that the connected topics receive themselves)?

Firstly, we create a function `centrality_measures` which will calculate the measures, then sorts them and prints the results. We also define a constant `LIMIT`--a maximum number of values to print (for visualization purpose). In our example, assigned value 25 will cover all the nodes of the graph:

```
LIMIT = 25
```

Function centrality measures take, as arguments, graph object G and all the labels that we defined previously:

```
def centrality_measures(G,labels):
```

We store the measures as in a list of tuples (`measure_name`, dictionary of centrality measures values):

```
centralities = []
centralities.append(('degree centrality',nx.degree_centrality(G)))
centralities.append(('closeness centrality',nx.closeness_centrality(G)))
centralities.append(('betweenness
centrality',nx.betweenness_centrality(G)))
centralities.append(('eigenvector
centrality',nx.eigenvector_centrality(G)))
```

For each centrality measure, we print the results for the `LIMIT` number of top elements:

```
for centrality in centralities:
    print(centrality[0]) #measure name
    print("\n")
    sorted_elements = sorted(centrality[1].items(), key=lambda x:
    x[1],reverse=True)
        for element in sorted_elements[0:LIMIT]:
            print('{} : {}'.format(columns[element[0]],element[1]))
        print("\n")
```

We obtain the following results:

```
degree centrality
data science : 1.0
machine learning : 0.8
big data : 0.6
data analysis : 0.6
difference data : 0.5333333333333333
data analytics : 0.5333333333333333
data mining : 0.5333333333333333
analytics data : 0.4666666666666667
algorithms data : 0.4666666666666667
science central : 0.4
cheat sheet : 0.4
```

```
r python : 0.4
learning algorithms : 0.3333333333333333
data data : 0.3333333333333333
data scientist : 0.2
infographic data : 0.13333333333333333
```

We can see that the most important topic by degree centrality is data science followed by machine learning and big data. Even graphically one could find the most number of connections being shared by three nodes. Degree centrality on smaller graph structures can be calculated quite easily by just counting the number of edges around the node.

```
closeness centrality
data science : 1.0
machine learning : 0.8333333333333334
big data : 0.7142857142857143
data analysis : 0.7142857142857143
difference data : 0.6818181818181818
data analytics : 0.6818181818181818
data mining : 0.6818181818181818
analytics data : 0.6521739130434783
algorithms data : 0.6521739130434783
science central : 0.625
cheat sheet : 0.625
r python : 0.625
learning algorithms : 0.6
data data : 0.6
data scientist : 0.5555555555555556
infographic data : 0.5357142857142857
```

The dataset based on our own Pins is small, so the most important topics by direct links follow the same distribution with respect to closeness. It means that the most important topics are at the same time the most central and closest to all the other topics:

```
betweenness centrality
data science : 0.3185714285714286
machine learning : 0.10634920634920636
data analysis : 0.031746031746031744
data mining : 0.028571428571428574
algorithms data : 0.026984126984126985
big data : 0.023333333333333334
science central : 0.022539682539682544
difference data : 0.009047619047619047
data analytics : 0.009047619047619047
data data : 0.004761904761904762
cheat sheet : 0.004761904761904762
r python : 0.004761904761904762
data scientist : 0.0
analytics data : 0.0
```

```
learning algorithms : 0.0
infographic data : 0.0
```

However, we can see an important difference in terms of the ability to connect other topics. Data analysis and data mining become linking hubs between our Pins. It is not surprising that these two topics are essential when connecting all the other topics, since, with the advancement in machine learning and big data, data analysis remains a vital component to give context to the results of advanced algorithms:

```
eigenvector centrality
data science : 0.530509121349612
big data : 0.35008269586274515
machine learning : 0.3263985242014839
difference data : 0.2808775587146514
data analytics : 0.2808775587146514
science central : 0.26129942683808993
analytics data : 0.2579541823300166
data data : 0.2076930432274413
data analysis : 0.19656423969734138
data mining : 0.1832926306043567
algorithms data : 0.16790428277928734
learning algorithms : 0.12754450847676477
cheat sheet : 0.11788600597586944
r python : 0.11788600597586944
data scientist : 0.07713131495155437
infographic data : 0.057367461630954804
```

The last measure gives us information on how well connected topics are that point to the main topic. In contrary to degree centrality measure results, big data becomes a more important topic on our Pinterest boards than machine learning.

As we have few nodes, we can summarize all the results in a heat map. Firstly, we need to create a new data structure inside the centrality_measures function. Then, we can show a heatmap.

In order to perform this task, we need to rewrite our function.

```
def centrality_measures_heatmap(G,labels):

    centralities = []
    centralities.append(nx.degree_centrality(G))
    centralities.append(nx.closeness_centrality(G))
    centralities.append(nx.betweenness_centrality(G))
    centralities.append(nx.eigenvector_centrality(G))
```

We have to store the results as a list of lists with measures for each topic.

```
measures = []
    for node in G.nodes_iter():
        measures.append(list(map(lambda f: f[node], centralities)))
```

Then, we transpose the list for a more readable visualization.

```
measures = list(map(list, zip(*measures)))
```

We also have to normalize the values in order to be able to compare the levels between different metrics.

```
#normalize
norm_measures = []
for measure in measures:
  norm_measures.append([float(element)/max(measure) for element in
measure])
```

Finally, we create a heatmap using the `matplotlib` library:

```
column_labels = labels.values()
row_labels = ['degree','closeness','betweenness','eigenvector']
ax = plt.subplot()
ax.set_xticks(range(0,len(labels)))
ax.set_xticklabels(column_labels, minor=False)
ax.set_yticks([0,1,2,3])
ax.set_yticklabels(row_labels, minor=False)
plt.xticks(rotation=90)
plt.imshow(norm_measures, cmap='hot_r', interpolation='none')
plt.show()
```

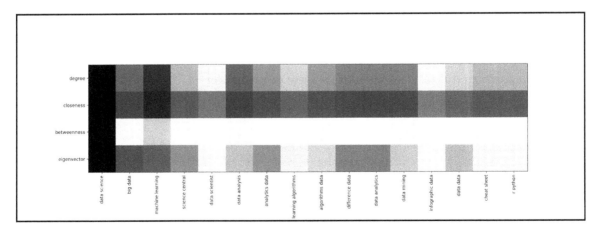

So what do we infer from this? We find that:

- Data science remains the strongest node on all four measures.
- Big data and machine learning are strong on closeness, degree, and eigenvector.
- Data analysis, data analytics, and data mining all have a better betweeness than the other nodes in the network.
- The graph network being a small one, the closeness is quite strong on all the nodes, highlighting the fact that overall all the nodes are close to each other. In a much larger graph it would be a different story.

Finding influencers

The aim of the second analysis is to find influencers by the popularity of topics they publish. In contrast to the most common social network, we will not deal with the number of followers or repins, but we will focus on created content.

We adjust function `centrality_measures` to generate bar charts instead of lists of results:

```
def centrality_measures(G,labels):

    centralities = []
    centralities.append(('degree centrality',nx.degree_centrality(G)))
    centralities.append(('closeness
centrality',nx.closeness_centrality(G)))
    centralities.append(('betweenness
centrality',nx.betweenness_centrality(G)))
    centralities.append(('eigenvector
centrality',nx.eigenvector_centrality(G)))

    for centrality in centralities:
        sorted_elements = sorted(centrality[1].items(), key=lambda x:
        x[1],reverse=True)

        chart_labels = []
        chart_measures = []
        for element in sorted_elements[0:LIMIT]:
            chart_labels.append(labels[element[0]])
            chart_measures.append(element[1])

        ax = plt.subplot()
        ax.barh(range(0,len(chart_labels)), chart_measures, align='center',
        color='blue', ecolor='black')
        ax.set_yticks(range(0,len(chart_labels)))
        ax.set_yticklabels(chart_labels)
```

```
ax.invert_yaxis()   # labels read top-to-bottom
ax.set_xlabel(centrality[0])

plt.show()
```

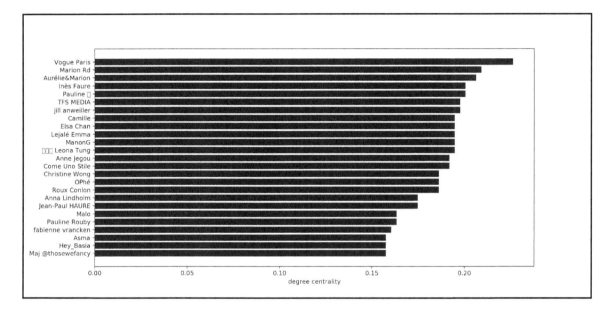

In our chosen topic of Fashion and from the search results analyzed, Vogue Paris emerges as the strongest in terms of connections. This is not very surprising, given Vogue's position as a leader of fashion content covering a large number of topics and with a large number of followers. Vogue Paris is followed by a lot of individual users (Marion Rd, Aurélie, Inès Faure, Pauline...). These users are interested in lots of fashion topics that they have pinned that emerge in the search results, so they are connected to a lot of topics.

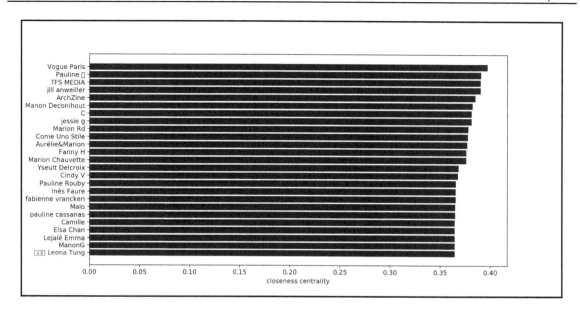

In terms of closeness centrality, Vogue Paris maintains the top rank. However, Pauline rises to the second spot indicating that the topics pinned by Pauline have connections to other users, making it a central user on the Fashion topic. Pauline is followed by TFS MEDIA and Jill Annweiller. Marion Rd, which had a lot of connections, drops in closeness centrality, which means that the user's topics are connected to many others but do not have a central position in the graph.

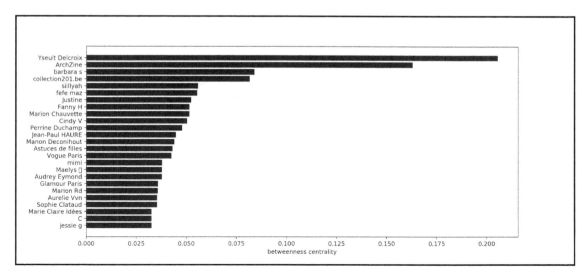

The betweenness of the users on the Fashion topic provides dramatically different results: The top users in the earlier metrics have dropped in position; other users, such as Yseult Decroix, ArchZine, and barbaras, are in the top three, which means that these accounts have content that bridges to other content, and so have a greater control in the overall content around Fashion. As seen in the following screenshot, the top account, Yseult Decroix, has a huge number of followers (421,144) making it a highly influential account!

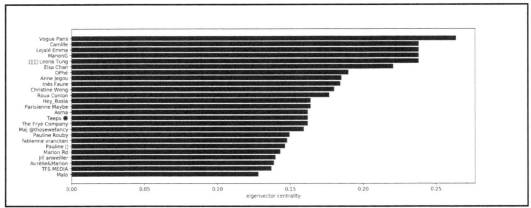

Vogue Paris, which is a well followed account (966,068 followers) makes a comeback at the top in the eigenvector centrality, followed by Camille, Lejalé Emma, and ManonG. As we can see from the preceding graph, that eigenvector centrality is a measure of influence of nodes in the graph. The conclusion is that these accounts have connections to nodes that have higher weights, making their overall influence greater than others.

Conclusions

The previous exercise on users around a specific topic gave us interesting results where a certain user, such as Vogue Paris, was a dominating account in influence and control, and, being a central account, scored high on all measures. The influence of the account was validated by seeing it has close to a million followers. On the other hand, other accounts had variance in their rankings, some being central in the overall graph, and others acting as bridges, due to their content variety or being more influential due to connections with higher weight. This shows how centrality measures can be used to perform network analysis and find influential nodes on a graph network. We have used Pinterest for this analysis but centrality could be applied to multiple social networks to compute the influence of users based on various factors. A very popular tool for measuring your social influence, Klout, is an interesting example of influence analysis from social media data. However, influence scores derived from such services should be used with caution, as it is strictly limited to interactions in the digital space and not a measure of influence in real life. Aa an analogy, great leaders such Mahatma Gandhi or Nelson Mandela, never used social media but were certainly more influential than today's social media influencers!

Community structure

Lastly, a great application of network analysis is the detection of communities. The graph we create using the relationship between multiple users allows us to figure out certain clusters that are grouped together in the overall network on specific criteria. Thereafter, these clusters can be examined in detail to find characteristics that describe them in commonality. Digging community characteristics is beyond the scope of the chapter but we'll show how algorithmically we can detect communities based on graph structures.

The objective of the last analysis section is to find communities of users who create pins about similar subtopics. To perform this task we use a library, `community`, which is dependent on the library `louvain`. You have to make sure that you have the most recent version which is compatible with Python 3.

We import all necessary libraries:

```
import community
import networkx as nx
import matplotlib.pyplot as plt
import random
```

Then, we use a method `best_partition` which finds the optimal clusters of communities:

```
#compute the best partition
partition = community.best_partition(G)
```

Finally, we visualize the graph:

```
#visualization
size = float(len(set(partition.values())))
pos = nx.spring_layout(G)
count = 0.
for community in set(partition.values()) :
    count = count + 1.
    list_nodes = [nodes for nodes in partition.keys()
    if partition[nodes] == community]
```

In order to use different colors for communities we generate random RGB colors using the `random.uniform()` method:

```
nx.draw_networkx_nodes(G, pos, list_nodes, node_size = 20, node_color =
(count*random.uniform(0, 1)/size,count*random.uniform(0,
1)/size,count*random.uniform(0, 1)/size))

nx.draw_networkx_edges(G,pos, alpha=0.1)
plt.show()
```

Finding users who pin content on similar subtopics and then plotting this on a graph gives us the following structure. The structure represents some interesting features, with multiple connections shared between certain nodes, and other nodes set towards the periphery with fewer but more targeted connections:

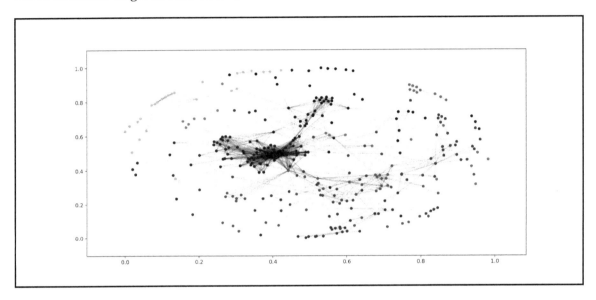

Each color on the graph corresponds to a different community of users who pin a particular subtopic. We can see that there is one central cluster (black dots) and multiple small communities in the outlying area.

Our example of community detection is around people pinning content on fashion on Pinterest. However, communication detection today covers serious subjects, ranging from a network of fraudulent websites who link to each other to finding electoral communities who are linked to each other based on their views and opinions. It is also used on e-commerce portals to find communities of users with similar shopping and browsing habits.

Summary

The last decade has seen an enormous growth of social media platforms, such as Facebook, Twitter, and Youtube. Since 2009, another platform with a different format and objective has grown - Pinterest. Unlike conventional social media, which is used as a communication tool, Pinterest is described as a "catalog of ideas". It allows users to create pinboards, and to organize and share content over the web, based on interests and ideas.

We've explored the use of the Pinterest API and also advanced scraping techniques, using Selenium and BeautifulSoup, to gather data for learning purposes. However, these have time constraints to be scalable. Therefore, we extracted the data from our own pinboard using the endpoints (user, board, and pins) and the search results on the topic of fashion. For data analysis, we used bigram analysis to extract a list of topics on our own pins and then visualized it in a graph structure using NetworkX (via `fruschterman_reingold_layout`). We then studied centrality metrics and four measures: degree, closeness, betweenness, and eigenvector. We applied these measures to our pinboard and found some interesting results. Then we extracted the topics on the data gathering from the search results on Pinterest on the subject of fashion. We used bigram analysis to discover some interesting results from trends, events, style, and clothes.

The next section was dedicated to finding user relationships on shared interests and topics, through graph relationships and community detection. We achieved this by first building a graph of the user network based on the similarity of pinned topics between all the users. Then we used the centrality measures to find out the most connected, central, and influential users. Finally, we provided an introduction to community detection using Python's community module, and visualized the community of users that shared similar sub-topics. We touched upon various important concepts including advanced data scraping, graph theory and visualization, centrality, and community detection.

These exciting concepts and skills lead us to the next and last chapter, *Social Media Analytics at Scale*, where we'll learn about several topics around distributed and parallel computing, Spark and Amazon Web Services. These will take your social media analytics skills to the next level!

9
Social Data Analytics at Scale – Spark and Amazon Web Services

In the age of big data we have to handle new problems for data handling that did not exist before in terms of the three **Vs** (**volume**, **variety**, and **velocity**). When we handle very large amounts of data, we have to change our approach entirely. For example, algorithms can no longer use exhaustive brute force, because this approach might just take years to complete. Instead, we would use intelligent filtering to reduce the search space. Another example is when we have very high dimensions; for example, in text analysis, where every word or combination of words in the vocabulary constitute a dimension we need to change algorithms to adapt to such scenarios.

Advances in cluster computing have given us a new tool to handle the challenge of big data. No longer do we think of performing an analysis on a single node (your computer), we have progressed to thinking in terms of clusters of resources. Of course, cluster systems existed before, but were not accessible to everybody. Now it is much simpler to set up a cluster for analysis purposes.

Scaling refers to the use of multiple computational resources to perform tasks. There are two fundamental types of scaling: vertical and horizontal.

Vertical scaling is where we increase the capacity of our current resources so that they are able to handle larger loads of data. For example, if our dataset is too large for our current node, we could increase the total disk space or the amount of **random access memory (RAM)** of the current node appropriately, to be able to handle more data. This approach is simpler because you don't have to handle problems of networking and node resource management. However, we will encounter limitations, because you cannot increase a single node's capacity infinitely, simply because such machines either don't exist or are too expensive.

Horizontal scaling is where we combine multiple nodes to increase the accumulated resources of the entire cluster. In the previous example, if our dataset was too large for our current node, instead of changing the type of current node, we could cut the dataset into multiple subsets (chunks), and assign them to different nodes. In the final step, we would combine the results of each subset to get the global result of the entire dataset. This approach potentially has no limitations, because depending on the size of the data we can increase the number of nodes in our cluster.

However, here we encounter a different set of problems, such as no single node having knowledge about the entire dataset, or combining results of subsets into the global context can be difficult. One of the early known problems of scaling up is the Google search engine, when Google invented the famous MapReduce algorithm. The idea behind this was simple. Instead of treating all the contents of the web in a single global context, the data is broken down into chunks, each chunk then maps out its results and finally the reduce stage combines the different chunks together to build the global context. Today, we have even more evolved systems like Spark that take MapReduce to yet another level.

In this chapter, we will focus on horizontal scaling and cover the following topics:

- Distributed computing on Spark
- Text mining with Spark
- Parallel computing
- Distributed computing with Celery

Different scaling methods and platforms

Let us look at some scaling methods on different platforms in detail in the following sections.

Parallel computing

Before the arrival of advanced systems, such as Hadoop or Spark, developers had to handle the problem of horizontal scaling. What are the methods they used?

The most basic form of horizontal scaling is multi-threading or multi-processing. These two approaches are similar, since both use multiple threads on a single machine to break the data into chunks and then execute the computation in parallel. The typical difference between a thread and a process is that threads (of the same process) run in a shared memory space, while processes run in separate memory spaces.

Parallel computation has one fundamental limitation: it is restricted by the resources of the single machine.

Let's see a hands-on example of parallel computation. For this we will use Python's native multiprocessing library.

```
from multiprocessing import Pool

def f(x):
    return x * x

number_of_processes = 3
data = [1, 2, 3]
p = Pool(number_of_processes)
print(p.map(f, data))
```

Here, the list represents the data and the f function represents the operation that has to be performed on the dataset. We use the Pool() function to create a pool of three different processes, then use the map function to map the data onto the different processes, where each process gets a single integer to compute and outputs the result.

But let us say the data had a million data points, and we wanted to stick to the same concept wherein we create enough processes so that every process gets a single data point to process. We would not be able to do that because the machine would not be able to create a million processes. If we fix the number of processes, and the analysis function had a high degree of complexity then again our time dimension is capped by the limits of the machine.

For example, let's say we have a machine of 40 cores and we want to extract the named entities in a dataset of a million sentences. On average, named entity extraction takes about 1.5 seconds to complete each sentence, due to the complexity involved. As our machine has 40 cores, creating more than 40 processes would be inefficient. Here we would be looking at a computational time of (1 Million / 40) * 1.5 Seconds. To complete the million lines it would take in total 37,500 seconds, which is about 10 hours!

How do we overcome this problem? To handle such scenarios, we see the birth of distributed computation, which is basically parallel-computation on multiple machines. In the next section, we will use Celery for distributed computation.

Distributed computing with Celery

Distributed computing is where we use multiple different machines to perform a task. For example, if we wanted to perform some operation on every sentence in a large file, instead of using a single process on a single machine, we could break the file down to many smaller files and assign those files to different machines to process in parallel.

As exciting as this sounds, distributed computing has its own set of problems. Shared memory is not possible as tasks are performed on completely different machines, synchronization between machines becomes a challenge, failure handling becomes more complicated, and so on. To ease our problems, we will use a software that makes the task of distributed computing much simpler.

The first distribution software is Celery (`http://www.celeryproject.org`). Celery is an asynchronous task/job queueing platform based on distributed messaging. What that means is that your application will communicate with the Celery job scheduler, the scheduler will add your job to a queue, and as soon as it has the resource available, it will schedule the job for execution.

To see this in action, we need to first install a few things to get Celery up and running. We will install everything on our machine (single node) to understand the concepts, but replicating this configuration on multiple machines is not complicated.

You should go through Celery's official *Getting Started* tutorial to get more in-depth knowledge before you attempt `http://docs.celeryproject.org/en/latest/getting-started/first-steps-with-celery.html`.

So, let's first install the Python package `celery`:

```
pip install celery
```

Now, Celery requires a solution to send and receive messages; usually this comes in the form of a separate service called a message broker. Celery uses ultra fast in-memory message brokers like RabbitMQ or Redis. For this example, we will use RabbitMQ as the message broker:

Here is a tutorial on how to install RabbitMQ `https://www.rabbitmq.com/download.html`, the following commands are to install and setup RabbitMQ.

Installing on an Ubuntu Environment:

```
sudo apt-get install rabbitmq-server
```

Next let's start the RabbitMQ server:

```
sudo service rabbitmq-server start
```

To verify, if RabbitMQ is running do the following:

```
sudo service rabbitmq-server status
```

You should get a response similar to this:

```
Status of node rabbit@d425a028a2da ...
[{pid,942},
 {running_applications,[{rabbit,"RabbitMQ","3.5.7"},
                        {mnesia,"MNESIA  CXC 138 12","4.13.3"},
                        {xmerl,"XML parser","1.3.10"},
                        {os_mon,"CPO  CXC 138 46","2.4"},
                        {sasl,"SASL  CXC 138 11","2.7"},
                        {stdlib,"ERTS  CXC 138 10","2.8"},
                        {kernel,"ERTS  CXC 138 10","4.2"}]},
 {os,{unix,linux}},
 {erlang_version,"Erlang/OTP 18 [erts-7.3] [source] [64-bit] [smp:2:2]
[async-threads:64] [kernel-poll:true]\n"},
 ...
 {uptime,80}]
```

Your RabbitMQ is running! To stop the service:

```
sudo service rabbitmq-server stop
```

Great, now that we have the message broker up and running, let's write some code to see it working.

In your home directory create a directory called `celery_app`:

```
mkdir ~/celery_app
```

Here we will create two scripts: `tasks.py` to define functions for the Celery workers, and a script `run_tasks.py` to delegate tasks to Celery. In the file `~/celery_app/tasks.py`, insert the following:

```
from celery import Celery

app = Celery(
'tasks',
backend='rpc://',
broker='amqp://guest@localhost//'
)

@app.task
def add(x, y):
    return x + y
```

So, we imported the `celery` module and created an `app` instance with the parameters `backend` and `broker`. The `broker` parameter configures Celery to use the RabbitMQ server at localhost (same machine) with the user as guest. Finally, we defined a function add and using the `app.task` decorator we declared to Celery to register the function. We can now create add tasks and Celery will know what we are talking about!

`backend` refers to the backend messaging broker. The backend messaging broker is used to return results once the job is finished. For this example, we will be using the `rpc` which refers to a temporary in-memory messaging service. However, to get better performance, it is advised to use a messaging broker like RabbitMQ or Redis for the backend messaging service. You can use the broker RabbitMQ server as the backend messaging service.

To use RabbitMQ as the backend messaging service replace `rpc://` with `amqp://guest@localhost//` like we set for the broker.

Next, in the `~/celery_app/run_tasks.py` file, insert the following:

```
from tasks import add

for _ in range(100):
    result = add.delay(4, 4)
    print result.get(timeout=5)
```

Here we import the function which is a Celery task, and we call the `delay` function on it passing our parameters. The `delay` function will run the add function asynchronously by sending a message through the messaging broker.

Before we can run this, we need to start the Celery worker, the component that listens to the messaging broker for task instructions.

```
cd ~/celery_app
celery -A tasks worker --loglevel=info
```

You should see the following output:

```
celery@localhost v4.0.2 (latentcall)

[config]
.> app:         tasks:0x1039aca50
.> transport:   amqp://guest:**@localhost:5672//
.> results:     rpc://
.> concurrency: 4 (prefork)
.> task events: OFF (enable -E to monitor tasks in this worker)

[queues]
.> celery            exchange=celery(direct) key=celery

[tasks]
  . tasks.add

[2017-06-12 17:38:35,416: INFO/MainProcess] Connected to
amqp://guest:**@127.0.0.1:5672//
[2017-06-12 17:38:35,426: INFO/MainProcess] mingle: searching for neighbors
[2017-06-12 17:38:36,449: INFO/MainProcess] mingle: all alone
[2017-06-12 17:38:36,482: INFO/MainProcess] celery@localhost ready.
```

This means that your Celery worker has successfully started, it has registered the task add, and is now ready and listening out for instructions!

Next, to schedule your jobs:

```
cd ~/celery_app
python run_tasks.py
```

On the Celery worker console, you should see tasks being accepted successfully:

```
[2017-06-12 17:38:35,416: INFO/MainProcess] Connected to
amqp://guest:**@127.0.0.1:5672//
[2017-06-12 17:38:35,426: INFO/MainProcess] mingle: searching for neighbors
[2017-06-12 17:38:36,449: INFO/MainProcess] mingle: all alone
[2017-06-12 17:38:36,482: INFO/MainProcess] celery@Arjuns-MacBook-Pro.local
ready.
[2017-06-12 17:43:28,271: INFO/MainProcess] Received task:
tasks.add[ad92630e-d3b7-4113-a13d-eca250e050dd]
[2017-06-12 17:43:29,128: INFO/PoolWorker-2] Task tasks.add[ad92630e-
```

```
d3b7-4113-a13d-eca250e050dd] succeeded in 0.0182580760011s: 8
[2017-06-12 17:43:29,132: INFO/MainProcess] Received task:
tasks.add[867a02a3-c5d6-4aab-b729-a4d82e248f6d]
[2017-06-12 17:43:29,153: INFO/PoolWorker-4] Task tasks.add[867a02a3-
c5d6-4aab-b729-a4d82e248f6d] succeeded in 0.0187370109925s: 8
[2017-06-12 17:43:29,155: INFO/MainProcess] Received task:
tasks.add[d0c24833-b187-4f35-939f-32282afc84d5]
[2017-06-12 17:43:31,113: INFO/PoolWorker-2] Task tasks.add[d0c24833-
b187-4f35-939f-32282afc84d5] succeeded in 0.000539859000128s: 8
```

That's how simple it is! Now you can create as complex a task as you wish. For example, I could make an HTTP call to get some information:

```
import requests

@app.task
def http_get(url):
    response = requests.get(url)
    # ... parsing the body ...

    return (response.status_code, result)
```

Alternatively, I could even get part-of-speech tagging for sentences:

```
import nltk

@app.task
def tag_pos(text, lang):
    tokens = nltkword_tokenize(text, lang)
    return nltk.pos_tag(tokens=tokens)
```

Now, let's see how to deploy Celery on multiple machines using Docker

Celery multiple node deployment

We will use Docker to simulate a multi-node environment for Celery. Docker is a software container platform, which means that Docker lets us create lightweight virtual machines to isolate and package our software and its environment. Docker is a very powerful tool for development because not only can you design your software, but also the environment that it runs in. This increases cross-platform compatibility and simplifies dependency management during deployment.

Before you proceed, make sure you have Docker installed and running on your machine.

So, for our simulation we will have the following Docker containers:

```
rabbitmq-service : The RabbitMQ broker agent
worker-1 : A celery worker
worker-2 : A celery worker
client : The client program that will delegate work to celery
```

Let's first build a Docker image from a simple Celery app. The only modification we need to make in the app is the address of the RabbitMQ service, as it will not be running on the same machine as the Celery app, but rather in a different Docker container.

In the file ~/celery_app/tasks.py change the following line:

```
app = Celery('tasks', backend='rpc://',
broker='pyamqp://guest@localhost//')
```

To this:

```
app = Celery('tasks', backend='rpc://', broker='pyamqp://guest@rabbitmq//')
```

So now the app will try to connect to the RabbitMQ service on the domain rabbitmq rather than localhost.

Next, create the following file ~/celery_app/requirements.txt file to install all dependencies in the Docker image:

```
cd ~/celery_app
touch requirements.txt
```

Add the following to the requirements.txt file:

```
requests
celery
nltk
```

Create the following file ~/celery_app/Dockerfile to tell Docker how to build the image:

```
cd ~/celery_app
echo "FROM python:2-onbuild" > Dockerfile
```

Now we will build the Docker image:

```
cd ~/celery_app
docker build -t test/celery .
```

This will build the Docker image and label it test/celery.

To run the app, we need to start the RabbitMQ service in a docker container:

```
docker run -d --name rabbitmq \
--hostname rabbitmq \
rabbitmq:3
```

Now we will create the two Celery workers and connect them to the container running the RabbitMQ server:

```
docker run -d --name worker-1 \
--link rabbitmq \
test/celery \
celery -A tasks worker --loglevel=info

docker run -d --name worker-2 \
--link rabbitmq \
test/celery \
celery -A tasks worker --loglevel=info
```

Finally, run the app to delegate the workload:

```
docker run --rm -it --name client \
--link rabbitmq \
test/celery \
python run_tasks.py
```

The app should start giving the same output as before, but now, when you check the logs of the two workers, you will see that the workload is being distributed equally to both the workers!

```
Logs of worker 1
docker logs -f worker-1

Logs of worker 2
docker logs -f worker-2

Voila !!
```

Distributed computing with Spark

Software like Celery is great for distributing relatively simple tasks, and especially great for scheduling asynchronous tasks. However, Celery is not the right choice for complicated tasks, for example, handling big data volumes for text analysis problems. For such problems we need a more advanced tool, like Spark.

Spark was inspired when Google developed the famous Hadoop. Hadoop is an open source software framework used for distributed storage and processing big data using the MapReduce programming model. However, we soon realized that the MapReduce pattern is very limiting for data analysis, and this realization gave birth to Spark.

Spark is an open source cluster-computing framework. Originally developed at the University of California, Berkeley's AMPLab. Spark is usually bundled together with Hadoop, where Hadoop provides the distributed storage system and Spark acts as the cluster computation framework. However, today we usually rely on cloud storage services from providers, such as Amazon, IMB-Bluemix, or OVH.

To get a feel for Spark, we will first install a cluster locally.

Download the latest version of Spark from `https://spark.apache.org/downloads.html`, for this example we will be using version 2.1.0.

```
wget https://d3kbcqa49mib13.cloudfront.net/spark-2.1.0-bin-hadoop2.7.tgz
```

Extract the files, and move the files to store them in the directory from where you want to use it:

```
tar -xzf spark-2.1.0-bin-hadoop2.7.tgz
mv spark-2.1.0-bin-hadoop2.7 /etc/spark
cd /etc/spark
```

Start the master component:

```
./sbin/start-master.sh
```

Go to `http://localhost:8080` to view the master interface:

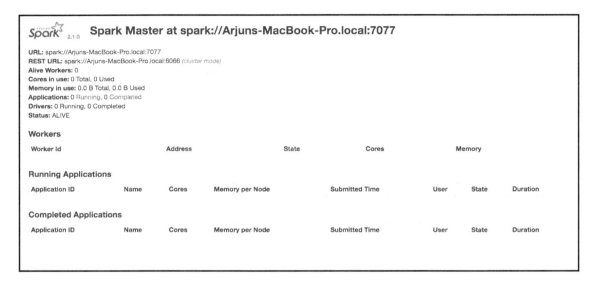

From the interface, we will take the master URL (in the preceding example, `spark://Arjuns-MacBook-Pro.local:7077`) and use it to start the worker instance.

```
./sbin/start-slave.sh spark://Arjuns-MacBook-Pro.local:7077
```

Now your master console will show a new worker component registered:

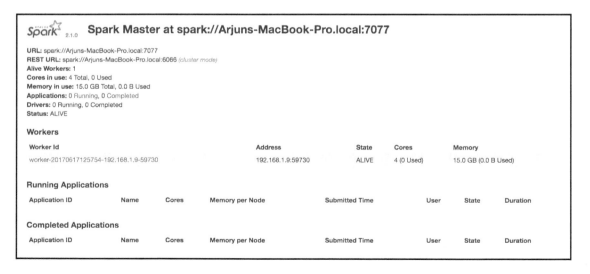

Now to check if Spark is working properly, we will connect using the Python Spark Shell:

```
./bin/pyspark --master spark://Arjuns-MacBook-Pro.local:7077
```

You should get an output like this:

```
Welcome to
      ____              __
     / __/__  ___ _____/ /__
    _\ \/ _ \/ _ `/ __/  '_/
   /__ / .__/\_,_/_/ /_/\_\   version 2.1.0
      /_/
Using Python version 2.7.10 (default, Oct 19 2015 18:31:17)
SparkSession available as 'spark'.
>>>
```

Just to check if the master is successfully connecting to the worker and back, we will create a simple list of integers, parallelize this list into multiple shards on the worker node, and square each entry in the list:

```
>>> list_integer = range(0, 10)
>>> sc.parallelize(list_integer).map(lambda _: _ * _).collect()
```

Great, everything works, so now let's handle a little more complicated problems using spark:

Text mining With Spark

Let's see some simple text mining techniques in Spark. For this example we will be using the packages nltk and pattern.

To install the required libraries, do the following:

```
pip install pattern nltk
```

In the next example we will take a list of sentences as our corpus, we then parallelize this list as a Spark RDD object, then we will pass the sentences through a standard textual preprocessing pipeline.

RDD is the standard data format accepted by Spark. On creation Spark, takes the input data and cuts it up into smaller chunks and distributes this data across the cluster. There are other formats offered by Spark as data frames, which resemble the pandas data frame, but for the moment we will stick with RDDs.

To work with Spark, now we will use Jupyter Notebook. Jupyter Notebook is an interactive notebook especially useful for experimenting with this new technology and/or new techniques.

To install Jupyter do the following:

```
pip install jupyter
```

Next we will create the directory ~/notebooks where we will store all the notebooks:

```
mkdir ~/notebooks
cd ~/notebooks
jupyter notebook
```

This is to launch the notebook server accessible at http://localhost:8888, and which should look something like this:

Next, use the **New** button to create a Python2 notebook. We will write and execute our code from this notebook.

To load the pyspark package we need to include the Python folder found in the Spark installed directory:

```
import sys
spark_home = '/etc/spark'
sys.path.insert(0, spark_home + "/python")

from pyspark import SparkConf, SparkContext

urlMaster = 'spark://Arjuns-MacBook-Pro.local:7077'

conf = (
    SparkConf()
        .setAppName('spark.app')
        .setMaster(urlMaster)
)
```

```
sc = SparkContext(conf=conf)
```

This creates a component of `SparkContext` for us, which is our communication gate to the `SparkMaster`.

Next we build the test corpus from `nltk.corpus.brown`:

```
from nltk.corpus import brown
sentences = brown.sents()[:1000]
corpus = sc.parallelize(sentences).map(lambda s: ' '.join(s))
```

Here we loaded a list of 1,000 sentences and, using the `SparkContext` object, we parallelized this object, instantly distributing the list as an RDD object.

Next, we will use the `pattern` package to chunk this sentence into noun and verb phrases:

```
from itertools import chain
from pattern.text.en import parsetree

def get_chunks(sentence):
    return list(chain.from_iterable(
            map(
                lambda sentence: sentence.chunks,
                parsetree(sentence)
            )
        ))

chunks = corpus \
    .map(get_chunks)
print chunks.take(2)
```

That should give you the following output:

```
[[Chunk('The Fulton County Grand Jury/NP'), Chunk('said/VP'), Chunk('Friday
an investigation/NP'), Chunk('of/PP'), Chunk('Atlanta/NP'), Chunk('recent
primary election/NP'), Chunk('produced/VP'), Chunk('no evidence/NP'),
Chunk('that any irregularities/NP'), Chunk('took/VP'), Chunk('place/NP')],
[Chunk('The jury/NP'), Chunk('further said/VP'), Chunk('in/PP'),
Chunk('term-end presentments/NP'), Chunk('that/PP'), Chunk('the City
Executive Committee/NP'), Chunk('had/VP'), Chunk('over-all charge/NP'),
Chunk('of/PP'), Chunk('the election/NP'), Chunk('deserves/VP'), Chunk('the
praise/NP'), Chunk('thanks/NP'), Chunk('of/PP'), Chunk('the City/NP'),
Chunk('of/PP'), Chunk('Atlanta/NP'), Chunk('for/PP'), Chunk('the
manner/NP'), Chunk('in/PP'), Chunk('which the election/NP'), Chunk('was
conducted/VP')]]
```

As you see, PySpark doesn't add much complexity to the usual process. If you are familiar with functional programming, you will feel right at home. Writing PySpark code is just as simple as writing functional Python code! The only new concepts are the RDD API: they are very simple but powerful tools that increase productivity.

For example, let's say we want to create a word count for all the nouns present in the corpus:

First, we will get all the noun-like words from the chunks:

```
def match_noun_like_pos(pos):
    import re
    return re.match(re.compile('^N.*'), pos) != None

noun_like = chunks \
    .flatMap(lambda chunks: chunks) \
    .filter(lambda chunk: chunk.part_of_speech == 'NP') \
    .flatMap(lambda chunk: chunk.words) \
    .filter(lambda word: match_noun_like_pos(word.part_of_speech)) \
    .map(lambda word: word.string.lower())

print noun_like.take(2)
```

That should give you the following output:

```
[u'fulton', u'county', u'grand', u'jury', u'friday', u'investigation',
u'atlanta', u'primary', u'election', u'evidence']
```

Next we will do a word count on the `noun_like` words:

```
noun_word_count = noun_like \
    .map(lambda word: (word, 1)) \
    .reduceByKey(lambda a, b: a + b) \
    .sortBy(lambda d: d[1], ascending=False)
print noun_word_count.take(10)
```

That should give you the following output:

```
[(u'state', 85), (u'city', 58), (u'administration', 52), (u'president',
52), (u'mr.', 52), (u'year', 46), (u'committee', 39), (u'bill', 39),
(u'states', 37), (u'county', 35)]
```

If you noticed here, we implemented the MapReduce pattern in Spark. There are many amazing things that can be achieved using Spark, and so we highly recommend further exploration of Spark.

Topic models at scale

For the final Spark example, we will do a simple topic modelling using MLLib (the Spark machine learning library) on our corpus.

We will use nouns as the features for our documents. First we will import the required classes:

```
from pyspark.mllib.clustering import LDA, LDAModel
from pyspark.mllib.linalg import Vectors
```

We will build the vocabulary from the noun word count RDD:

```
vocabulary = noun_word_count.map(lambda w: w[0]).collect()
```

Next, we need to transform the chunks corpus into a list of nouns per document:

```
doc_nouns = chunks \
    .map(lambda chunks: filter(
            lambda chunk: chunk.part_of_speech == 'NP',
            chunks
        )) \
    .filter(lambda chunks: len(chunks) > 0) \
    .map(lambda chunks: list(chain.from_iterable(map(
            lambda chunk: chunk.words,
            chunks
        )))) \
    .map(lambda words: filter(
            lambda word: match_noun_like_pos(word.part_of_speech),
            words
        )) \
    .filter(lambda words: len(words) > 0) \
    .map(lambda words: map(
            lambda word: word.string.lower(),
            words,
        ))
```

Next, we need to transform the doc_nouns RDD into a vector representation, where the size of the vector is the size of the vocabulary, each index corresponds to the vocabulary item's index.

So, if we have the vocabulary: [paris, tokyo, world], and we have the sentence: Hello World! This is Paris Calling!, the sentence would have the following vector representation: [1, 0, 1]

```
def get_vector_representation(nouns, vocab):
    return  Vectors.dense(map(
```

```
        lambda word: 1.0 if word in nouns else 0.0,
        vocab
    ))

doc_vecs = doc_nouns \
    .map(lambda nouns: get_vector_representation(set(nouns), vocabulary)) \
    .zipWithIndex().map(lambda x: [x[1], x[0]])
```

 The `zipWithIndex` will create unique ID numbers of each document. The ID will be their index value in the RDD.

Next we train the LDA Model:

```
ldaModel = LDA.train(doc_vecs, k=3)
```

Let's see the features for each topic:

```
print("Learned topics (as distributions over vocab of " +
str(ldaModel.vocabSize()) + " words):")
topics = ldaModel.topicsMatrix()
for topic in range(3):
    print("Topic " + str(topic) + ":")
    topic_words = sorted(map(
        lambda d: (topics[d[0]][topic], d[1]),
        enumerate(vocabulary)
    ), reverse=True)
    for word in topic_words[:10]:
        print("{}: {}".format(word[1], word[0]))
    print '-----------'
```

That should give you the following output:

```
Learned topics (as distributions over vocab of 2279 words):
Topic 0:
state: 27.6350480347
city: 18.9516713343
mr.: 17.5439356649
president: 16.8568307883
year: 15.4074257761
committee: 14.0324129502
administration: 13.9553862346
bill: 12.960995307
election: 11.6073234867
house: 11.5578186886
-----------
Topic 1:
```

```
state: 26.203168362
administration: 18.269679186
year: 16.2404114273
president: 16.0424256301
city: 14.5047677994
bill: 13.728963992
committee: 13.6235523038
mr.: 13.6074814177
tax: 12.0525070432
states: 11.6004234735
-----------
Topic 2:
state: 27.1617836034
city: 17.5435608663
president: 16.1007435816
mr.: 15.8485829174
administration: 15.7749345795
states: 14.7379675751
year: 13.3521627966
house: 12.5135762168
election: 12.140906292
united: 11.8705878794
-----------
```

That's it! We have created three clusters using the LDA and nouns extracted from our list of sentences plus this process was completely distributed and scalable!

Spark on the Cloud – Amazon Elastic MapReduce

Finally, now that you have learnt about Spark, let's finally look at potentially limitless scaling! We will learn how to use cloud services to deploy Spark clusters. There are many big data and data analytic service providers, such as Google or IBM Bluemix, but we will concentrate on Amazon for this chapter. We will provide screenshots of the process because sometimes such platforms can get a little overwhelming. The following are the steps for the process:

1. First, we need to create an Amazon Cloud account if you don't already have one. Go to `https://aws.amazon.com` and click on create a free account:

2. Provide your credentials and click on **Create account**.

3. Next, we have to create a Key Pair. Key Pairs are the basic authentication method on Amazon.

4. First, we need to go the EC2 services dashboard:

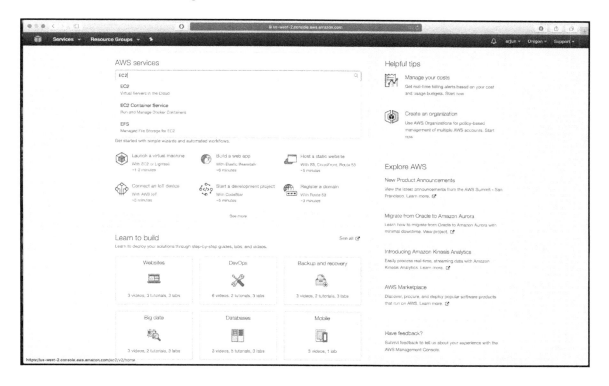

5. Then, click on **Key Pairs** in the side menu.

6. Click on **Create Key Pair** and name it `test-spark`.

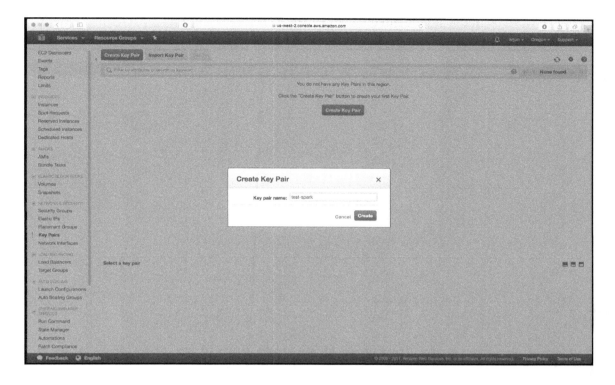

7. Next, we need to give our user some special permissions, so on the Header Menu hover on your name, from the drop-down menu click on **Security Credentials**, and from the side menu click on **Users**.

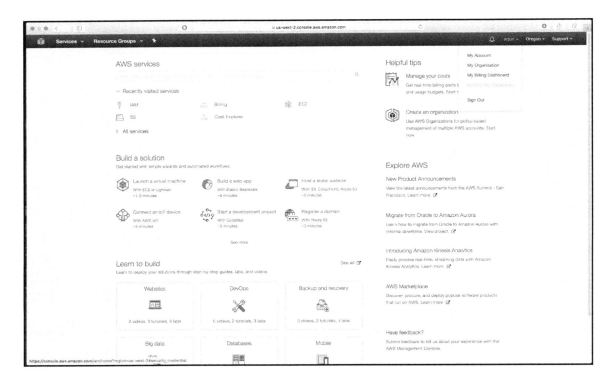

8. Next, click on your user, then click on **Add permissions**.

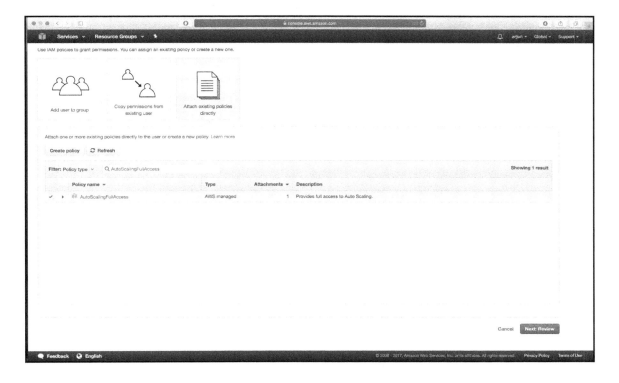

9. Choose the option **Attach existing policies directly** and search for `AutoScalingFullAccess`. Finally, click on **Next: Review** and click on **Add permissions**.

Your user permissions should look like this:

AutoScalingFullAccess will give your user the right to use services like Amazon Elastic MapReduce to automatically commission servers to form clusters.

10. Next, go back to the AWS Console home screen and we will choose the service **EMR (Elastic MapReduce)**:

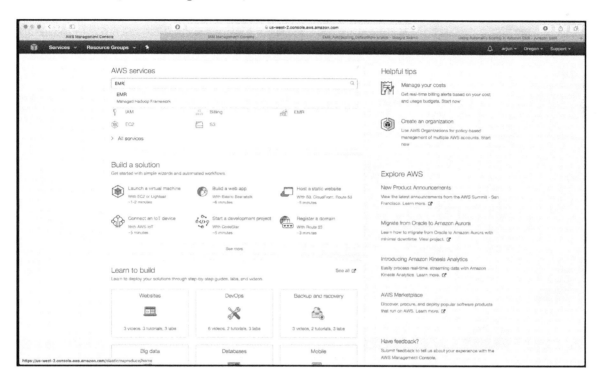

11. Click on **Create cluster**, which should land you on the following screen:

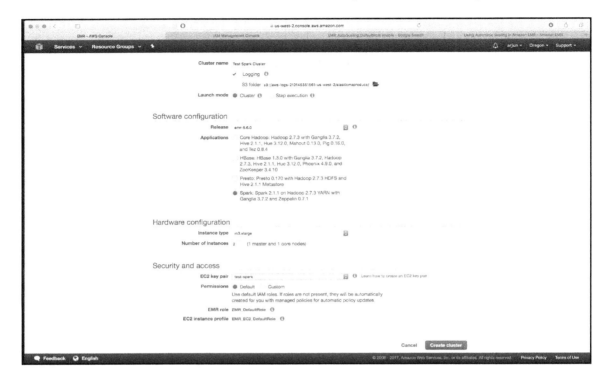

12. We will name the cluster `Test Spark Cluster`, and choose the number of nodes we desire in the cluster. For testing purposes, we will choose only two (one master and one slave). Finally, select the EC2 key pair that we created previously and click on **Create cluster**.

    The cluster will take about 10 minutes to be ready, but once it is ready you should see the following on your screen:

13. The cluster services are only accessible from the master node, so we will SSH into the master node to get access to the cluster. To do so, we need to add our IP address in the **Inbound Rules**.

14. To do this, return to the AWS Console home screen and choose the service **EC2**. When open click on **Security Groups** from the side menu, and you should see the following:

15. In the table under **Group Name** you will find **ElasticMapReduce-master.** Right-click on it and click on and select **Edit inbound rules**:

16. Add a new rule and choose the choose **SSH** as the type of rule, and **My IP** for the address, and save the list of inbound rules:

17. Next, return to the cluster in the EMR services dashboard and, next to the **Master public DNS**, click on **SSH**. This will open a pop-up window with instructions on how to connect to the Master Node:

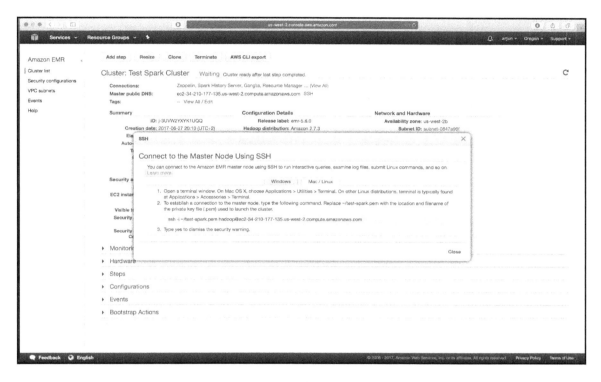

18. Copy and paste that in your terminal, indicating the right location for the `test-spark.pem` file.

    The command should look like the following:

    ```
    >> ssh -i test-spark.pem hadoop@ec2-34-210-177-135.us-west-2.compute.amazonaws.com
    ```

19. Next, when logged in, simply open the PySpark shell

    ```
    >> pyspark
    ```

20. Just like that you are connected to your Spark Cluster. Next, do a simple test to make sure everything by running the following:

    ```
    >> sc.parallelize(range(10)).map(lambda _: _ * _).collect()
    ```

That should return a list of integers as result.

Here we've created a cluster with just two nodes, but Amazon EMR allows to to scale up to as many nodes as you need. With a simple click, you could scale up to hundreds or even thousands of nodes.

Summary

Ten or twenty years ago, we did not need to scale up, except in very specific domains. Today, with the boom of digital, data volume is increasing exponentially. In today's world we need to be able to scale. Scaling brings about more new challenges than simple sequential programming, but its benefits largely outweigh the challenges.

Social media analytics also require the processing and analysis of massive amounts of unstructured data, so the ability to scale our algorithms and analysis is indispensable.

In this chapter, we looked at the basic methods of speeding up programs, like multi-threading and multi-processing. These methods are great when we have a powerful machine and a moderate sized data. If we are working on a small machine with, for example, four to eight cores then we will be limited on the extent to which we can parallelize our code. However, of course, if we only have a single machine with such resources, installing Spark on it is pointless. At the same time, let's say we have a single very powerful machine with say 40-80 cores and our program is not very complicated, then using Celery might be more beneficial than Spark, because with Celery we would have less major code adaptations and, we could launch multiple Celery workers on the machine.

Big data analysis platforms like Spark are not optimal on small datasets because the overheads of master to slave communication and data distribution might themselves consume more resources than a slower sequential program. The power of such platforms is seen when processing large datasets, which a sequential program might take days to compute, whereas Spark with adequate resources can do in minutes!

The biggest decision when scaling up is to choose the right approach for your problem. In some situations, multi-processing can be a better choice than Celery or Spark; it all depends on the problem in hand. The complexity of our problem viz-a-viz the availability of resources, such as the budget, the available processing power, and the number of machines available, are to be carefully considered before coming to a decision.

This chapter is meant to be a beginner's guide to scaling up. There are of course many things left to learn, but we hope that this chapter has demonstrated the potential of what can be achieved when we master cluster computing for social media analytics.

Index

www.ingramcontent.com/pod-product-compliance
Lightning Source LLC
Chambersburg PA
CBHW062108050326
40690CB00016B/3251